Conversations with Tom Robbins

Literary Conversations Series
Peggy Whitman Prenshaw
General Editor

Conversations
with Tom Robbins

Edited by Liam O. Purdon and Beef Torrey

University Press of Mississippi   Jackson

Publication of this book was made possible in part through the support of Doane College.

www.upress.state.ms.us

The University Press of Mississippi is a member of the Association of American University Presses.

First printing 2011

∞

Library of Congress Cataloging-in-Publication Data

Robbins, Tom, 1936–
  Conversations with Tom Robbins / edited by Liam O. Purdon and Beef Torrey.
      p. cm. — (Literary conversations series)
  Includes index.
  ISBN 978-1-60473-826-1 (cloth : alk. paper) — ISBN 978-1-60473-827-8 (pbk. : alk. paper) 1.
Robbins, Tom, 1936-—Interviews. 2. Authors, American—20th century—Interviews. I. Purdon,
Liam O. II. Torrey, Beef. III. Title.
  PS3568.O233Z46 2011
  813'.54—dc22   2010015536

British Library Cataloging-in-Publication Data available

Books by Tom Robbins

Another Roadside Attraction, New York: Doubleday & Company, 1971.
Paperback released by Ballantine.
Even Cowgirls Get the Blues, New York: Houghton Mifflin, 1976, released
simultaneously in hardcover and paperback editions. Mass-market
paperback released by Bantam Books, 1977.
Still Life With Woodpecker, New York: Bantam Books, 1980.
Jitterbug Perfume, New York: Bantam Books, 1984.
Skinny Legs and All, New York: Bantam Books, 1990.
Half Asleep in Frog Pajamas, New York: Bantam Books, 1994.
Candy from a Stranger: A Tom Robbins Reader, New York: Bantam Books,
1994, a special ABA commemorative edition of one thousand copies,
each signed and numbered.
Fierce Invalids Home From Hot Climates, New York: Bantam Books, 2000.
Villa Incognito, New York: Bantam Books, 2003.
Wild Ducks Flying Backward: The Short Writings of Tom Robbins, New
York: Bantam Books, 2005.
B Is for Beer, New York: Ecco Press/HarperCollins, 2009.

Contents

Introduction

Tom Robbins is as intellectually engaging in a literary conversation as his perfectly crafted sentences are thrilling to read. Though perhaps wary at first, he soon adjusts to the interview format. His eloquence both startles and cajoles interviewers, and, when least expected, makes one rethink previously held assumptions. All the while, his interview responses entertain and inspire joy and wonder. He is, after all, a world-class storyteller, as well as an expatriated Southerner.

In each of the interviews comprising this collection, which spans nearly the breadth of his four-decade writing career, readers are invited to learn a number of things about Robbins the man and Robbins the writer, which can be loosely organized under four instructive headings: 1) how formative experiences in his youth directly affect his later thinking as a writer, 2) what this fearless voice in contemporary American literature has to say about his work as he reaches each new milestone in his literary career, 3) how his imagination works, weaving pyrotechnic language, pestled quips, evocative images, and distillations of the counter-idea in his fiction as well as his essays, and 4) why he remains devoted, even after all this time, to re-creating through his fiction, not the bourgeois notion of the counterculture, but rather the postmodern anarchistic idea of the thought of the Other and the imaginative space most conducive to its expression.

Almost without exception, interviewers inquire about Mr. Robbins's origins to seek connections between his childhood or adolescent experiences and themes appearing in his prose. Invariably, they are informed about his Southern Baptist heritage and upbringing in North Carolina and Virginia, his parents' involvement in his early education, and his waggish adolescent ways. Nothing appears in the interviews to suggest he did not enjoy his youth, which offered him enviable opportunities, while concealing his precocious interest in language and books. Nor are any excuses offered to conceal the fact that throughout his teenage years and early adulthood he repeatedly brushed against institutional authority culture—in school, at college, in the military (where he served as a meteorologist), and finally at the professional level as a journalist and art critic. However, two illuminating anecdotes about the magic of transformation in his youth—both told more than once in this collection—enable readers to appreciate fully the connection between his childhood experience and the imaginative function that magic plays in his art, a function illuminated by him in *Even Cowgirls Get the Blues* when, distinguishing it from mysticism, he defines magic as the art of making "something permanent out of the transitory," of coaxing "drama from the colloquial."[1]

The first of these anecdotes has to do with the transformative effect a traveling circus, perhaps the Beers and Barnes Traveling Circus, had on his impressionable nine-year-old imagination and heart in the early 1940s when it suddenly appeared overnight, as if by magic, in a neighboring vacant schoolyard in Burnsville, North Carolina. In establishing the context for Robbins's account of his response to this marvel, Peter O. Whitmer describes the early-morning scene as one of "an oasis of flapping canvas tents, strange odors, weird animals, and exotic people."[2] Wide-eyed, Robbins lost little time making his way to the big top, the center of that enchanting and quirky rural mutation of Southern culture's inherent paganism, to offer his services as youthful roustabout in return for free admission. Given a job, he worked assiduously, watering llamas, setting up the menagerie, and scraping moss off the back of a six-foot alligator. In exchange, he got to behold adoringly—and was quickly transformed by—Bobbie, the daughter of the sideshow tent's scantily-clad "Indestructible Woman":

> I met . . . [her] . . . and just fell totally in love. She was the most exotic thing I had ever seen. She had waist-length, brilliantly blond hair. She wore black, patent-leather riding boots and riding britches. She had this pet black snake and scars on her arm where it had bitten her. I have always been a romantic, one of those people who believes that a woman in pink circus tights contains all of the secrets of the universe.[3]

The second of these anecdotes enabling readers to understand further how experience established the basis for Robbins's conceptual appreciation of magic, both literary and otherwise, calls attention to an annual event that occurred before and around him in the little town in which he was born, Blowing Rock, North Carolina. As he tells Larry McCaffery and Sinda Gregory,[4] the town was really no different from other small, rural Southern towns of that era except for one thing that happened to it in the summer of each year. Almost like clockwork, from the beginning of June until Labor Day, that little, ordinary Mayberry was transformed, as if by magic, into an extraordinary Coney Island for the rich and famous:

I grew up in small Southern towns. I was born in Blowing Rock, North Carolina, a very interesting place because nine months of the year it was like Dogpatch. Literally. It was Appalachia all the way, impoverished, ignorant, populated by men who beat their wives and drank too much—a rather *mean* place, abounding with natural beauty and colorful characters, but violent, snake-pit [sic][5] and sorrowful, over all. In summer, it became transformed into a wealthy resort, and from June through Labor Day there was nothing on the street but Cadillacs and Rolls-Royces and Mercedes and Lincoln Continentals. There were high fashion boutiques there, whose owners were from Paris and Palm Beach. Glamorous men and women who wore diamonds and played tennis and golf. There was a movie theater that for three months showed first-run films as soon as they opened in New York and Los Angeles; the other nine months, it was closed. So every June there would be this dramatic transformation, and the dichotomy between the rich, sophisticated scene and the hillbilly scene affected me very much. It showed me how the ordinary suddenly could be changed into the extraordinary. And back again. It toughened me to harsh realities while instilling in me the romantic idea of another life. And it left me with an affinity for both sides of the tracks.[6]

What Robbins has to say coincident to his latest literary accomplishments is treated in nearly all of the interviews he has offered, from the first he gave in 1976 until this volume's concluding piece. Though always willing to promote his work through readings and signings, Robbins refuses to explicate his text, despite energetic requests from his loyal, long-time readers. It is not that he has been made cautious by repeated critical attempts to pigeonhole his narrative fiction, or that he worries about being defined by a particular era (the 1960s) or movement (the Beat Generation, drug culture, the Counterculture). Nor is his reluctance motivated by an effort to cultivate a mystery about his style of living, to effectively create a cult of personality around himself, as occurred spontaneously after the publication of *Even Cowgirls Get the Blues.* No, his reluctance to interpret his prose simply reflects a conviction that his readers encounter his work uninterrupted by external commentary, whether by him or other writers attempting to explicate his intentions. He wants the reading experience to maintain the purity of vision that existed when the work was being painstakingly created at his writing desk.

This distinction is not to suggest, however, that he has nothing to say about his work as a writer. On the contrary, as this volume reveals, he has much always to offer in the way of wisdom, partly to illuminate his style and themes, but especially to prepare or reorient the thinking of his readers in relation to his fiction. This interest in having a hand in how his readership responds to his works, often the basis of accusations of preaching leveled against him by his detractors, reveals a continuity of thinking between his fiction and his philosophical outlook that is sometimes not fully anticipated or understood even by sympathetic readers or interviewers. Michael Rogers's expression of perplexity over Robbins's lack of interest in a purportedly serious work by an East Coast academic novelist, which appears in the first interview included in this collection, serves to illustrate this point. While Rogers assumes Robbins will praise the novelist as others have, he is taken aback to discover no such response is forthcoming, and even more startled to learn next from Robbins it is because the book in question has little wisdom to offer since it lacks humor:

> But it wasn't *supposed* to be funny, I say. That was the *point.*
> Robbins shakes his head again, almost as if puzzled. "But if there's any wisdom in it, it's *bound* to be funny."[7]

This interest in reorienting his readers' thinking is also evidenced by Robbins's readiness to address taboo subjects that appear in his fiction. In *Fierce Invalids Home From Hot Climates*, the novel's protagonist Switters provides just such a subject through his celebration of the vagina, which is expressed by his encyclopedic knowledge of all the words that exist for that particular part of the female anatomy. When Robbins is asked by Russell Reising whether it is fair to compare this conspicuous interest in female genitalia with that of *Hustler* magazine's editor Larry Flint, who has been known to justify the single-most distinct feature of the pictorial content of his publication by saying, "This is where we all come from and where we all want to return, so I'm going to show it to you as clearly as I can," Robbins's rather energetic and somewhat lengthy response not only clarifies the very serious purpose of Switters's seemingly frivolous, exotic knowledge, but also, more importantly, readjusts general assumptions about Flynt's unabashed explanation of his particular art form's purpose:

> Flynt probably didn't realize it, but he was propagating an essentially tantric idea. One of the major differences between us, though, is that I want to present the vagina in a way that reinforces rather than dispels its mystery. Uh, let me violate my principles here and lapse into autobiography for a moment.
> When I was growing up, my father moved us a lot, usually from one small southern town to another. And for some reason, we always seemed to land next

door to a family with little girls. These female playmates taught me plenty, especially in the realm of sensitivity, a realm no southern male child would dare visit in the company of his daddy, his uncles, his brothers, or his peers. Anyway, we moved to Burnsville, North Carolina, when I was eight, and the family next door to us was named Angel, and they had two daughters. Angel girls. I'm not making this up. Barbara Angel was ten and the most sophisticated female I'd ever met, and Helen Angel was seven. There was an older brother, Jack, who'd survived polio, and the father had built Jack a steel aboveground swimming pool so that he could exercise his withered legs. Well, one summer afternoon while I was taking Jack's waters, I turned to see Helen squatting on the rim of the tank. She was in a short cotton dress and wearing no underpants. You get the picture? It was totally innocent, but there she was, there *it* was, not twenty inches from the tip of my nose. The pretty little treasure. The vertical smile. The mollusk pried open by an undine's salty thumb. Raw and moist and fresh and sweet and crimped and apertural; unobscured as yet by a single hair; as pink as one of these radishes and more mysterious than the Appalachian forests by moonlight. I was absolutely mesmerized.

Before long, Barbara tapped Helen on the shoulder to alert her to her indiscretion, and the way that Barbara acted so protective and Helen became so embarrassed, well, it just magnified my fascination. The secret enfolded flesh flower that had suddenly bloomed before my eyes was not merely mysterious, it was forbidden. Forbidden! A taboo, and therefore sacred. The next time I eyeballed one of those tidewater orchids, both it and I were more fully developed, but the experience was no less vivid and no less unforgettable. And why would we, any of us, want to forget our introductory encounters with nature's most supercharged attractants? It isn't that often in the modern, civilized world that something has the power to galvanize and enrapture us on such a primal level.[8]

Most reassuring about Robbins's readiness to readjust his readers' thinking is the emphasis he places on the importance of remembering what is fundamentally meaningful to their lives. For his immediate American reading audience, this act of remembrance frequently has to do with what it is to be an American. This emphasis is heard repeatedly in the interviews that follow, but most instructively in the dialogue he has with Michael Strelow. It is in that exchange about Bernard Mickey Wrangle, protagonist of 1980's *Still Life With Woodpecker*, that he helps his readers understand the profundity of Bernard's refusal to compromise the integrity of who he is and what he believes:

. . . The Woodpecker is a man who refuses to suffer. Or perhaps I should say, the Woodpecker suffers as all of us must, but he refuses to let it warp him. Or trivialize him by making him cautious or bitter.

When social institutions wall him in, he blows down the walls with dynamite, metaphoric or literal. So, he arouses in me a sense of my own individual liberty, how precious it is, how threatened it is, to what extremes I must be prepared to go to protect it.

As he himself says in the novel, the Woodpecker stands for "uncertainty, insecurity, surprise, disorder, unlawfulness, bad taste, fun, and things that go boom in the night." Viewed collectively and in a positive light, these items define a philosophy of life that I much admire, a philosophy that encompasses the rewards of cutting against the grain, the giddy exhilaration of moving against the flow, the boldness of deliberately choosing the short straw, the crazy wisdom involved in taking the advice of the Spanish poet Jiménez when he said, "If they give you ruled paper, write the other way."

Jiménez's statement could have been the Woodpecker's motto, but I doubt if the Woodpecker sensibility could have developed in Spain, or anywhere except the United States. He is quintessentially American. I admire that, as well. I despise the government of the United States, as any intelligent, honorable person must, but I love the land, the people, the culture with all my heart. A Russian cab driver in Los Angeles said to me recently, "This is a good country with bad mistakes." How true.[9]

Robbins ever so succinctly recasts this point about the need for collective perceptual correction or reorientation, in response to a question posed to him by Nicholas O'Connell:

. . . If we want to change things, then *we* have to change. To change the world, you change yourself. It's as simple as that, and as difficult as that. Politics is not going to make anything any better. There are no practical solutions. Sooner or later, we have to have the guts to do the impractical things that are required to save the planet.[10]

How Robbins goes about creating his literary magic is the question most frequently asked by his interviewers, admirers, and detractors. In these interviews, Robbins reveals how his writing process begins and, once begun, how it is refined.

As Robbins reveals, few of these imaginative situations are ever begun with any kind of plan whatsoever. As he tells Michael Strelow:

My formula is to try to avoid formula, to remain open and spontaneous, to allow images and ideas to marinate in the unpredictable but vital waters of the sub-conscious imagination, and to keep myself cleansed of preconceived notions of what a novel should or should not be. Critics maintain such preconceptions, which is why, by and large, they are an impediment rather than an impetus to the evolution of meaningful literary expression.

I'm not implying that I don't revise. My typing finger moves so slowly that if it fell off a cliff it would still be going only two miles an hour. It revises as it creeps along. I try never to leave a sentence until it's as memorable as I can make it, although sometimes that's about as memorable as a line from an Arabic drinking song. Using that slow, painstaking method, it can take me up to three years to complete a novel, but when it's done, it's done. There is no second draft.[11]

For Robbins, the writing always involves an alteration of the act of literary representation itself, an alteration *always* to make it more his own. As he explains and implies in several interviews that follow, this process has to include at least two things. The first is resolving the problem of the illusion of realism effectuated by the abstractionism of two-dimensional, conventional narration. This is done by him, as he suggests to Sinda Gregory, by presenting the real through language on the page in much the same way Jackson Pollock presents the real through pigment on the canvas.[12] The narrative technique employed by him to make this happen, he indicates, is through repeated and tactical collapsing of the distinction between two-dimensional, abstract and three-dimensional, experiential narrative in the storytelling by incorporating intrusive acts such as those of discursive philosophizing, genealogy, and meditation.

The other thing that has to be included in this process of alteration, Robbins tells several of his interviewers, is to create the imaginative space where language can happen[13] so that shape may be given to the postmodern anarchistic counter-idea or the thought of the Other. Preservation of this imaginative space is so important, he insists, because it is where the subjectivity of any one of his characters will be constituted, unhindered, *through the practice of the self.* Accordingly, this is where a postmodern anarchistic, anti-humanist feminine consciousness comes alive in a number of ways in American literature starting in the early Seventies; where a reactionary humanistic feminine consciousness as warning against materialism's ineluctable taint, in the mid-Nineties, nearly scares the pants off us, showing us how close to the abyss of cruelty and inhumanity we have come; where an anti-corporatist-thinking, postmodern anarchistic masculine consciousness in the early Ought's emerges resoundingly, as corrective, to reassure us by giving us hope that things still can be otherwise; where even Huckleberry Finn's consciousness brashly steps forward again, all growed-up and back from the territories—this time wearing the store-bought's of postmodern anarchism's Foucaultean mutation—to throw, at the dawn of the Eighties, a lit stick of dynamite into the midst of our picnic lunch of smug cultural complacency; and where finally, just recently, innocence in the full bloom of its sweetness—far removed imaginatively from the deleterious effect of consensual reality's illusionism—is given the refreshing opportunity to understand how its own very reality—its sweetness—is the basis of consciousness.

Why Robbins continues to engage audiences in this way is a general concern addressed by interviewers. For Robbins there are three principal reasons. The first is that the reading experience of any one of his novels should always lead readers to the moment of awakening. He wants everyone to wake up from the mindlessness and complacency of consensual reality.[14] While the cynical might scoff at the seeming banality of this objective since *every* writer hopes for this sort of reaction, crossing over this cognitive threshold is a necessary preliminary action for Robbins, for it makes one capable of expanding consciousness and experiencing wonder anew.[15] An example of this occurs when readers are confronted, in *Skinny Legs and All*, with the performance function of Turn Around Norman. His actions, implies Robbins, should inspire one to recollect suddenly the wonder of the planet they inhabit. Robbins's sincere hope is that, through his fiction, everyone can reach this point of being *turned on* to full consciousness and, with that consciousness, become joyful.[16]

The second reason Robbins writes, he remarks, is to enable awakened readers, once *tuned in* or in harmony with the world about them, to deal effectively with consensual reality. This fighting the good fight of liberation, as Robbins identifies it for Stefania Scateni,[17] entails three things: 1) comprehending liberation is not from despotic control but rather from thinking of simulation *as* reality; 2) realizing that humor is a doorway to deeper reality, and play is a kind of psychic survival.[18] (When engaged in effectively, both always say yes to life, and no to any kind of shamming or illusion being used to divert attention from what is essential.) Finally, 3) looking out for anomalies always apparent in everyday life, for they call attention to breaches in the continuum of consensual reality.

Two such anomalies are of special importance to Robbins and are mentioned in the following interviews and elsewhere. The first can be heard in

Larry Diamond's account—in *Half Asleep in Frog Pajamas*—of the Malinese Bozo tribe's five-thousand-year-old detailed astronomical knowledge of a star system invisible to the naked eye, a subject discussed by Jessica Maxwell and Robbins.[19] The second can be found in Wiggs Dannyboy's theorizing in *Jitterbug Perfume*. There the function of the brain's cerebrum is presented to indicate a new phase of the evolution of the entire species—rather than to show the end of the brain's evolution as neurological structure.

Robbins's final purpose, as he sees it, is to show how to take control of one's own life—how to *drop out* or gracefully select to be actively detached in regard to consensual reality. This orients the audience to the fiction's value they have in hand, and to its application in the form of practical action in their own lives. The former becomes apparent when they realize fiction is the enchantment that replenishes the wasteland of the mind.[20] The latter becomes apparent when they translate that understanding into an effective means of outwitting fate, turning the tables on despair, and finding fun and meaning in a corrupt world.[21] The Beer Fairy's hierophantic distinction between the explicit and implicit worlds of human epistemological experience is made clear at the end of *B Is for Beer*: "The Ordinary world is only the foam on the top of the real world, the deeper world."[22] This statement may be dismissed by consensual reality's proponents as nothing more than fanciful romanticizing of the stuff of brewskies, but those who take beer seriously know that it is always its bittersweet taste that really quenches thirst, by making palatable what often is not in one's day or even one's life.

To know how to thank adequately all who have been instrumental, one way or another, in helping this volume of interviews come to completion is an art exceeding our present ability. Forgive us, then, if we resort here to simple expressions of gratitude: to you, Mr. Tom Robbins, novelist of the real, for the perfect taco of all your help, genius, insights, and razzle-dazzle, in over half a year of email back-and-forth's; you, magical Alexa, for capturing the exquisite image of Maestra's Maestro that adorns this publication; you, beautiful Dianne, who give it all meaning and leave me right; you, dearest sister Nan and brothers Arty, Malc, and Julian, who are but of memory now; you, Paul, Karen, Zu, Theo, Liz, Jim, Dana, Al, Roy, Kathy S and Kathy L, Stanley and Deb, little Carly, dear friends all; you, other special friends Jill Hagemeier, Jan Seng, Susan Mead, for continued support and encouragement—and still many more, not to forget little-big Jos; you, Tammy, for all your invaluable help, and the rest of the library staff always ready when assistance was needed; you, newly met interviewers and publishers and others who granted permission to reprint the interviews selected for this volume; you, Walter Biggins, our editor, and the rest of the UPM staff, including Shane Gong and Anne Stascavage; you, Jayne Uerling, for special assistance and believing in the value the present volume would offer the *Literary Conversations* series; and, finally, you, Doane College, for offering generous grant support to enable completion of this most enjoyable scholarly endeavor.

LP
BT

Notes

1. (New York: Houghton Mifflin, 1976), 302.

2. With Bruce Van Wynegarden, "The Post-Modernist Outlaw Intellectual," in *Aquarius Revisited: Seven Who Created the Sixties Counterculture That Changed America* (New York: MacMillan, 1987), 240.

3. Ibid. Mr. Robbins has informed us he remains unsure if it was the Beers & Barnes Circus that offered him this early transformative experience. He is certain, however, that he worked some years later in Warsaw, Virginia, as an adolescent roustabout for the Hunt Bros. Circus, where two of his many duties were to scour the back of an alligator and water the llamas.

4. See "Tom Robbins," in their *Alive and Writing: Interviews with American Authors of the 1980s* (Urbana: University of Illinois Press, 1987), 222–39.

5. In our correspondence, Mr. Robbins requested we remind his readers he was using the old baseball term "snake-bit," not "snake-pit," when responding to Sinda Gregory's question at this moment in the interview.

6. McCaffery and Gregory, 226.

7. "Taking Tom Robbins Seriously," *Rolling Stone*, November 17, 1977, 68.

8. "An Interview with Tom Robbins," *Contemporary Literature* 42 (2001): 478–79.

9. "Dialogue with Tom Robbins," *Northwest Review* 20 (1982): 98–99.

10. "Tom Robbins," in his *At the Field's End: Interviews with 20 Pacific Northwest Writers* (Seattle: Madrona, 1987), 276.

11. "Dialogue with Tom Robbins," 99–100. Mr. Robbins asked us to make certain that an answer he gives in the same interview about what a novel must do—that is, that it "make me think, make me laugh, make me horny, and awaken my sense of wonder" (98)—be emended to read (in order that proper attribution of its source be made): "Echoing something a fan wrote to me recently, I ask four things of a novel: that it make me think, etc." Though he offers a correction himself in 2001 at the end of his interview with Russell Reising (484), we are happy to oblige him here by adding that the author of this insight was a "stranger, a woman in the scientific field" who had written to him some time after the publication of his first or second novel.

12. McCaffery and Gregory, 229.

13. Liane Hansen, "Tom Robbins," in *The NPR Interviews, 1995*, ed. Robert Siegel (New York & Boston: Houghton Mifflin, 1995), 18.

14. Jay MacDonald, "Fame and Fortune: Tom Robbins," Bankrate.com, 2007, 4.

15. Stefania Scateni, "Interview with Tom Robbins" [though published in *L'Unitá* (March 1995), available only in manuscript, pagination of which is used here], 3.

16. Rogers, 67.

17. "Interview with Tom Robbins," 3.

18. Gregory Daurer, "The Green Man," *High Times*, June 2000, 67, and Reising, 469.

19. "Tom Robbins's Book of Bozo," *Esquire*, 1995, 18.

20. Daurer, 67.

21. Strelow, 98, and Daurer, 67.

22. (New York: HarperCollins, 2009), 125.

Chronology

1932*   Born Thomas Eugene Robbins on July 22 in Blowing Rock, North Carolina, to George Thomas and Katherine Robinson Robbins.

1937   Robbins writes first short stories, dictated to his mother.

1939   Robbins's four-year-old sister, Rena, dies. He publishes first fiction, a story in the newspaper of the consolidated grades 1–12 Blowing Rock School.

1940   Robbins's twin sisters, Mary Katherine and Marian Elizabeth, are born.

1941   Robbins's family moves to Burnsville, North Carolina, where a new kind of "magic" enters his life when he is allowed to perform odd jobs for a traveling circus, possibly the Beers and Barnes Circus.

1943   Family relocates to Virginia; briefly in Urbana, then Kilmarnock, finally settling in Warsaw, where he does odd jobs for the Hunt Bros. Circus.

1946–49   Robbins attends Warsaw High School, where he plays basketball, is Class Scribe, and is voted Most Mischievous Boy. Covers high school and semi-pro sports for *Northern Neck News*, a weekly paper serving four counties.

1950   Robbins graduates from Hargrave Military Academy, where he is sports editor of the paper and wins Senior Essay medal.

1951   Robbins enters Washington and Lee University, majoring in journalism and writing for college newspaper along with upperclassman Tom Wolfe.

1952   Robbins leaves Washington and Lee at end of sophomore year after failing to win letter in basketball and being reprimanded by his fraternity for bad behavior.

1952–53   Hitchhiking up and down East Coast, Robbins stops briefly in Greenwich Village where he "pretends" to be a poet. Works for

---

* The discrepancy between Mr. Robbins's year of birth appearing in the Library of Congress Cataloging-in-Publication Data and the Chronology above results from previous inaccurate reporting and an LoC rule prohibiting correction of CIP data. Mr. Robbins has assured us his mother first laid eyes on him in 1932.

	Virginia Electric & Power Company, constructing and maintaining substations.
1953	Robbins marries Peggy Waterfield. He enlists in U.S. Air Force to avoid the draft, and is trained in meteorology. He wins Air Force short story contest at Pine Castle Air Force base in Florida. The story is entitled "A Change in the Weather."
1954	Shortly after son Rip is born, Robbins is sent to Korea, where he teaches weather observation to South Korean air force. Traveling frequently to Japan, he develops a lifelong interest in Eastern philosophy and aesthetics.
1955–56	Working in Special Weather Intelligence, Robbins is stationed at Strategic Air Command headquarters in Nebraska. Writes liner notes for regional jazz ensemble, "The New York Jazz Workshop," an ensemble composed of expatriated New York jazz musicians, and wins another Air Force short story prize for a story entitled "A Touch of Red." Divorces Peggy Waterfield.
1957	Honorably discharged from Air Force, despite not receiving customary reenlistment pep talk, Robbins enrolls at Richmond Professional Institute of the College of William and Mary, primarily known as a professional school of art, drama, and music; now it is part of Virginia Commonwealth University.
1958	Robbins writes a weekly column and is named editor-in-chief of college newspaper. He works part-time first for Cokesbury Book Store, then on the sports desk of the Richmond *Times-Dispatch*, Virginia's leading metropolitan daily. Marries Bunnie Roy.
1959	Robbins works full-time for the *Times-Dispatch* while carrying eighteen hours of classes. He begins writing about art and drama. Son Kirk Kerrington is born. Robbins graduates with honors, degree in social science, and accepts job on the copy desk of the *Times-Dispatch*, specializing in international and entertainment news. Reads *On the Road* by Jack Kerouac, a transformative intellectual experience introducing him to ideas of the Beat Generation.
1960	An integrationist in a racially segregated city, Robbins spends his days off secretly doing civil rights work in King William County, while continuing to hang out with artists and bohemians at Richmond's now legendary Village Inn. Begins extensive reading of French avant-gardists, including Rimbaud, Jarry, and Breton. Divorces Bunnie Roy.

1961   Robbins travels to Mexico. Gets into trouble at *Times-Dispatch* for ignoring warnings and selecting photos of black entertainers to illustrate Earl Wilson's nationally syndicated show-business column.

1962   On a whim, Robbins marries Susan Petway Bush, a young woman he had met only once, and drives with her to Seattle where he had been accepted in graduate school at the University of Washington's Far East Institute. Susan has a two-year-old daughter, Kendall, from a previous marriage, and Robbins and Kendall develop a lasting bond. Within days after arriving in Seattle, Robbins is hired by the daily *Seattle Times*, where he works first as a feature editor and later as a critic, specializing in art but also reviewing theater and films. His flamboyant, take-no-prisoners approach to reviewing wins him both friends and detractors. The associate director of the Seattle Art Museum labels him "the Hells Angel of art criticism." This may be partially due to the fact that Robbins is frequently seen riding to art galleries and theaters on a black motorcycle, with little Kendall perched on the back. He also covers Seattle arts for the *Christian Science Monitor*. Overworked, he drops out of graduate school prior to the end of the first quarter in order to concentrate on exploring modern art, including the Northwest school of "mystic" painters which had partially attracted him to Seattle in the beginning. He also develops an interest in hunting wild mushrooms and is a fixture at the Blue Moon Tavern, the Seattle equivalent of Richmond's bohemian Village Inn.

1963   In late summer, in a conducive setting, he ingests 300 micrograms of pure lysergic acid diethylamide-25 (LSD). Later, he would describe that day as "the single most rewarding day" of his life.

1964   "Transformed" by psychedelics, Robbins experiences dissatisfaction with the "straight" world. Separating from Susan and, in autumn, quitting the *Seattle Times*, he moves to New York City, intending to research and write a dual biography and appreciation of the painters Jackson Pollock and Chaim Soutine. He is to complete the research but never to write the book. In New York, he meets Allen Ginsberg and Timothy Leary for the first time.

1965   Moves back to Seattle. There he becomes increasingly involved with the art world, producing a monthly column on the arts for

Seattle Magazine, contributing essays to national magazines such as *Art in America* and *Artforum*, and writing catalogs for museum exhibitions. His monograph on painter Guy Anderson is published by Gear Works Press. No longer impressionistic, his criticism is now hard-nosed, analytical, and formalistic. He divorces Susan Petway Bush.

1966   Robbins works part-time on copy desk of the Seattle *Post-Intelligencer*; hosts a late-Sunday-night radio show, "Notes from the Underground," on KRAB-107.7; and stages happenings (performance pieces), one of which gets him arrested for obscenity, although charges are dropped. Covers the world's first LSD conference, in San Francisco. Enthralled by the Haight-Ashbury scene, he is to become for several years an enthusiastic participant in the West Coast psychedelic counterculture.

1967   Robbins is assigned to review a Doors concert for the *Helix*, an underground newspaper. While writing the review in the wee hours of morning, he has a "literary epiphany." Inspired, he abruptly pulls up stakes and moves with his new girlfriend, Terrie Lunden, to a rural area of Washington to begin writing *Another Roadside Attraction*.

1968–70   Robbins works on his novel, commuting weekends and holidays to the *P-I* copy desk. Marries Terrie Lunden. He finishes *Another Roadside Attraction* in winter of 1970, moves to La Conner, Washington, a fishing village and long-time art colony, in April. With a small advance for his novel, he flies to Japan where he travels for one month.

1971   *Another Roadside Attraction* is published by Doubleday, and is praised in galleys by Lawrence Ferlinghetti and Graham Greene. First review of this work appears in the January 26 issue of the *New Republic*, page 29. Later described by *Rolling Stone* as the "quintessential Sixties novel," it has remained in print. Son Fleetwood is born.

1972   Paperback rights to *Another Roadside Attraction* are bought by Ballantine.

1974   Robbins contributes to *The Story So Far 3*, edited by David Young.

1974–75   Robbins buys back his contract from Doubleday. Phoebe Larmore becomes his agent and negotiates a deal with Bantam Books for his second novel, a work still in progress. Divorces Terrie Lunden.

1976   *Even Cowgirls Get the Blues*, Robbins's second novel, is published by Houghton Mifflin simultaneously in hardcover and
paperback editions, and is lauded by Thomas Pynchon. A year
later, Bantam's mass-market paperback becomes a phenomenal
publishing success. Ted Solotaroff, senior editor at Bantam, excerpts a chapter from *Cowgirls* and issues it in his journal *American Review*. An excerpt from *Cowgirls* also appears in the June
issue of *High Times*.

1977   Robbins is invited to be a contributor to *The Best American Short
Stories 1977*, edited by Martha Foley, and published by Houghton
Mifflin. The first scholarly treatment of Robbins's works appears in
Robert L. Nadeau's "Physics and Cosmology in the Fiction of Tom
Robbins" (*Critique: Studies in Modern Fiction*, vol. 20, no. 1).

1978   Robbins and singer-songwriter James Lee Stanley pay an unau-
thorized visit to Cuba, where, during two weeks in Havana, they
stage short impromptu street concerts, mostly for children.

1979   Robbins's fiction is treated for the first time as subject of a dissertation study. Patricia E. Cleary Miller's Ph.D. dissertation, "Rec-
onciling Science and Mysticism: Characterization in the Novels
of Tom Robbins," is completed in partial fulfillment for her Ph.D.
degree at the University of Kansas, Lawrence. Included in this
work is also an interview with Tom Robbins.

1980   *Still Life With Woodpecker*, Robbins's third novel, is published
by Bantam, and reaches #1 on the *New York Times* trade paperback best-seller list. *Esquire* magazine devotes entire front cover
of its July issue to the book.

1981   Robbins contributes to *The Great American Writers' Cookbook*,
edited by Dean Faulkner Wells, and published by Yoknapa-
tawpha Press. "The Genius Waitress," a tribute essay, appears in
Playboy.

1983   Along with Norman Mailer, Ken Kesey, et al., Robbins is guest
at *Esquire's* 50th Anniversary celebration in New York. Receives
modeling assignment for *Sportswear International*, featured in
September issue.

1984   *Jitterbug Perfume*, Robbins's fourth novel, is published by Bantam. It stays on the *New York Times* best-seller list for several
months.

1985   "The Day the Earth Spit Warthogs," an account of Robbins's raft-
ing and hiking adventure in Africa, is published in *Esquire*, a
magazine in which he is frequently published.

1987   Robbins appears in Alan Rudolph's *Made in Heaven* as a toymak-
        er, a part his friend Debra Winger convinces him to play. Along
        with Hunter S. Thompson, William Burroughs, Allen Ginsberg,
        Ken Kesey, Timothy Leary, and Norman Mailer, Robbins is iden-
        tified as one of the seven principal figures who defined Sixties
        counterculture thinking and the counterculture movement in
        *Aquarius Revisited: Seven Who Created the Sixties Countercul-
        ture That Changed America* by Peter O. Whitmer, with Bruce
        VanWyngarden. Robbins marries Alexa Ann Beyers.

1988   Robbins's tribute essay, "Redheads," appears in *GQ*.

1990   *Skinny Legs and All*, Robbins's fifth novel, is published by Ban-
        tam, and becomes a national best seller. Robbins's "Introduc-
        tion," for Bruce Villick's *A Kiss Is Just a Kiss*, is published.

1991   Robbins publishes *Ginny Ruffner*, an introduction to an exhibi-
        tion catalog for the Linda Farris Gallery, Seattle.

1993   Release of the unabridged audiotape version of *Even Cowgirls
        Get the Blues*, read by Michael Nouri, Dove Audio. Release of
        feature film adaptation of *Even Cowgirls Get the Blues*, directed
        by Gus Van Sant, with narrative voice-over by Tom Robbins.

1994   Tom and Alexa Robbins appear in the brothel scene of Alan Ru-
        dolph's *Mrs. Parker and the Vicious Circle. Half Asleep in Frog
        Pajamas*, Robbins's sixth novel, is published by Bantam. Released
        in limited edition, Bantam publishes *Candy from a Stranger: A
        Tom Robbins Reader*. Robbins contributes to *EdgeWalking on
        the Western Rim, New Works by 12 Northwest Writers*, published
        by Sasquatch Books, Seattle. Tom and Alexa travel to Timbuktu
        to see and experience the legendary city and much-dreaded des-
        tination. It is Robbins's fourth trip to Africa. Throughout the late
        eighties and nineties, he goes on white-water rafting adventures
        all over the globe.

1995   Robbins goes to Australia to attend the Melbourne Writer's Fes-
        tival, October 16–22, and is featured as a speaker at the festival
        and in an interview in the October issue of *She* magazine. At
        the singer's request, Robbins writes the liner notes for *Tower
        of Song*, Leonard Cohen's thirty-year tribute album. Robbins's
        short story, "Moonlight Whoopee Cushion Sonata," appears in
        After Yesterday's Crash: The Avant-Pop Anthology.

1997   Robbins receives the much-coveted Bumbershoot's Golden
        Umbrella Award for "lifetime achievement in the arts." He ap-

pears in the documentary film, *Anthem: An American Road Story*, directed by Shainee Gabel and Kristin Hahn, the complete transcript of which is published by Avon Books under the same title.

1999   Fernanda Pivano, legendary Italian critic, refers to Robbins as "the most dangerous writer in the world." Robbins appears on CD by Gang, an Italian rock group; has speaking part in Alan Rudolph film *Breakfast of Champions*, and is featured in *1 Giant Leap*, a widely circulated film and media event produced by the British rock band of the same name.

2000   *Fierce Invalids Home From Hot Climates*, Robbins's seventh novel, is published, and features Robbins's first male protagonist. Robbins is named on *Writer's Digest* millennial list of "best writers of the 20th century."

2001   Robbins is guest of honor at the *Festival du Livre et du Vin* in Saumur, France. He is interviewed on French radio and TV, and is writer-in-residence for one month at the famed Café Deux Magots in Paris. He wins an Audie for best audio recording of a novel (*Fierce Invalids Home From Hot Climates*), and is honored by the Willamette Writers Association, Portland, Oregon, as "distinguished Northwest writer."

2002   Robbins is included as a subject of biography by Brian Kent in *American Writers: A Collection of Literary Biographies*, Supplement X, edited by Jay Parini.

2003   *Villa Incognito*, Robbins's eighth novel, is published. It becomes number one best-seller in Australia.

2004   Robbins's essay, "In Defiance of Gravity," is published in *Harper's* magazine.

2005   *Wild Ducks Flying Backward: The Short Writings of Tom Robbins*, a collection of works spanning his writing career, is published.

2006   Robbins is named lifetime laureate at Seattle's prestigious Rainier Club. He is nominated for the Dublin Prize, awarded to the best foreign translation of an English language novel (Czech edition of *Villa Incognito*). Writes the introduction to Susan Bernofsky's new translation of Hermann Hesse's *Siddhartha: An Indian Poem*.

2007   Robbins is writer-in-residence at the Seattle *Post-Intelligencer*.

2008   A three-day festival is organized wholly around *Fierce Invalids*

	Home From Hot Climates in San Miguel de Allende, Mexico. Robbins attends, gives keynote address, and teaches workshops.
2009	*B Is for Beer*, Robbins's ninth novel, is published. Inspired by a cartoon in the *New Yorker*, this novel is a children's book for grown-ups and a grown-up book for children.
2010	Robbins delivers the annual English Department–sponsored Lucille Cobb Memorial Lecture at Doane College, Crete, Nebraska.

Conversations with Tom Robbins

Taking Tom Robbins Seriously

Michael Rogers/1976

From *Rolling Stone*, November 17, 1977, pp. 66–71. © Rolling Stone LLC 1977. All Rights Reserved. Reprinted by Permission.

Tom Robbins has already managed two remarkable feats during his brief career as a novelist. His first book, *Another Roadside Attraction*, became, with almost no publicity, an underground classic among a generation not terribly inclined toward the novel form in the first place—perhaps because, in many ways, *ARA*, is the quintessential counterculture novel.

Robbins's second book, *Even Cowgirls Get the Blues*, has found a similarly appreciative audience. And it has also suggested a new way to reach that audience: an object lesson couched in solid sales figures that could help change the nature of American fiction publishing.

Not, in all, a bad track record for a novelist whose previous fiction experience was limited to childhood fantasies and one first place win in an Air Force short story contest. But even so, Robbins remains a relatively mysterious figure; rumors abound among his fans as to his lifestyle and whereabouts, and it took considerable arm-twisting simply to coax him out of his Washington state retreat to do a handful of interviews and appearances for *Cowgirls*.

When Robbins agreed to do a *Rolling Stone* interview, it sounded ideal. Not only did he promise to be an interesting fellow, but from the nature of his novels—unalloyed wordplay and a rich, almost hedonistic use of language—he would probably also be a cinch interview. A counterculture Brendan Behan: just switch on the Sony and let him expound.

What Robbins fan would ever have expected that the new king of the extended metaphor, dependent clause, outrageous pun, and meteorological personification would turn out, on first meeting, to be just about as talkative as a Puget Sound clam?

We meet in San Francisco and drive over the Golden Gate Bridge to see a little-known, found art/curiosa headquarters in Mill Valley: an ideal Robbins oddity dubbed the Unknown Museum that features, among numerous bizarre attractions, an automobile entirely encrusted with sequins.

There are two immediate surprises in our meeting. The first is that Robbins—consummate counterculture novelist—is at least a couple of decades older than his hard-core following. But then he doesn't look to be into his forties; dressed in florescent green track shoes, blue jeans and faded work shirt, he is slim, well-proportioned and just a few inches and ten pounds over the category of "slight." He has an immediately likable, diffident air that persists even with friends; a sense that he's always a touch puzzled by his surroundings—even though it soon grows clear that he knows exactly what's going on and just what he wants to have to do with it.

The second surprise is that by the time we reach Mill Valley, Robbins has managed to utter no more than five or six complete sentences.

My vision of the quick and clean Q&A evaporates in the Marin County sunshine. "I'm not sure," Robbins says, "that I'm *verbal* enough to do a Q&A."

I agree immediately. We're both, I think, in a lot of trouble. He offers that he has just spent the morning with a writer from *People*, and that during those three hours had done more talking than he had done, in total, during the previous three months. He was burned out. "You know," he says softly as we pull into Mill Valley, "I don't think we can do this sitting in a hotel room."

Four weeks later I drive into the small Puget Sound community, an hour and a half north of Seattle, that Robbins has called home for seven years. It is a tiny town, population 650, and surrounded by one of the largest tulip-growing regions on the planet; an area that exports bulbs even to Holland. Each year the fields briefly blaze with color—red, white, yellow, variegated. Briefly, because the blooms are cut as quickly as possible, lest they rob energy from the more profitable bulbs below.

Robbins lives in the heart of town, in a tiny, well-weathered house set back from a narrow side street. The front porch is reached by means of a series of massive granite stepping stones, and the porch itself is almost totally obscured by an aged, thick-set maple.

The town—favored decades ago by a group of painters—is now in transition to a more costly resort for well-heeled weekenders and, in turn, a hangout for long-haired artisans. Longtime residents can be heard to complain that the place is getting to be just a bit too much like Woodstock during the summers.

Robbins tries not to notice. His house is one of the oldest in town—nearly one hundred years—and his writing studio is a house trailer, constructed by a Boeing Company employee and now permanently perched in Robbins's backyard. When Robbins writes, he locks himself into the trailer and hangs a warning sign on the gate. And if summer visitors inquire as to his whereabouts, the locals simply reply that he's gone to, say, Arabia.

"Then the person goes home to L.A. or Missouri," Robbins says, "and writes me to say that 'I came to your house, but you were in Arabia.' I get the letter, but I never know who told them that."

Tom Robbins is a cult writer. And while he doesn't know exactly how that's defined, he knows what it means. It means, for starters, at least four long letters each day from fans, many of whom aver that Robbins's writing has changed their lives. "It's a little embarrassing, and kind of scary," he says, "and you don't know what to say in return. Do you know," he wonders, "if Updike gets letters like that?"

Women write Robbins regularly to say that they *are* Amanda—earth-mother heroine of *ARA*—and that, moreover, they are coming to visit. And another generation is already under way: five or six people have already named their daughters Amanda, in honor of the character. Seven or eight commercial establishments have been named "Another Roadside Attraction," ranging from a vegetable stand in Washington to a California yoga center.

But the final certification of Robbins's cult status is that his fiction inspires offerings. They may come through the mail, they may be left at the door, but however they arrive, they are profuse. His house is already filled with myriad representations of hot dogs (a significant motif in *ARA*) in every medium from polyethylene and plaster to cookbooks and posters. The fallout from *Cowgirls* has just begun, but already it ranges from a bumper sticker that proclaims COWGIRLS NEED LOVING TOO to a cellophane package that hangs unopened over Robbins's writing desk and contains a giant slip-on rubber thumb complete with gaudy red thumbnail, neatly titled "The Motorist's Delight"—an apt representation of the thumbs that adorn *Cowgirls'* heroine.

"I'm going to have to be very careful what I write about in the future," Robbins says. "I just hope I can stay ahead of them. I want to be permanently corruptive and subversive, but it's really *hard*."

Robbins's living room, while fully sixteen feet high, is nonetheless nearly overwhelmed by exceedingly healthy plants. In one corner, a hanging Boston fern enshrouds the back of a wicker chair. A wandering Jew trails down from the ledge of Robbins's sleeping loft so profusely that it brushes the sofa ten feet below. In another corner, some manner of trailing plant has virtually engulfed the right channel speaker of the stereo. And in yet another corner, a spindly avocado has, in a prodigious feat, nearly touched the ceiling.

Did he start that from a pit? Someone asks.

Robbins nods solemnly. About, he says, five years ago. He studies the plant for a moment, squinting up at the apex which now nearly brushes the ceiling. "I suppose," he says, "that I'm going to have to figure out some way to pinch it off."

It is a living room almost cinematically befitting the author of what is, probably, the quintessential counterculture novel. And to have written such a novel is no small achievement—because from 1967 on, authors of every age and stripe have tried and failed to capture the special, elusive feel of the Sixties.

All seemed to founder on the same technical problem. The language and style of the counterculture was so fluid and so wired into the electronic media that by the time a novelist of manners depicted the manners, they had changed. Vocabulary had become passé, and the telling observation had turned embarrassingly obvious. It was enough to make young novelists wonder if McLuhan had been right; they seemed locked into a lively culture that defied successful novelization.

But then Tom Robbins came along. Robbins not only embraced the printed word—he positively smothered it with kisses. *ARA*, over three hundred pages long, was almost nonstop wordplay. Similes and metaphors and personifications and free-hand analogies poured off the pages. And those literary pyrotechnics were wrapped around a collection of larger-than-life characters—from Amanda, the ultimate earth mother, to John Paul Ziller, a bizarre distillation of the stylish desires for primitive lifestyles. And those outlandish characters were deployed in an even more outlandish plot, involving, among other things, the discovery and theft of the body of Christ from the basement of the Vatican and its subsequent reappearance in a small roadside zoo in the American Northwest.

And, most outlandishly of all, the book actually worked. *ARA* begins with a meandering narrative that seems to promise more than it can possibly deliver—yet by the time fifty pages have passed, most readers are hooked.

Robbins's success was his realization that the essence of the counterculture was not manners, but fantasy. And so, while *ARA* contains counter-culture trappings galore—drugs, food, music, fashions, vocabulary—it takes each out to the edge of the mythology that, for one brief moment in the Sixties, looked almost possible.

The long cold Seventies have now cast a far more realistic light on that fantasy. But *ARA* was not, in the first place, a realistic novel. It has, in fact, very little to do with reality. And in the end, that is why it will probably remain the most realistic of the counterculture novels.

Fantasy is, in fact, at the heart of both Robbins's life and work. "I've always wanted to lead a life of enchantment," he says, "and writing is part of that. Magic is practical and pragmatic—it's making connections between objects, or events, in the most unusual ways. When you do that, the universe becomes an exciting place.

"I'm a romantic, and I don't apologize for that. I think it's as valid a way of looking at life as any. And a hell of a lot more fun."

Someone in the room compares the level of reality in Robbins's fiction to that of musical comedy—the reason that people like musical comedy, she says, is that in real life people don't walk down the street and burst into song.

"Not only that," Robbins says immediately, "but it promises that someday people are going to *start* bursting into song when they walk down the street. People like it because they wish they could do it. And I think they *will* do it."

Once Tom Robbins was caught in a telephone booth on the Lower East Side of New York City, surrounded by thugs who clearly meant him harm. His call didn't go through, but he faked a conversation for at least half an hour, waiting for the thugs to depart. They didn't. Finally it got ridiculous—his arm had even fallen asleep—so he hung up the telephone, rushed out of the booth, and started shaking the first thug's hand, pumping it up and down and asking, in slightly hysterical tones, "Do you believe in *angels*?" He rushed over to the second thug, and then the third, repeating the performance. "Do you believe in angels?" The thugs, says Robbins, were so taken aback by this performance that they promptly turned and walked away.

Robbins shared that Lower East Side neighborhood with several indigenous gangs, and one day, while he was walking down the street, he saw a group of Puerto Rican teenagers writing "Duchmen" on a wall.

Robbins walked over, grabbed the chalk, and corrected the spelling. "Oh, boy," he thought then, "spontaneity can get you in a lot of trouble." But the gang members simply said "thank you," and soon thereafter Robbins became something of a street-gang cultural arbiter. "These guys hang around in doorways looking threatening," he says, "but they're really talking about a *lot* of things."

After a day or so in Washington, it grows clear that stories like the above are standard Robbins fare—and if, in the midst of them, one occasionally questions their verisimilitude, in the end it really doesn't matter. Most fiction writers tend to embroider reality a bit, and more often than not, outrageously.

And Robbins's anecdotes are hardly outrageous. In fact—for all his emphasis on spontaneity—one soon suspects Robbins's personal revelations are not exactly off-the-cuff. Robbins talks only when he feels like talking—and even then, in the same brand of well-turned sentence and apt phrase that marks his prose. He continues to apologize for the fact that he is not articulate—that's why, he says, he writes—but it seems more the case that he only articulates when he feels like it—and when he's certain about what's going to come out.

"I don't think writers should talk anyway," he says, and then mentions a recent Nobel Prize winner. "Look at him—ever since he won that award he's been spouting off like some junior college professor on beer and diet pills. He's said that people in our culture should stop listening to intellectuals. Since when have people listened? There hasn't been an intellectual in a position of leadership in this country since Thomas Jefferson. Since Andrew Jackson, in fact, the government has been entirely in the hands of hillbillies and yokels and urban thugs. So who are these intellectuals we're supposed to be listening to?"

Apparently not literary critics—because best-selling Robbins has been treated, thus far, less than kindly by the book review establishment. *ARA* netted good reviews in only a handful of publications, and while *Cowgirls* was more widely reviewed, it received more sneers than raves.

Robbins doesn't seem concerned. He tells a story about a former girlfriend who, in the midst of walking down the street, turned abruptly and announced that, "the trouble with you, Tom, is that you have too much fun."

Robbins suspects that the literary establishment feels the same way. At one point I mention a highly praised novel by an East Coast academic novelist. Robbins shakes his head. The problem, he says, was that it wasn't funny.

But it wasn't *supposed* to be funny, I say. That was the *point*.

Robbins shakes his head again, almost as if puzzled. "But if there's any wisdom in it, it's *bound* to be funny."

Critics complain, he says, that he doesn't write about rootlessness, despair, sexual frustration—but what's wrong, he wonders, "with writing about joy? Why is that any less serious?"

According to Robbins, one book review editor at a major newsweekly refused to review *Cowgirls* altogether—because he could not take it seriously as literature. (The editor subsequently said he decided not to review it because no one on the staff thought it sufficiently interesting.)

"Well," Robbins shrugs, "this delights me, and there's no sour grapes there. If I'm not writing literature, then I don't have the burden of a literary past on my shoulders. I'm free to do whatever I want. And I'm very comfortable in that role."

On our first afternoon in town, Robbins drives us out to a small beach facing the fir-covered islands that dot Puget Sound. We sit, eating a garlicked cheese washed in Idaho river water (that Robbins swears was once the favorite of western badmen), drinking Rainier Ale, and watching Tom's young son, Fleetwood, sink plastic superhero figures into the mushy tan sand at water's edge.

With inexorable Rainier-fueled logic, the conversation proceeds directly to psychedelics. "July 16th, 1963," Robbins says, "was the most rewarding day of my life, because that was the first day I took acid."

In those days, Robbins was newly engaged in hunting edible mushrooms in the forests around Seattle. At about the same time, *Holiday* magazine published an article describing the peculiar consciousness-expanding properties of a mushroom called *Psilocybe*.

Robbins was curious, so he approached an older woman in Olympia, with whom he had hunted fungi and who had, moreover, written a mushroom guidebook. "She looked exactly like Margaret Rutherford," he says. "Knee socks and tweed skirts, and she didn't want to have anything to do with psychedelic mushrooms."

She suggested, however, a nearby university professor conversant with the subject. The professor demurred also, but referred Robbins to a pharmacology professor.

This was pay dirt. The pharmacology professor was an amateur painter, and at the time Robbins was an art critic. They met for lunch, and finally Robbins popped the question.

Forget the mushrooms, the professor answered. There's something else, called LSD-25.

Okay, said Robbins, if I can't have peach pie I'll take apple.

Not so fast, said the professor. This is strong stuff and I need to know you better.

So they met for lunch again, and then the third time they met at a local art gallery and the professor passed on three tablets of what was then perfectly legal Sandoz LSD.

Robbins ate, sat down in a chair, and didn't move again for eight hours, except to visit the bathroom. "And that," he says, "was an odyssey."

"It was so intense that for the first time in my life I couldn't read. I taught myself to read when I was five, because I loved books so much. But all of a sudden I had no interest in either reading or writing. That lasted for about six months, and then I read *Steppenwolf*, and it was the first thing that made any sense at all."

Why?

Robbins smiles. "Hesse has denied that he had any knowledge of psychedelics, but I'm not convinced. I've heard there was a castle in Switzerland where Paul Klee, the painter, and Henri Micheux, the painter and poet—along with several noblemen and noblewomen—used to gather and eat mescaline, I think in the Thirties. And Hesse was around that area and he was a friend of Klee's."

Robbins stares out at Puget Sound briefly. "And so I'm almost certain," he says, "Hesse *had* to be in on that."

In the publishing trade, Tom Robbins is known as a phenomenon—a designation which refers not to the nature of his writing, but rather to its marketing.

In 1971, *Another Roadside Attraction* was published in hardcover by Doubleday and met, as one trade journal politely put it, "an indifferent public." What that meant was that by late 1975, when the hardcover edition went out of print, it had sold only 2200 of the 5000 that had been printed. Even for a first novel, this is the kind of performance that disheartens publishers.

But even as the hardcover version of *ARA* was crashing and burning, a remarkable thing was happening to the Ballantine paperback edition: it was slowly but surely, with the benefit of nothing but word-of-mouth advertising, starting to sell like crazy on campuses and in any city where long-haired, drug-consuming young people gathered. Selling so well, in fact, that by now the paperback of *ARA* has sold over half a million copies.

While *ARA* was starting to soar in paperback, Tom Robbins was at home in Washington, working on a second novel and sufficiently destitute that much of his nutrition derived from midnight raids on local truck farms. One might well think that some astute publisher would have noticed the curious marketing pattern on Robbins's first book and the significant lesson it offered. But it was, finally, Robbins's literary agent who approached Bantam Books and offered to sell them paperback rights to the unfinished second novel.

Selling paperback rights to a "serious" novel before hardcover rights had been sold was unconventional, but Bantam went for it—resulting in an advance sufficient to see Robbins through the book ultimately titled *Even Cowgirls Get the Blues*.

By the time *Cowgirls* was completed, Robbins had, by means of the paperback *ARA*, become an underground celebrity. Anyone who had read *ARA* was, almost certainly, enthusiastically awaiting the second Robbins novel. And so Bantam decided to approach some hardcover publishing houses with the rights to *Cowgirls*. There was, clearly, some money to be made out there.

But almost no one was interested. For starters, the whole deal turned the traditional publishing hierarchy—hardcover first, then paperback a year or so later—upside down. "They said," according to Ted Solotaroff, Robbins's influential young Bantam editor, "that they'd like to *sell* it to Bantam, not *buy* it from Bantam."

But at last a Boston house, Houghton Mifflin, agreed to publish both a small hardcover edition (still necessary to attract the attention of book reviewers and to fill library orders) along with a "quality" or "trade" paperback edition—a midsized book, on nice stock, with a heavy paper cover and a price considerably below hardcover.

It was the first time Houghton Mifflin had done such a thing, but it will likely not be the last. By the time Bantam published their mass-market edition of *Cowgirls*—a smaller version at $2.25—Houghton Mifflin had already moved 170,000 $4.95 *Cowgirls*. And that's not bad business. Past that, there's little to add, besides the fact that Bantam has already purchased rights to Robbins's third novel.

Does Tom Robbins have a life plan, I wonder? Some kind of career set out?

Robbins hesitates. "Not really. If I ever started to think about writing being my career, it would probably stop being fun." He pauses again. "Someday," he says, "I'd like to be a photographer and take still lifes of small toys."

The next day he adds an amendment. He would also like to open a roadside zoo, and while it would necessarily be cheap and tawdry, he would also have two young mathematics prodigies on view, who would stage math contests three times a day.

Tom Robbins was raised in the South, where, by the time he was a teenager, he'd been pulled out of public school on the grounds of general naughtiness and sent to a military academy that bore the motto "Making Men Not Money." Robbins graduated directly into Washington and Lee University in Lexington, Virginia—a Southern gentleman's school often called the Princeton of the South.

Robbins lasted two years at Washington and Lee, until "it finally became apparent that I didn't have the makings of a Southern gentleman"—having, among other transgressions, already been ejected from his fraternity for throwing biscuits at the housemother. Robbins went on the road—hitchhiking and doing construction work—and finally ended up, at age twenty, in Greenwich Village.

He wanted to be a poet. "Which was really pretty laughable. Here I was, twenty years old, from a little town in the South. My pants cuffs were probably way above my ankles, and I thought an Alexandrian couplet was something from which Egyptian babies drank."

Robbins spent his first tenure in New York trying to decide whether to become a beatnik or an advertising man, until the federal government finally suggested a compromise in the form of avoiding the draft by enlisting in the Air Force.

The Air Force taught him meteorology and then sent him to South Korea to teach it to the South Korean Air Force.

"But the South Korean Air Force had no interest whatsoever in meteorology," Robbins says. "If they came to a thunderstorm, they'd fly right through it. No circumnavigation at all; it wasted gas. So we operated a black-market ring instead, dealing in soap and toothpaste and cigarettes. Later I found out that most of it was going to Red China, so I figure that for about thirteen months I was supplying Mao Tse-tung with all his Colgate."

After the Air Force, Robbins went to an art school that no longer exists. "I went back there summer before last, and all three places I'd lived were parking lots. Two places where I lived in Seattle are now parking lots. I feel like someone is going around behind me with an eraser. I just hope they don't catch up."

From art school, Robbins went to work for a Richmond, Virginia, newspaper. "They were very conservative," he says, "and kept their foot on my head pretty well. They wouldn't let me write anything but headlines."

But then a movie star intervened, in the unlikely form of Sammy Davis Jr. "One of my duties at the paper was to edit the Earl Wilson column. Every day I had to pick someone he'd mentioned and go in the library and get a photograph of them, so there'd be a little picture in the column each morning.

"One day, without thinking, I chose Louis Armstrong—hell, everybody loves Louis Armstrong, right? But not in Richmond, Virginia, in the early Sixties. They got some really nasty letters about it, and the managing editor called me in and said: 'Don't run any more gentlemen of color.'

"Well, I thought about that for a couple of weeks and, as I'm a generally rebellious person, I finally slipped in Nat 'King' Cole. And this time they got very angry, and I got very chewed out.

"I waited a couple of months more, until I decided that it was time to get out of the South. It just so happened on that particular day, I read the Earl Wilson column and he mentioned Sammy Davis Jr.—who had just married a Scandinavian actress.

"Perfect. I slipped him in, and that was that. Two weeks later I left for Seattle."

On the day we arrive at Robbins's house, a millionairess from the Southwest is buried in her Ferrari. Robbins—who seems to collect this kind of lore like a magnet—merely nods at the news. "Good hunting," he says, "for the archaeologists of the future."

How, someone wonders, would Robbins like to depart?

Robbins doesn't hesitate. "I would like to be shot out of a circus cannon, like the Great Zacchini, into an open grave. I'd like streamers of flowers tied to my feet, and everybody sitting around the open grave eating watermelon."

And somebody selling popcorn?

Robbins shakes his head seriously, emphatically. "No commercialism."

So how did a naïve southern boy wind up in Washington?

"Seattle was the farthest place from Richmond on the map without leaving the country. And I couldn't afford to leave the country."

Robbins studies me briefly, from the corner of his eye, to determine whether I'm content with that answer.

"That wasn't the total reason," he continues after a moment. "I'd studied in art school about Morris Graves and Mark Toby and the other painters from this area, who were collectively called mystic. And I was intrigued about what kind of landscape could produce a school of mystic painters.

"It was a wise choice. Everybody else I knew who left the South for the West came to San Francisco. I was obstinate enough not to do that. Seattle is really a sweetheart of a city, and because I was from the East, and they were self-conscious about their culture, I found I could do anything I wanted."

Robbins drove into town on a Friday night and the next Tuesday started working at a local paper, reviewing everything from painting and sculpture to opera, symphony, ice shows, circuses, hootenannies, and rodeos. Robbins was really only qualified in painting and sculpture, but he leapt into the other areas with such gusto that the conductor of the Seattle Symphony soon invited him to a dinner party just to see what sort of person could get so worked up about Rossini. "Actually," Robbins says, "the only reason I liked Rossini was because he looked so much like Robert Mitchum."

"I love it," Robbins says, "when people say the novel's dead, because I feel so free—sort of necrophiliac."

If it's dead, it can't hurt you.

"That's right. You can just have fun with it. And it can't hurt you either."

But Robbins, obviously, doesn't really think the novel is dead. "Shaw said fifty years ago that the future of the novel depended on how well it transcended the tyranny of plot. Since then, lots of people have written boring, plotless novels that only the friends of the authors have read.

"But then Brautigan came along and wrote *Trout Fishing in America*, which had no plot, no character development, none of the things that are taught as necessary to the novel—and yet for many people it was as hard to put down as a suspense thriller. I think that was a real milestone in Western literature.

"My books have plot but they don't *depend* on plot, and I think this is important. If you're only interested in plot, it's much easier to go to TV or the movies."

As a transplanted Virginian, Robbins did art criticism for the *Seattle Times* for two and a half years—and then, following his encounter with the psychedelic products of the Sandoz firm, he quit, in rather the same fashion as the young psychiatric intern Dr. Robbins quits his job in *Cowgirls*: "I called in well one day. 'What do you mean, well?' Well, I've been sick ever since I've been working there, and now I'm well, and I won't be coming in anymore."

Robbins returned to New York and the Lower East Side, and chipped away at a book on Jackson Pollock. But after a year or so, he found himself reading *Sometimes a Great Notion* while lying on a cot in his tenement. "I started to hear the raindrops beating on the ferns," Robbins says, and shortly thereafter he was back in Seattle.

In Seattle he wrote a column for *Seattle Magazine*—a space over which he ranged freely, ultimately including, among other things, neon signs, posters, and greeting cards.

Robbins considers those columns his first good criticism, and indeed they led, in short order, to a letter from Luther Nichols, the West Coast editor for Doubleday.

"I've always had this fantasy," Robbins says, "of going to a mailbox and taking out this letter and having it change my life." In retrospect, Luther Nichols's letter probably qualifies, because Nichols had a simple question: was Robbins interested in writing a book?

Robbins was, indeed, but when the two met, it became clear that Nichols was interested in a book about art. Robbins said he was more interested in writing a novel. Nichols asked what that novel might be about. And then Robbins launched into a description of a bizarre story involving the theft of Christ's body from the Vatican catacombs.

That sounds intriguing, Nichols said. When can I see it?

Robbins told him it was still a little rough—and promptly went home and started writing.

"Nature is tantric," Robbins suggests one afternoon as we're driving north in his convertible. "The water on earth exists because hydrogen, with only one electron, is lonely and needs oxygen."

The observation leads promptly to a discussion of the chemical concept of oxidation-reduction reactions, and Robbins listens carefully to an explanation of that process from the science student in the car. "So is that what bonds hydrogen and oxygen?" he asks finally.

"No," says the science student. "That's when charge is transferred between two atoms."

"They are in love?" Robbins wonders.

"Well," she says, with some hesitation, "it's like they both need something. One has too much and one has too little."

Robbins nods, satisfied. "That's what I said."

When Robbins received his advance check for *ARA*, he quit his job and went to Japan to see the famous white cranes. He was disappointed. The entrance to the reserve was in the center of the largest Coca-Cola billboard he'd ever seen.

Mt. Fuji was an immense pile of Fanta grape cans. "And," Robbins says, nodding toward the photographer in the room, "you'd save a lot of money on developing film in Tokyo. You'd just have to hang it out on the line overnight. The air is photochemical."

Near the end of his visit to Japan, Robbins walked into a Zen temple and asked the caretaker if he could meet the priest. "There's no priest here anymore," the caretaker replied, and only after Robbins departed did he realize the caretaker *was* the priest.

"Jung," Robbins says, "said the one thing all his patients had in common was the lack of spiritual life. Maybe the lack of a real spiritual life is why the West is so neurotic. (Although we're no more neurotic than the East anymore—Japan's worse.)

"After some investigation, I was flabbergasted to find that Christianity isn't really our religious heritage—paganism is. And it all stopped somewhere back about four thousand years ago—or at least the matriarchies did. Paganism didn't really stop until the birth of Christ.

"I think maybe the carnival—the kind they had in the rural South—and the circuses were really the last vestiges of pagan celebrations. A dull, boring, vacant lot would suddenly fill with these strange people, and tents and banners and flags, and that night it would light up with neon. It was a magical transformation, and I loved it.

"I really believe I'm a pagan at heart, and when this next book is finished, I plan to go to the British Isles and devote a couple of years to Nordic and pre–Anglo Saxon paganism.

"I don't believe in going back—I think that retreat into the past is both sentimental and dangerous. But I think we left something back there—the thread of identity, perhaps—which we might go back and pick up again."

Even Cowgirls Get the Blues is the story of Sissy Hankshaw, a young woman gifted with outsized thumbs that immediately earn her a place in the pantheon of great American hitchhikers. But the thumbs also create considerable difficulty for Sissy, and after much personal travail, she joins a group of self-sufficient cowgirls on their ranch in the Dakotas—only to find herself involved in the benign kidnapping of the last remaining flock of whooping cranes.

Cowgirls has received far more attention, and far more criticism, than *ARA*. Many readers feel that *Cowgirls* wanders too far from the leisurely plotting that made *ARA* a gentle, but irresistible, page turner—and that Robbins's stylistic flamboyance has crossed over into self-indulgence.

The consistent exception to that reaction is among women. Women, rather more than men, appreciate *Cowgirls*, and that's probably only fair—because Tom Robbins, clearly, appreciates women.

Robbins is a connoisseur of the female, in the nicest sense, and it is in fact difficult to keep precise track of the various women who populate Robbins's life story. "I'm much closer to woman than to men," he says. "It's easier to be playful with women, because women aren't under the pressure that men are to be serious—because we all know they're dumb, and et cetera . . . ." The narrator's unrequited yet unstinting love for earth-mother Amanda in *ARA* seems pure Robbins—and in the last paragraph of that book, Amanda's ambiguous deification reads almost as a twist on the old joke about the fellow who's seen God: "Well, first of all, *she's* . . . ."

Before Fleetwood was born, Robbins hoped dearly for a girl—afraid that he would find it difficult to relate to a boy. Robbins had even selected girls' names—the leading contender, as he recalls, being Cinema. When the nurse told him the baby was male, he cried.

But it's clear that a special bond has developed between Robbins and Fleetwood, who is now six. "He was my Zen master," Robbins says. "They can do that, you know. At about four months or so, they start making these motorboat sounds," Robbins smiles. "Beautiful music."

Robbins no longer lives with Fleetwood's mother, but they share joint custody. Now, Robbins says, he always wants to have a child around—and he finally understands why Picasso was still making babies at seventy.

"My mother has stories that I wrote when I was five," Robbins says, "that I dictated to her in a Snow White and the Seven Dwarfs scrapbook. She still has it in her cedar chest.

"I found one of those stories recently. I can't remember the title, but it was about a pilot who crashed on a desert island, and there was a cow on the island. A brown cow, with yellow spots.

"The pilot was starving to death, because there wasn't anything to eat. So he considered eating the cow. But he'd actually gotten to like the cow so well that he couldn't eat it. And so they trained themselves to eat sand together, and they lived on as friends.

"I wouldn't find that story out of place in what I'm doing now, and so I guess I haven't changed all that much. I had a very rich fantasy life as a child. And I still do as an adult."

While Robbins is the perfect host during our Puget Sound stay, it's clear by the end of our visit that he's said everything he's going to say.

We occupy his living room for three or four additional hours, but during those hours the people talking are the visitors. Robbins listens with interest, but he shows little tendency to reciprocate.

Finally we excuse ourselves and go out onto the street, to walk down the hill to our inn. Robbins follows us out, and farewells are exchanged.

And it's only then—once we've passed over the granite stepping stones, stooped under the boughs of the massive maple, and stepped out onto the tiny side street—that Robbins deploys his parting line.

"Listen," he calls from the porch. "You can tell people that my goal is to write novels that are like a basket of cherry tomatoes—when you bite into a paragraph, you don't know which way the juice is going to squirt."

I pause briefly on the dusty Washington street. That's a transparently obvious, carefully prepared closing quote—delivered, moreover, just at the closing. And despite the fact that I kind of like it, I resolve firmly that I'm simply not going to use it in this story.

Dialogue with Tom Robbins

Michael Strelow/1981

From *Northwest Review* 20 (1982): 97–102. Reprinted by the permission of *Northwest Review*.

Michael Strelow: How did you get started as a novelist?

Tom Robbins: I started before I was old enough to know any better. My muse was a cradle-robber, a child-molester. She seduced an innocent, blue-eyed, tow-headed, pre-literate tot and turned him into a paragraph junkie. By the time I was four I had written all of the works now attributed to Hermann Hesse. That's a lie, of course, but by four I truly was in love with books. I couldn't decipher them yet but I liked the way they looked, felt and smelled, and my idea of ecstasy was to have my parents read out aloud.

When I was five, somebody gave me a Snow White and the Seven Dwarfs scrapbook. Instead of pasting pictures in it, I put in stories. I dictated the stories to my mother and she wrote them in. Not long ago, my mother told me that when my muse would visit, she'd have to interrupt her ironing, cooking, whatever she was doing, and take dictation. Sometimes she'd rephrase a sentence to make it, in her opinion, "sound better," but I always remembered verbatim what I'd dictated and if so much as one word had been altered I'd throw a tantrum until my mother changed it back to the way I had it originally. When I mentioned this recently to my editor at Bantam, he said, "My God, Robbins, you haven't changed in thirty years!"

As a child, I wrote the beginnings of countless novels. In adolescence I stopped creating fiction and channeled all that energy into basketball and cheerleaders, still two of my favorite things in this world. Fashions come and go, come and go, but the length of the cheerleader skirt remains constant, and it is upon that abbreviated standard that I base my currency of joy. Yes, yes, but I digress. Later, I expanded my interest to include journalism, painting, mythology, psychedelic drugs and mysticism. Then, in my late twenties, I ran into my old love, the novel, and we have been inseparable ever since.

Strelow: How does the process of a new book start now?

19

Robbins: If authors aren't writing enough of the kind of books one wants to read, then one has to write them oneself. That might be the only good reason for ever writing a novel. Otherwise, why bother? Unless you're Sidney Shelton contracting to manufacture another best-seller so that you can install a nuclear reactor on your yacht.

Personally, I ask four things of a novel: that it make me think, make me laugh, make me horny, and awaken my sense of wonder. If many months have passed in which I've not encountered such a book, I know it's time to try to write one. I take out a sheet of blank paper and simply commence.

Strelow: What calculations, thinking, goes into making a character work—come alive? Are they based on people you know?

Robbins: My major characters tend to be the sort referred to as "larger than life." Some waggy reviewer once suggested that when we say "larger than life" what we really mean is "unbelievable." I disagree. I'm fortunate enough to know personally people who are larger than life. And I believe in them more than I believe in people who are merely life-sized. Some of those people I have used as *partial* models for characters, and there is a little of my own personality in every character, male or female, that I create, but for the most part, they are products of my imagination.

Strelow: Which of your characters submit to their fates most graciously? (Is it cunning? resilience? grandly perpetuated illusion? what? that makes us succeed or fail at being alive?)

Robbins: I prefer characters who outwit their fates. Outwit rather than submit to. If we must submit, however, do let it be graciously. And a grandly perpetuated illusion is probably preferable to a mediocre reality.

We succeed at being alive only when we enjoy life. Anyone except certain existentialists and guilt-ridden liberals can enjoy life when it is easy. The trick is to enjoy it when it is hard. Fate gave Sissy Hankshaw (in *Even Cowgirls Get the Blues*) abnormally large thumbs. She didn't submit to her deformity, she turned the tables on it, exploited it, made it work for her, had fun with it, was fulfilled by it, pushed it all the way to glory. That's successful living. That's wisdom.

Strelow: What emotions does the Woodpecker character arouse in you?

Robbins: Those emotions associated with the power—the elation—of positive thinking. The Woodpecker is a man who refuses to suffer. Or perhaps I should say, the Woodpecker suffers as all of us must, but he refuses to let it warp him. Or trivialize him by making him cautious or bitter.

When social institutions wall him in, he blows down the walls with dynamite, metaphoric or literal. So, he arouses in me a sense my own individual liberty, how precious it is, how threatened it is, to what extremes I must be prepared to go to protect it.

As he himself says in the novel, the Woodpecker stands for "uncertainty, insecurity, surprise, disorder, unlawfulness, bad taste, and things that go boom in the night." Viewed collectively and in a positive light, these items define a philosophy of life that I much admire, a philosophy that encompasses the rewards of cutting against the grain, the giddy exhilaration of moving against the flow, the boldness of deliberately choosing the short straw, the crazy wisdom involved in taking the advice of the Spanish poet Jiménez when he said, "If they give you ruled paper, write the other way."

Jiménez's statement could have been the Woodpecker's motto, but I doubt if the Woodpecker sensibility could have developed in Spain, or anywhere except the United States. He is quintessentially American. I admire that, as well. I despise the government of the United States, as any intelligent, honorable person must, but I love the land, the people, the culture with all my heart: A Russian cab driver in Los Angeles said to me recently, "This is a good country with bad mistakes." How true.

Strelow: What things, conditions, etc. can injure your writing?

Robbins: Talk hurts. One can talk all the juice out of one's prose. Literary conversation not only drains energy, it can generate a mephitic smog of self-consciousness. That's one reason why I seldom speak with interviewers.

Aside from loose talk and the inescapable interruptions of daily life, the thing most injurious to my writing is a shortage of good cigars.

Strelow: Is there any formula you follow to be the best writer you can be? i.e. constant revision? looking for what in revision?

Robbins: My formula is to try to avoid formula, to remain open and spontaneous, to allow images and ideas to marinate in the unpredictable but vital waters of the sub-conscious imagination, and to keep myself cleansed of preconceived notions of what a novel should or should not be. Critics maintain such preconceptions, which is why, by and large, they are an impediment rather than an impetus to the evolution of meaningful literary expression.

I'm not implying that I don't revise. My typing finger moves so slowly that if it fell off a cliff it would still be going only two miles an hour. It revises as it creeps along. I try never to leave a sentence until it's as memorable as I can make it, although sometimes that's about as memorable as a line from an Arabic drinking song. Using that slow, painstaking method, it can take me up to three years to complete a novel, but when it's done, it's done. There is no second draft.

Strelow: Rain, blackberries, mushrooms, caves, ranches, etc.—things Northwest—abound in your novels. Why have you used these so extensively as opposed to, say, the stuff of the East, your childhood, your university days?

Robbins: I suspect that very little happens during one's university days that is worth writing about. It is in every respect a transitional time, a generally superficial and secondary rite of passage that has little or no connection to that iridescent wolf's head we call "soul."

The university experience can be valuable, to be sure, but it is insular and fairly predictable. And as Robert Bly said, not many of us have any consciousness until we're past the age of twenty. If you don't eventually get out of academia, you may never have any. Student writing seems to be bound by *Holden Caulfield at Princeton* on one side and *Animal House* on the other. Going to the campus for a novel is like going to a barber college for a haircut. Of course, a good writer, one who can make ideas dance and language sing, can write interesting prose about anything. A telephone pole, a watermelon, the dean's wife, *anything*.

Events, images, characters and places from my southeastern childhood do pop up in my novels occasionally. Generally, though, the stuff of the West is a wilder stuff. It speaks to my imagination more directly and with greater poetic authority.

Let John Updike write about what it's like to go through a divorce in upper middle-class Connecticut, let Richard Price write about what it's like to pick cockroach legs out of spaghetti sauce in the Bronx. For better or worse, I'll build my literary house from cedar root and cloud totem and Zen yo-yo and mushroom dream—and pray that I have enough sense to turn off the neon sign on the roof when the structure starts to rot and slide into the slough.

Strelow: Do you have any movie plans for your books? Or, more broadly, can you conceive of other forms coming out of any or all the three novels—plays, theater of any sort, even collaborations? That is, are you willing to let go of the literal word for any of the hard-won blank pages you've filled with very successful novels?

Robbins: Each of my novels has been optioned by film companies and there is a lot of talk about going into production, but I've learned that Hollywood is 99 percent talk, so I'll believe it the night I have to decide what to wear to the premiere. I would enjoy the money and I'm curious about the process, but I'd be just as happy if no novel of mine is filmed.

Of all the ways that we can spend our hours on this little planet, reading is among the most satisfying and magical. In my books I try to provide a reading experience, one that cannot be duplicated in any other medium. Despite their abundance of visual imagery, my books rely upon literary effects. There is the book and then there is the plot. I strive to keep the plot secondary to the book itself. My books have plots but they don't *depend* on plots. That is what is different about them. To translate such a novel into cinema or theater would be no easy task, and major alterations would be required. Unlike many writers, I'm not bothered by the prospects of such changes—provided they were done artistically—because I recognize that literature and cinema are vastly different media. In my heart, however, I'd prefer that the size of Sissy's thumbs never be pinned down by a camera. Certainly, I'd never write the screenplay.

Strelow: A question about technique and writers you read and admire. You create special definitions by catalog (moon, p. 4; sexual love/security, p. 14; Sunday and the Sunday papers, pp. 22–23—all in *Still Life With Woodpecker*) and these definitions come back and make the story move in a narrative way. Shakespeare does this; Homer, too, I suppose. But is there some author, maybe of this century, whose work you admire and return to to get pumped up again. And did you get this definition by catalog from someone? the author you admire?

Robbins: "Definition by catalog" is not something I've ever thought about. I guess it's just something I naturally do. If I was influenced in that technique by another writer, it was entirely unconscious.

There are dozens of writers whom I admire, and there are some to whom I often turn to prime the pump, to arouse me and get the fluids flowing. I'm thinking now of Norman Mailer (I'm at odds with him philosophically, but nobody muscles words around quite like Mailer), Blaise Cendrars, James Joyce, Anaïs Nin (the early pages of *Seduction of the Minotaur*), Ishmael Reed and the Spanish poets. First and foremost, though, would be Henry Miller. The establishment critics hate Miller. They deny his magnificence because he is an active threat to their values, both personal and literary. I would like to think that I might be capable of presenting a similar threat. To be eternally subversive, that should be my goal.

Strelow: Other questions come readily to mind, but we agreed to keep this short. Is there anything you'd like to add?

Robbins: One thing. Saul Bellow has been sneering in public at those writers who, in his words, "have succumbed to pop reality." I suppose I am one of them. I have not the slightest objection to being linked to "pop reality" and I'd like to tell you why.

With the exception of Tantric Hinduism, every religious system in the modern world has denied and suppressed sensuality. Yet sensual energy is the most powerful energy we as individuals possess. Tantric saints had the genius and the guts to exploit that energy for spiritual purposes. Food, drink, drugs, music, art, poetry, and especially sex, are used in Tantra in a religious manner. Tantrikas perfect the techniques of sensual pleasure and use the energy released as fuel for their God-bound vehicle, their rocket ride to enlightenment.

Pop culture, in somewhat the same way, may be exploited for serious purposes. Pop reality has great energy, humor, vitality, and charm. When it comes to liberating the human spirit, sensitizing experience and enlarging the soul, pop reality has one hell of a lot more literary potential than Bellow's earnest moralizing, all stuffy and dour.

Strelow: One final question, please. Are you concerned with immortality? How important is it that your books live on after you are gone?

Robbins: In the next life I hope to be concerned with far more important things than whether or not people are reading my novels. Did you know that after you die, your hair and your nails continue to grow? It's true, they do. But your phone calls taper off.

An Interview with Tom Robbins

Larry McCaffery and Sinda Gregory/1982

From *Alive and Writing: Interviews with American Authors of the 1980s* (Urbana: University of Illinois Press, 1987), 222–39. Copyright 1987 by the Board of Trustees of the University of Illinois. Used with permission of the University of Illinois Press.

Some writers make piles of money, others are canonized by the literary establishment, but very few are as beloved by their audience as Tom Robbins. His fans embrace his books with a devotion and fervor that writing these days rarely elicits. The source of this adoration comes mainly from the philosophy that permeates his fiction, a philosophy that celebrates the power of human consciousness to find laughter, transcendence, and something of interest in everything we come in contact with. Robbins's philosophy is unabashedly exuberant and joyful, full of play and the sense that the universe is filled with all sorts of mysterious harmonies and passions that Western rationalism—with its emphasis on consistency and logic—trivializes and distorts.

Although this effervescent quality has led some critics to dismiss his novels as pop fare for adolescents, Robbins's work is deceptively sophisticated both in terms of its central thematic concerns and in its relentless drive to develop an aesthetic appropriate to its vision. All of Robbins's novels can be shown to explore many of the most basic issues that define our existence: What is the nature of sexuality, and what is the relationship between the male and female aspects we all share? How can people break free of the systems (political, spiritual, social) that repress our natural passions and sense of play, that rigidify belief into dogma, that encourage us to stop personal exploration? Robbins's method of presenting these issues—with its nonstop verbal pyrotechnics, its digressive structure, its authorial intrusions, and its general refusal to "contain" events within the usual framework of causality and linearity—*is* playful and full of surprises; but such methods emerge naturally from Robbins's conviction that the real enemy facing most people today is the threat of standardization and manipulation. "We all have the same enemy," as one character puts it in *Even Cowgirls Get the Blues*. "The enemy is the tyranny of the dull mind."

Despite a generally positive critical reception, Robbins's first novel, *Another Roadside Attraction* (1971), was only a modest success until the paperback edition gradually found its audience (primarily among college students). The book's outlandish plot—the mummified body of Christ is discovered in the basement of the Vatican and is subsequently sent into the stratosphere in a hot-air balloon piloted by the philosopher/proprietor of a roadside hot dog stand—contains myriad digressions and diversions. But here, as in later work, the plot itself is of secondary importance to its manner of presentation. One of Robbins's characters explains this emphasis on style by noting, "Those folks who are concerned with freedom, real freedom . . . must use style to alter content. If our style is masterful, if it is fluid and at the same time complete, then we can re-create ourselves, or rather, we can re-create the Infinite Goof within us. We can live *on top* of content, float above the predictable responses, social programming and hereditary circuitry."

Even Cowgirls Get the Blues (1976) found a much larger audience at once, partially due to the irresistible appeal of its protagonist, Sissy Hankshaw, a young woman with a monstrously large thumb and a taste for the open road and high adventure. As she hitchhikes the country looking for intellectual and sexual enlightenment, she conveys the spirit of spontaneity and the willingness to explore the eccentric that characterizes the maverick hero and heroine of Robbins's next novel, *Still Life With Woodpecker* (1980), a book about redheads, pyramid power, and the boundless mystery inherent in the most ordinary objects. In all three of these novels, as well as in *Jitterbug Perfume* (1984)—which takes as its modest theme the search for immortality—there is a fascination with the infinite variety of shapes into which reality is constantly transforming itself. Robbins offers his readers a vision of life as a glorious but ultimately mysterious adventure—"Mystery is part of nature's style," says a character in *Another Roadside Attraction*. "Behind everything in life is a process that is *beyond* meaning. Not beyond understanding, mind you, but beyond meaning." Life, then, is a short but exciting trip, especially rewarding for those willing to take the metaphysical outlaw's pledge to "stand for uncertainty, surprise, disorder, unlawfulness, bad taste, fun and things that go boom in the night."

Because his fiction is so full of acrobatic, slaphappy energy, we were expecting Robbins himself to be a pretty wild character. When we met him at his home in a small fishing village outside Seattle in June 1982, we found a reflective, soft-spoken individual, still possessing a trace of a North Carolina accent he acquired as a boy. While we admired the artwork in his living room (Andy Warhol prints of Mao and of Marilyn Monroe, along with several of his own paintings) and bathroom (a framed cover of the *National Enquirer* featuring the headline "Vatican Considers Sainthood for Elvis"), Tom finished taping some Beatles music for an upcoming trip to Mexico, concluded a conversation with two young visiting writers, opened us all some beers, and generally puttered about, probably giving himself a few minutes to get a feel for us. It wasn't an easy conversation for him or for us at first, but after we exchanged some pleasantries about his beloved Seattle Sonics, our beloved San Diego Padres, and our mutual passion for rock and roll, we were ready for literary topics and a delicious salmon dinner at the local seafood restaurant. Gradually it became clear that, beneath the shy, boyish demeanor, Tom Robbins *is* a wild character ever ready to take off on whatever adventures the Infinite Goof has in store for him.

Larry McCaffery: What's a successful popular writer like you doing living in a remote fishing village up here in the Northwest?

Tom Robbins: I suppose I could live anywhere in the world and do what I do, so apparently I live here by choice. Here's one reason: In the summer, during the relatively warm months, I can work until 4:30 or 5 in the afternoon, get my sleeping bag and a quart of ale and some bread and cheese, go out walking across the fields until I come to what used to be an island—it's landlocked now—and walk into the woods and work my way up across the crown of this island; eventually I come out on the other side on a grassy cliff and spread my sleeping bag down in the soft grass overlooking a deep-water slough. When the moon rises, I can watch beavers playing in the moonlight, slapping their tails in the water; minks frolicking and large salmon jumping. There's a great blue heron that roosts on a dead tree spar almost above my head. Nobody's around, it's like wilderness, and yet it has only taken me twenty or twenty-five minutes to walk to this spot. And the next morning, in the same amount of time, I can be back at my desk writing; or I can drive to Seattle and within an hour and a half be going to galleries, eating in fine restaurants, seeing first-run movies, shoplifting lingerie or objets d'art, girl-watching, kicking the gong around, whatever. It's the best of both worlds.

Sinda Gregory: The rainy season doesn't get you depressed?

TR: Great weather for ducks? No, contrary to popular opinion, ducks don't like rain, but it's ideal for writers. It reduces temptation. During the rainy months you're forced to stay indoors. You turn inward. It's a cozy feeling, very comfortable and introspective. In life as in literature, I prefer wet to dry. And, of course, living out here in Monsoon Central, I can be as secluded as I need to be.

LM: Do you feel you need this sense of seclusion to write?

TR: Yes, very much so. I think it's important to live far from the centers of ambition, to keep away from literary politics and the sort of social contacts that can put the wrong emphasis on one's work.

SG: Do you mean emphasis on the commercial aspects of writing?

TR: Maybe "commercial" is not the right word. I don't object to commercialism unless it compromises a writer's personal truth or native style. Trevanian's *Shibumi* is an absolutely delicious novel and it's commercial to its core. Have you ever noticed that nothing upsets an intellectual as much as discovering that a plumber is enjoying the same book he or she is? The literati are too insecure to ever admit liking a book that isn't inaccessible or esoteric. At any rate, I'm not talking about commercialism so much as egoism, the pathetic desire to be more highly regarded than one's peers, the neurotic need to be lionized at cocktail parties and favorably reviewed in the correct periodicals. When we are trapped in the ego, our finest energy goes into these foolish competitive things instead of into our work, or, more importantly, into the development of our higher consciousness. When a writer is more interested in the reaction to his words than in the words themselves, he's a victim of misplaced emphasis.

LM: It's surely no coincidence that so many West Coast writers—you, Ursula Le Guin, Gary Snyder, and others—have concerned yourselves with counterculture values and Oriental philosophy and religion. Do you ever think of yourself as a regional writer?

TR: Not really. You know the painter Jacques Louis David had a room, a studio, that overlooked the square where the major guillotine was located in Paris before the Revolution. And he would sit up there all day and watch heads being lopped off, blood flooding the cobblestones. Then he would turn to his easel and paint those very sweet portraits of members of the court. Now there was a man who was rejecting his environment. Most artists have a more direct dialogue with their environment than David, and so do I. But while there is a sense of place in my work, and that place is the Northwest, I see myself not as regional but American.

SG: Wouldn't you agree, though, that people living out here on the West Coast are more likely to be influenced by Oriental ways of thinking and living?

TR: Well, the Northwest is, after all, perched on the Pacific rim facing the

Orient rather than Europe, and that's bound to affect people in all sorts of ways. A lot of my orientations are Asian rather than European—but they were leaning that way before I moved here. Maybe that's one of the reasons *why* I moved here. Somebody suggested that my penchant for writing episodically came from the influence of Kurt Vonnegut, but I never read Vonnegut until after I wrote my first novel. In fact, that abbreviated, episodic style of writing came to me, in part, from the Zen koan, through John Cage. Back in Virginia, I read *Silence*, in which Cage made use of the Zen koan form, and that influenced me in that direction early on. Later, out here, the Tibetan concept of Crazy Wisdom became fairly central to my way of thinking, and so did aspects of Taoism and Tantra. I'd say that anyone who lives out here who *isn't* influenced by the Far East is behaving a bit like David.

SG: You grew up in the rural South. What was that experience like?

TR: I grew up in small Southern towns. I was born in Blowing Rock, North Carolina, a very interesting place because nine months of the year it was like Dogpatch. Literally. It was Appalachia all the way, impoverished, ignorant, populated by men who beat their wives and drank too much—a rather mean place, abounding with natural beauty and colorful characters, but violent, snake-pit* and sorrowful, over all. In summer, it became transformed into a wealthy resort, and from June through Labor Day there was nothing on the street but Cadillacs and Rolls-Royces and Mercedes and Lincoln Continentals. There were high-fashion boutiques there, whose owners were from Paris and Palm Beach. Glamorous men and women who wore diamonds and played tennis and golf. There was a movie theater that for three months showed first-run films as soon as they opened in New York and Los Angeles; the other nine months, it was closed. So every June there would be this dramatic transformation, and the dichotomy between the rich, sophisticated scene and the hillbilly scene affected me very much. It showed me how the ordinary suddenly could be changed into the extraordinary. And back again. It toughened me to harsh realities while instilling in me the romantic idea of another life. And it left me with an affinity for both sides of the tracks.

SG: Did growing up in the South have any specific effect on your writing?

TR: From my perspective today I can see that the *juice* of my fiction comes out of the South, but I felt so repressed in the South that I'm not sure that if I had remained there I would ever have found a way to channel that juice. Virginia, where I spent a lot of time in my youth, is a fairly repressive place.

---

* Mr. Robbins asked us to remind readers that he was using the old baseball expression, "snake-bit," here instead of "snake-pit."

LM: You've said elsewhere that even as a kid you had the sense of being an outsider. Was that sense one of the things that helped lay the foundation for the "metaphysics of the outlaw" that you develop in your fiction? I gather that even as a young man you were already something of a rebel.

TR: I feel completely at home in the world, I like it here, but from the beginning I've insisted that my stay here be on my own terms and not society's. In that sense, I've been more allied with the outlaw than the outsider. I don't know if it helped shape the unbaked cookie dough of my talent, but one thing that was a *beacon* for me as a boy rebel was a roadhouse just outside Blowing Rock, a joint named The Bark because it was sided with cedar shakes that still had the bark on them. At The Bark, folks drank beer and danced. Can you appreciate the fact that among fundamentalist Southern Baptists drinking and dancing were major sins? My mother taught a Baptist Sunday school class for an age group of about sixteen to twenty-three, and once a week, Wednesday nights, this class would meet at our house. It was partly religious, partly social, but they did a lot of gossiping, and the hottest items of gossip always involved The Bark. "So-and-so was seen leaving The Bark Saturday night." "No! Well, I'll be!" Now, I was a little kid, seven, eight, nine, while this was going on, but they made The Bark sound so attractive, so fascinating! I just loved eavesdropping on those shocked conversations about the evils of that roadhouse. My little pals and I were all over those hills, and we frequently passed by The Bark, it was on a route between one of our hideouts and another, and we'd always stop and stare at it. We'd see men coming out the door with "floozies" on their arms, and they'd be smoking cigars and sporting tattoos, and they'd climb on a big Harley-Davidson and roar out of the red clay parking lot. I was so attracted that all I wanted to do was grow up to be old enough to go to The Bark, to drink beer, squeeze floozies, dance, get tattooed, smoke cigars, and ride a motorcycle. We moved to Virginia when I was ten and I never got back to The Bark, but I eventually *did* do all those other things. And they were every bit as good as I had imagined them.

LM: Was The Bark an early version of the roadside attraction in your first novel?

TR: No, The Bark was a zoo of a different order. But there were lots of roadside attractions in the South on the tourist highways that led to Florida.

SG: You were also an avid reader as a kid, weren't you?

TR: I read the stuff that most kids read—the kids who read at all—except for an atlas. One of my favorite playthings as a child was a world atlas that I read from cover to cover. I knew the capitals of all the countries until that frenzy of independence in the '60s, when all those new nations in Africa emerged; then I lost track. But I also devoured adventure and mystery stories—the Hardy Boys and all that—and comic books, too. I was always reading as a kid; I taught myself to read when I was five years old because I couldn't wait to get into books. In a way, books were more magical to me than The Bark, although The Bark was forbidden fruit and books were not—my mother always encouraged me to read and she read to me from the time when I was in the cradle.

LM: You ended up in a school of music, art, and drama—the Richmond Professional Institute. Were you interested in becoming a performing artist or a painter?

TR: No, I was interested in writing about art. I had earlier spent two years at Washington and Lee University and then I was out of school for four years. I was kicked out of my fraternity for lobbing biscuits at the housemother. Being expelled from a fraternity at Washington and Lee was tantamount to being expelled from the university itself, because it was the epitome of the preppie college and there was hardly a student there who wasn't in a fraternity. So I hitchhiked around the country for a year, landed in the air force for three years, and then I returned to school. While I was in the air force I met some painters, and that was quite a magical thing. Not only had I never seen a real painting, rather than a reproduction, but to actually go into a studio and smell turpentine, actually see people painting pictures for a living— well, this experience blew my mind and I became friends with these wild bohemian artists and grew very interested in art. At college I took mostly theory courses—I didn't learn how to play an instrument or anything, and although I did take a course in play direction and some courses in painting, I didn't really accumulate much in terms of practical technique. I wanted to write about art. I never thought I could create it.

LM: But you did some painting later on, didn't you?

TR: Yes, I have painted for years, when I've had the space. I used to write during the day and paint at night because they were such opposite disciplines that I found it very relaxing to paint after a long day at the typewriter. Lately I haven't had enough space to do any painting, so I've worked with rubber stamps. I design many of my own stamps, and recently I've made little rubber-stamp and watercolor collages.

LM: Just now, when you said that painting and writing were "such opposite disciplines," what did you mean?

TR: For one thing, they are physically opposite, at least in the way I practice them. I can get very tense at the typewriter—I end up with a sore neck at the end of the day. Writing is harder physical labor than digging ditches, at least for me, because I have rotten typing posture and don't deal well with machines. So to go then and paint and just move that brush around—well, it's a lyrical, fluid, liberating feeling; it's more like a dance, swinging and lifting and dipping your muse, rather than trying to knead some words out of her.

LM: Several of my favorite writers—Coover and Barthelme, for example—worked closely with painting while they were developing as writers. Did your experience with painting affect your views about writing?

TR: Probably. It may have heightened my visual sense, my passion for color and texture and shape in language. Language is alive for me, in my eyes as well as in my ears, and painting must have contributed to my good fortune in this regard. It probably also contributed to my appreciation of objecthood. I'm very interested in inanimate objects and in the mysterious network of connections—in terms of the poetic, psychological, and historical associations they inspire, as well as in terms of the energy fields—by which all objects are joined. I believe that every object leads a secret life of its own, although it isn't necessary to delve into those secrets to appreciate the object. Does this sound kooky? Is Claes Oldenburg kooky? Oldenburg understands the rich, complex life of the common object, and in a less profound way so does Andy Warhol. The pop artists deepened my relationship with objects, but so did the "old-fashioned" still-life painters such as Morandi and Cezanne.

SG: Were you interested in realistic painting or in nonrepresentational art?

TR: I consider the art I'm interested in realistic, but then I consider Jackson Pollock a realistic painter and Andrew Wyeth an abstract painter.

SG: Could you explain?

TR: Well, Wyeth's paintings are two-dimensional reductions of the three-dimensional world. Thus, they're abstracted from the external world. They are pictures *of* things. Pollock's paintings don't refer to things, they *are* things: independent, intrinsic, internal, holistic, *real.* Now, in a sense, books are abstractions in that they refer to countless things outside themselves. In my books, when I interrupt the narrative flow and call attention to the book itself, it's not cuteness or self-consciousness but an attempt to make the novel less abstract, more of a real thing.

LM: That's interesting, because I suspected that that strategy of reminding readers that they're reading a book, reminding them that the author is inventing what's going on, was designed, in part, to expose all forms of knowledge as subjective—that is, to remind the reader that mimetic fiction is another illusion, just as scientific and mathematical descriptions are metaphoric.

TR: I believe that reading is one of the most marvelous experiences a human being can enjoy. Being alone in a room with a book is so intimate, so individualistic, so kaleidoscopically imaginative; it's erotic to me, sacred. What I want to do with my fiction is to create an experience peculiar to reading alone, an experience that could not be duplicated in any other medium, something that can't be done in the movies, can't be done on television, on stage, record, or canvas. What this means, on the one hand, is devaluating plot to a certain extent, because if it's only a story you're after, how much easier it is to switch on TV or go to a film. Reading requires more from an audience than television or film; the audience has to participate more fully. Keeping plot secondary to "bookness" helps to make it a reading experience, a literary experience, an experience that could only be derived from words on a page. I also have wanted to avoid the escapism that frequently results from a mimetic approach. What I've wanted to do was to break into the narrative and say, "Look, this is a book—you're just reading a book. But it's nice, isn't it? It's still entertaining, isn't it? I still have your attention, don't I? Even though I'm popping through the page and pointing my finger at what I'm doing, even though you're not caught up in the belief that you're living on Tara plantation."

LM: What they're caught up in is reading words on the page.

TR: That's right—and it's still fun, and it's still serious, and it's still believable, and you're going to keep on reading, aren't you? Because the art of reading is as valid and interesting and real as anything else.

SG: Did you do much fiction writing before you started on *Another Roadside Attraction*?

TR: No. I was waiting for the right moment to begin.

LM: You mean *Another Roadside Attraction* was actually the first piece of fiction you'd ever started? You had no apprentice pieces at all?

TR: Oh, I'd been writing stories off and on since I was five years old, but nothing I wanted to show anyone, and I'd never begun a novel or anything like that. I concentrated on nonfiction. I was waiting to find my voice. Once I found it, I was off and running. But I felt that I couldn't start writing fiction before my voice evolved. One of my art teachers was always encouraging me to go out and become another Faulkner, but that was the last thing in the world that appealed to me. By that I don't mean any disrespect toward Faulkner—I simply didn't aspire to *become anybody else.* So I really didn't want to write, and certainly not to publish, until I was certain my own voice had evolved.

LM: What was it that helped you find that voice? Was there a specific event that helped you crystallize your sense of voice?

TR: I think that the times—the '60s—had a lot to do with it. I was very much caught up in that whole psychedelic revolution, and I quickly realized that no one was going to write about it in an appropriate way. I could see that writers were going to *describe* it rather than *evoke* it. And as a matter of fact, that's exactly what happened—almost no good novels came out of the '60s dealing with the kinds of things we were experiencing then, because most writers described them in a reportorial, journalistic manner that was inadequate to reproduce the essence of what was going on. But I realized that I could capture this experience from the inside out, partly due to my experience with LSD. I based my first novel, *Another Roadside Attraction*, on a psychedelic model. Some people complained that *ARA* had no structure, but that book was carefully structured, I spent two years structuring it, although it was not structured in any usual way. There had been plenty of previous books that were nonlinear, but not nonlinear in the way that *ARA* is nonlinear. I don't think there has ever been a book quite like *ARA*, either in content or in form. It may not be great, but it is definitely one of a kind.

LM: When you said that *ARA*'s form is based on a "psychedelic model," what did you mean?

TR: Simply that its structure *radiates* in many directions at once, rather than progressing gradually up an inclined plane, like most novels, from minor climax to minor climax to major climax. There are lots of little *flashes* of illumination strung together like beads. Some of these flashes illuminate the plot; others merely illuminate the reader.

LM: Could you talk a little more about the effects that drugs had on your aesthetic sensibility?

TR: Mainly, psychedelics left me less rigid, intellectually and emotionally. Certain barriers just melted away. Reality is not a fixed thing, and I learned to move about more freely from one plane of existence to another. The borderlines between so-called reality and so-called fantasy, between dream and wakefulness, animate and inanimate were no longer as distinct, and I made some use of this newfound mobility in my writing. Also, there's a fairly narrow boundary between the silly and the profound, between the clear light and the joke, and it seems to me that on that frontier is the most risky and significant place an artist or philosopher can station himself. Maybe my psychedelic experiences prepared me to straddle that boundary more comfortably than most. Or maybe you'd say that, as a writer, I'm a borderline case.

SG: Larry and I find that most of our favorite artists share an ability to be serious and funny at the same time.

TR: Like the universe, you mean?

LM: What?

TR: Quantum physics has taught us that the universe is a balance between irrevocable laws and random playfulness. We've learned that part of the evolutionary process is purposeful and part of it is merely an adventure, a game. I don't know why I said "merely." Games are serious, too. And playfulness, when the player's consciousness is fully operative, can be profound. We could define life as the beautiful joke that is always happening—and find support for that definition in advanced science.

LM: The literary community is usually suspicious of playfulness.

TR: Isn't it a pity? The greatest weakness of the intelligentsia in this culture has been its inability to take comedy seriously. That's changing in science, at the higher levels. Maybe it'll change in literature as well.

LM: But a lot of comedy, or playfulness, if you prefer, *is* merely frivolous, isn't it? I assume you feel there are different ways of laughing at things, of playing with them, some of which *would* be frivolous.

TR: Yes, I do—although we must remember that, to the unenlightened, the god-laugh always seems frivolous. There is, however, a distinction between important humor and unimportant humor. Important humor is liberating and maybe even transformative. Important humor is also always inappropriate. If you go to a funny movie and you know it's going to be funny, you can enjoy yourself and laugh and have a fine evening, but nothing *liberating* happens to you. But a joke in the *wrong* place at the *wrong* time can cause a leap in the consciousness that is liberating to the human spirit. So it is this inappropriate area of humor in which I work, or at least aspire to work. But I should emphasize that I'm not praising the cynical, cruel, nihilistic humor too often typical of *Saturday Night Live.* There's nothing liberating about that, either. We need to be able to make fun of things, anything, even the reputation of Christ, as I did in *ARA,* but there has to be in the mocking some sense of respect for life, in all of its crazy and necessary manifestations.

SG: How did you happen to choose the particular subject matter for *ARA*— the demythologizing of Christianity?

TR: The idea of the discovery of the mummified body of Christ had been kicking around in my head for six or seven years. I was fascinated by the fact that Western civilization is based upon the divinity of Christ in a lot of crucial ways. So what would happen if we were to learn conclusively that Christ was *not* divine? What would this say about the future of Western civilization? Could we continue to lead moral and ethical lives if Christ proved to have died and stayed dead? I had that idea in mind for a long time, and I did a lot of research into the life of Jesus and the history of religion. Actually, however, I didn't demythologize Christianity, I *re*mythologized it. As Joseph Campbell has pointed out, a major problem with Christianity is that it interprets its myths historically rather than symbolically.

SG: Obviously *ARA* takes a pretty dim view of organized religion in general and Christianity in particular. Was there a special incident that had made you react against your religious upbringing?

TR: Yep, it was seeing Johnny Weissmuller for the first time. For years I had attended Sunday school. I also was subjected to a lot of Southern Baptist training at home. So I knew that Jesus was supposed to be "the big man," my hero. But then I saw my first Tarzan movie, and after that Jesus just didn't cut the mustard. I continued to like Jesus, and I still admire the myth—he's still a sort of hero of mine. In *ARA* I have a dialogue between Tarzan and Jesus which was an attempt to resolve, I suppose, all those conflicts in my early years when Jesus and Tarzan were competing—Jesus quite unsuccessfully, as it turned out—for being my main man. You know, religion is organized spirituality. But there's an inherent contradiction there, because the moment you try to organize spirituality, you destroy its essence. So religion is spirituality in which the spiritual has been killed. Or at least diminished. Spirituality doesn't lend itself to organization. The whole process is rather like Heisenberg's uncertainty principle. That was one of the messages of *ARA*.

SG: Your second novel, *Even Cowgirls Get the Blues*, also had its spiritual side—the spiritual side of feminism, modern woman's connection to the goddess, and so forth. And in *Still Life With Woodpecker*, where you were dealing with romantic love and outlawism . . .

TR: And objecthood.

SG: Yes, and objecthood. You managed to find a spiritual side to those things as well. Does *Jitterbug Perfume* have a spiritual theme?

TR: From one perspective, the perspective of subatomic physics, where matter and energy merge and become one, *everything* is spiritual. Including poodles with rhinestone collars. But, yes, *Jitterbug Perfume* concerns itself with immortality, which is the basis of most spirituality and all religion.

LM: Do you develop a theory of the afterlife?

TR: Not exactly. Whether there is an afterlife or not, beyond the pure energy level, is something that can't be known unless you die. Meanwhile, a rigid belief in an afterlife can be very harmful. A belief in Heaven can cause Hell. As long as a population can be induced to believe in a Heaven or a Nirvana, it can be controlled and oppressed. People will put up with all sorts of tyranny and poverty and ill treatment if they're convinced they'll eventually escape to a stress-free dude ranch for eternity. And then they're much more willing to risk their lives for their governments. Also, these old men who run our governments, as long as they believe that life is just a trial for eternal life after death, they will be less hesitant about leading us into a nuclear conflict. I'm convinced that, if we want to end war, then we've got to put all thoughts of an afterlife out of our minds. To emphasize the afterlife is to deny life. And denial of life is the only unpardonable sin. Amen.

SG: I'd like to take you back to something you said a minute ago about objecthood. Could I ask you about the Camel cigarette pack in *Still Life*? Did that idea occur to you in the midst of your work, or did you know from the beginning that you wanted to bring it in?

TR: This is a case where I had something specific in mind early on. At the beginning of that novel my ambition was to write about objects in a way in which they had never been written about in a work of fiction. People had previously used objects symbolically, of course, and had done so very beautifully and very effectively. But I wanted to write about objects *for their own sake*, to write about the object as if it had a life of its own—which I think inanimate objects do have. In order to get this out of the whole broad social context, I decided I wanted to find some way to put one person alone in an empty room with three objects. Well, that didn't quite work out, for reasons that are still pretty unclear to me; so I decided to concentrate on a single object. And it occurred to me that better than some natural object—like a snail's shell, or a pine cone, or a seashell, something that lends itself to poetic interpretations—would be a popular object, because I have an affinity with popular objects. So I decided to take something out of the supermarket and use it, hopefully in a profound way. I began mulling over our common objects, and by far the richest was the Camel pack. There is a whole mythology and lore about the Camel pack that has gradually evolved in this century. Jokes and riddles have been invented by prisoners, by sailors, by men bored and alone. There are far more of these stories than I mention in the book; I just used a fraction of them.

SG: You must have gone out and researched this area once you figured out you were going to use the Camel pack.

TR: I did some research, although I knew some of the lore already. When I first thought of the Camel pack, I figured, this has got to be my object, because there is no other package design, no other common object, no other supermarket artifact that has that amount of richness and resonance.

LM: So you chose the Camel pack and the basic situation and then worked the plot of *Still Life* around these things?

TR: Right. I wanted to use the Camel pack, and I wanted to use the idea of one person locked in a room with the Camel pack, having to relate in a way in which we don't usually relate to inanimate objects.

LM: *ARA* seemed like a strikingly original novel when it appeared; but there were a number of other experimental works appearing during that same period with which your book shared certain affinities. Were there any writers you were reading during that period who did have some impact on you while you were working on *ARA*?

TR: Not any fiction writers. During that period I was mostly reading Alan Watts, Gary Snyder, Timothy Leary, Yogananda, people like that. The only fiction writer who spoke to me then was Hermann Hesse, and he certainly didn't influence my style.

LM: When I saw that reference to Bokonon in *ARA*, I assumed it was a kind of playful homage to Vonnegut.

TR: That was a curious incident. People who read my manuscript in progress kept mentioning Vonnegut to me, but I had never read him. A friend of mine stacked up her whole collection of Vonnegut novels and said, "Now I know you don't want to read these now, but when you're finished with your book, here they are." Well, I was reading an issue of *The Realist*—Paul Krassner's newspaper—and there was an article in there by Wavy Gravy in which he used as an epigraph the quote, "Certain travel suggestions are dancing lessons from God," and attributed the quote to Bokonon. Of course, that was from Vonnegut's *Cat's Cradle*, but I didn't know that. I liked the quote so much that I worked it into *ARA*, attributing it, again, to Bokonon. I actually looked up Bokonon in a religious encyclopedia, thinking he might have been some Persian cult figure or something. But I never found him. And this is even more interesting: One day I stopped off to see that friend who was the Vonnegut fan, and while she was getting ready to go to lunch with me, I picked up *Cat's Cradle*, which was on the top of the stack of Vonnegut books that she had waiting for me. And I very absentmindedly leafed through it and found that she had underlined one sentence—one and only one—and it was that very same sentence that I had already used in *ARA*.

SG: Brautigan's work is also frequently linked to your own. Did his fiction offer you any specific inspiration?

TR: When I finally got around to reading *Trout Fishing in America*, it encouraged me greatly. It was the first modern novel to successfully do away with plot. By "successfully" I mean it remained accessible and compelling. It's a landmark book. But I was well along with *ARA* before I ever read a word of it. People are always comparing me to Brautigan and Vonnegut and I can't understand it. The only thing I have in common with Brautigan is the use of imaginative, fanciful, outrageous metaphors and similes, but I was using them before he was and I can prove it. I'm not suggesting that he was influenced by me, either, because he wasn't. And Vonnegut, well, we've both employed an episodic structure, and once in a while our ideas dovetail, but I'm obsessed with the poetics of prose and he clearly is not, I'm optimistic and he's pessimistic, I'm complex and he's simple: His sensibility is much more middle aged and middle class. Vonnegut and Brautigan are far more interesting and important than most of those safe and sane ivory-carvers who get all the awards and "serious" acclaim, but anybody who's concerned with my influences had better look elsewhere.

LM: To where?

TR: To James Joyce, for openers. Next, to Alfred Jarry and Günter Grass. Then to Blaise Cendrars, Henry Miller, Claes Oldenburg, George Herriman, and the Coconut Monk.

LM: George Herriman?

TR: The creator of *Krazy Kat.*

SG: Who's the Coconut Monk?

TR: He was some outrageous Buddhist monk who buzzed around Saigon on a motorbike during the war and was forever presenting ripe coconuts to foreign diplomats and military leaders as an emblem of peace. He had a habit of saying something eccentric and beautiful and then vanishing into the jungle. His laugh could be heard all over the Mekong Delta.

LM: OK, speaking of laughter, let's talk some more about comic writing. As I'm sure you know, there are some critics and readers out there who don't take your work seriously because you are so playful and comic; and because, despite your frequent poignancy and the often savage satiric thrust of your books, you seem fundamentally optimistic. How do you respond to this kind of charge?

TR: I don't feel any need to respond to it at all. I suppose I *ought* to be discouraged. Comic writing is not only more profound than tragedy, it's a hell of a lot more difficult to write. There seems to be almost a conspiracy against exploring joy in this culture; to explore pain is considered not only worthy but heroic, while exploring joy is considered slight. This kind of attitude strikes me as nearly insane. Why is there more value in pain than there is in joy? This is not to say that pain, anger, alienation, and frustration can't inform us or shouldn't be explored, but only to ask why these emotions should be explored while joy is excluded. Part of this is due to a prevailing sensibility, particularly rampant in academic and journalistic circles, that it is simply not hip to be life-affirming or positive. Some critics prefer books that reflect their own neuroses, their own miserable lives. The buzzword in New York reviews these days is "gritty." A gritty book is a book to admire. How do you explain this hunger for the sabulous? Where I come from, only chickens and turkeys deliberately consume grit.

LM: Does this neurosis, as you call it, show up both in criticism and in fiction? And is it a matter of content alone, or does it affect style?

TR: All of the above. When Jim Harrison strayed from the dark side into the light side with his novel *Warlock*, the critics who had been washing his feet (and rightly so) now began to dice them with razor blades. He was punished for going AWOL from Camp Desperation. Yet *Warlock* is just as tough and true, in its own way, as Harrison's earlier work. *The World According to Garp* started out fine, the first twenty pages were absolutely marvelous, but the neurosis of the content gradually overtook John Irving's style, infected it, made *it* neurotic, so that sixty pages into the book the style had been reduced to morbid manipulation, to obscene hack writing. Scott Spencer's *Endless Love* suffered an identical fate. After a riveting, lyrical beginning it became so permeated by neurosis that toward its end Spencer was totally out of control. Not out of control in the exhilarating, hallucinogenic way of Hunter S. Thompson, but out of control emotionally. Hysterical, in the worse sense of the word. A vile, wimpy, whining, scab-picking display.

LM: There must be other contemporary writers you admire or feel affinities with.

TR: Lots of them. Too many to list. There is a tremendous amount of literary talent on the planet right now. For that matter, anybody who sits down daily and faces the terror of the blank page has my respect, and that includes Irving and Spencer. Bless them.

LM: How about younger, promising writers?

TR: There's a ripe crop of them, too. Ted Mooney, John Calvin Batchelor, and Eve Babitz. Todd McEwen wrote a sweetheart of a first novel called *Fisher's Hornpipe*, although his outrageous protagonist was whining at the end. (A sop to the reviewers, maybe?) David Payne is a born writer. And Francisco Goldman may be the best of the bunch, if he doesn't go Hollywood on us.

LM: Do you have any advice for younger writers?

TR: Maintain a pitch next to madness, but never take yourself too seriously. There are a few things in life that are more important than literature, but your career is *not* one of them.

SG: Could I ask you something about women? In all of your books you have a main admirable heroine who winds up meeting what is essentially a male mentor. This seems to suggest that men and women have crucial differences that need to be shared with each other, and runs against the idea that men and women are basically the same.

TR: They *are* different, and *vive la différence*! Men and women are not alike, and blacks and whites are not alike, and French and Germans are not alike, and gays and straights are not alike. One thing I really hate is the tendency today toward homogeneity. These differences among people are important and we're all enriched by them. The fact that a man is different from a woman enriches the life of both the man and the woman in ways that would be lost were we to become truly unisexual. This doesn't mean that either the man or the woman is limited by sexual definition. But to keep the gene pool from dwindling, to keep options open, to keep life bright and free and interesting, it's imperative that we have variety and maintain differences. It's important that the gypsies not be assimilated into the mainstream, and that certain aspects of black culture remain black. This idea of all of us becoming the same is a greater threat to our survival than nuclear warfare—it's a threat to our psychic existence. Every man has a woman in him, just as every woman has a man in her. Every black has many things in common with every white, just as every white has many things in common with every Oriental. These similarities are good, they're connections, they can help us live peacefully with one another. But the differences are more important than the similarities because the differences give life its fizz, its brew. Everything that makes life really challenging and interesting emerges out of these differences. The similarities form a good foundation, create a structure, a glue to hold us all together. But the really important things in life are a result of the tensions that arise from a balance of opposites.

SG: Once you actually sit down at your Remington, do you have a clear idea about where your novel is going to go? That is, do you work from an outline, have extensive notes about the characters and what's going to happen, that sort of thing?

TR: Not this pig. I begin with a general sense of the plexus of effects I wish to produce, but I try not to let the concept solidify too quickly or to let the picture fix. I want it to marinate in my imagination, I want to connect the dots a few at a time. When I can surprise myself every day, it makes it easier to go to my desk. If I'm going to sit at a desk six hours a day, five days a week, it's necessary for me to surround the act of writing with an atmosphere of drama and discovery.

LM: Your books are filled with an incredible amount of esoteric information, a bit like Pynchon's novels. How does this information find its way into your works? Do you write along and find something interesting and then decide to research it? Or is most of it available to you beforehand?

TR: I do research my subjects. For *ARA* I read seventeen books on the life of the historic Christ. For *Jitterbug Perfume* I haunted perfume shops and read everything available on perfuming. For *Still Life With Woodpecker* I actually meditated on a Camel package for days, alone in an empty room. But much of the esoteric information just bubbles up when required. I have a ravenous curiosity and a pretty fair memory, especially for cosmic details such as the rectal temperature of a hummingbird.

SG: Which is . . . ?

TR: A hundred and four, point six. Under normal conditions.

LM: Do you have any predictions for the future?

TR: Of literature or of life?

LM: Both.

TR: Well, I predict a period of accelerated growth in the evolution of human consciousness. But if there is a new Messiah, he won't walk down from some Asian mountaintop, he—or she—will climb out of a hot tub in California. And I predict that I'm gonna regret opening my big mouth in this interview. Let's unplug this machine and take a voyage up the Amazon.

Will the real Robbins please stand up?

Randy Sue Coburn/1984

From *Atlanta Journal-Constitution*, sec. B, November 14, 1984. Reprinted by the permission of PARS International Corp.

LA CONNER, Wash. — When Tom Robbins answers his door wearing a rubber alligator mask, it's obviously just a little joke. Yet he seems sincere as he shakes hands and says in a soft Southern accent muffled by the mask, "You can interview me all you want, just don't ask me any questions."

It's true Robbins doesn't like talking about himself. But the best-selling author has said on several occasions that his novels (the underground classics *Another Roadside Attraction* and *Even Cowgirls Get the Blues*, the somewhat less daring *Still Life With Woodpecker*, and his latest, *Jitterbug Perfume*) are merely the tip of his iceberg, the public expression of his being, and that what transpires in his private life is what is really important.

The few who have been allowed to peek into that private life have come away with conflicting observations. Some say Robbins is an introverted mystic dabbling in ancient magic and claiming membership in strange secret societies with names such as The Union of Mad Scientists and Friends of the Missing Link. There are those who believe that the time away from his writing desk is divided between playing competitive volleyball with his team, the Fighting Vegetables, and hanging out with his thirteen-year-old son, Fleetwood.

Others report that his free hours are devoted exclusively to the romantic entertainment of young women, while still others seem convinced that he spends his evenings home alone, dressed in an old satin smoking jacket and puffing huge Havana cigars as he reads quantum physics and Spanish poetry.

Is Robbins an athlete or a scholar, a doting father, a mystical recluse or a backwoods bon vivant? Probing the true persona of a forty-eight-year-old novelist wearing an alligator mask would not be easy. It comes as something

43

of a relief when, in an apparently symbolic gesture, Robbins removes the mask—"See, just another pretty face"—and asks, "You want to know what I am? That's simple.

"I'm an ordinary, sweet, witty guy who happens to possess a luminous cosmic vision and a passionate appreciation of fine sentences. There. Now let's talk about books. Let's talk about life, death, and goofiness. Best of all, let's talk about lunch."

If Robbins had his way the story would end there, over a sandwich made from a perfectly ripe, late season tomato. Like Robbins, the tomato grew up in Virginia: it was hand-carried to La Conner by an East Coast friend. "Tomatoes grown out here taste like wet Kleenex," Robbins explains, slathering mayonnaise onto Wonder Bread. It almost seems like bad manners to interrupt such wholeheartedly culinary nostalgia by reminding the press-shy author that his career has sometimes been a controversial one.

Robbins emergence as a so-called "cult" writer was gradual. No one paid much attention to the 1971 publication of *Another Roadside Attraction*, a book that's about the Second Coming as it occurs at a highway hot dog stand, sort of. Hardcover copies, now collector's items, sold poorly. But Robbins ultimately drew plaudits for the metaphorical intoxication of his writing, his buoyant inventiveness.

When *Cowgirls* heightened Robbins's profile in the mid-Seventies, selling well over 159,000 copies before it appeared in mass market paperback, critics began paying closer attention, alternately hailing him as a dazzling prose stylist and condemning him for mannered, self-indulgent excess. Again, his plot was philosophically oriented and hardly conventional, centering around Sissy Hankshaw, a hitchhiking heroine with tremendously outsized thumbs.

Like other writers before him, Robbins began to be judged for his audience, then perceived as largely youthful and female, and for his press, which seldom knows what to make of a West Coast author claiming playfulness as his preferred form of wisdom. Dubbing Robbins "Prince of the Paperback Literati," a 1976 *New York Times Magazine* article indicted him along with Pynchon, Vonnegut, and Brautigan as the literary equivalents of bunco artists.

In his new novel, *Jitterbug Perfume*, Robbins takes a gentle swipe at such detractors, noting that critics "must laud polish and restraint" and "attack what is quirky and disobedient." Any author who says, as Robbins does, "I believe in a literature that sings in the shower," falls effortlessly into that latter category. But Robbins is dead serious about the celebratory nature of his work. Although it doesn't seem to bother him that he'll never be confused with Saul Bellow, he's impatient with the notion that despair amounts to profundity.

"When your attitude is intelligently optimistic," he says, "it's hard to be taken seriously by people who find that to be a soft position. I'm not some shallow, frivolous person who's never suffered. There have been deaths in my family: two of my best friends died in the last five years. I've had two divorces, many economic setbacks, and chronic eye problems. I could lament these things page after page, novel after novel. But where's the growth in that? The point is, if you're a healthy human being, there's joy in spite of everything."

In La Conner, a fishing village sixty-five miles north of Seattle, Robbins's modest house is tucked away on a side street. Financial success has extended its boundaries, adding on an airy study, a bedroom, and a Jacuzzi where there used to be a backyard and the glorified tool shed in which Robbins once wrote.

Years ago Robbins was an art critic, contributing erudite reviews to professional journals. But as his living room walls attest, his taste is hardly academic. There are three Andy Warhol Campbell soup cans plus a painting by Seattle cartoonist Lynda Barry blaring out the *National Enquirer*–style headline, "Demons From Hell Force Woman to Shed Unwanted Pounds."

Robbins's son, whose mother lives a few miles away, is spending the weekend with his father. In preparation for their upcoming trip to Italy, Robbins has mastered the phrase, "What time does the ice skating begin?" Much as Robbins may enjoy the romantic entertainment of young women, he lives alone and has kept steady company for the past several years with another La Conner resident, Donna Davis.

After dinner that night at a local restaurant ("Woody Allen has Elaine's and I have my own table at The Black Swan"), Robbins will retire early in preparation for his first seasonal volleyball practice. "To improve my game," Robbins says, "I plan to grow an additional inch in the next year." It's not always clear if laughter is the appropriate response to such pronouncements, for when dealing with the public domain, Robbins seems to follow an old Tibetan dictum: If you're going to do anything serious, make sure you've got the tourists laughing: when they stop laughing, let the humor begin.

As usual, Robbins is not writing about ordinary people in *Jitterbug Perfume*. "It's been said that characters who are larger than life are unbelievable," he says. "But I happen to be fortunate enough to have met a number of people who are larger than life, and let me tell you, I believe in them more than I believe in people who are only life-size."

This time Robbins's cast includes a one-thousand-year-old janitor, a genius Seattle waitress, the shabbily genteel proprietress of a New Orleans perfumerie, and a Timothy Leary–type character named Dr. Wiggs Dannyboy, who's established the Last Laugh Foundation to explore immortality and brain science. The lusty goat god Pan, a minor presence in each of Robbins's previous novels, is a full-fledged character here, showing up at Descartes's funeral to declare, "I stink, therefore I am."

Robbins has done his homework. Touring Greek mythological sites with the poet Robert Bly, he explored an Arcadian cave in which Pan was worshiped. Robbins has also accompanied mythologist Joseph Campbell on a similar trip, studying the nature of ancient Central American gods and goddesses.

Robbins was not performing research when he attended the Hollywood premiere of *Ghostbusters* with actress Debra Winger, who expressed interest in portraying the Princess Leigh-Cheri in a movie version of *Still Life With Woodpecker*. Like his first two novels, *Woodpecker* has been optioned by Hollywood. The movie versions of his books are continually entangled in typical film-land snafus, but Robbins doesn't mind; the option checks keep rolling in.

One thing's for certain: Mrs. Robbins's boy Tommy was not brought up to lead this kind of life. But then, Southern Baptist upbringings sometimes have a way of backfiring.

Born in Blowing Rock, North Carolina, and raised in Warsaw, Virginia, Robbins studied journalism at Washington and Lee University, known for producing Southern gentlemen. Robbins proved he did not have the makings of one by pelting his fraternity house mother with biscuits. Expelled from his fraternity and thereby consigned to social Siberia, Robbins quit school and hit the road, hitchhiking around the country.

After a stint in the Far East as an Air Force meteorologist, he graduated from the Richmond Professional Institute, a school of art, drama, and music. In the early sixties, he quit his copy editing job at the Richmond *Times Dispatch* after consistently defying his superior's segregationist attitudes: whenever possible, Robbins would illustrate Earl Wilson's show business column with pictures of black entertainers.

He went to Seattle to obtain a graduate degree in Eastern philosophy but wound up the *Seattle Times'* art critic instead. Those early reviews display

Robbins's distinctive style but, according to him, not much else. "I was not a good critic," he says, "because that takes a hell of a lot of knowledge. I worked at it, though. I studied and studied and after about three years, I was pretty good."

Good enough to impress Luther Nichols, a Doubleday editor, who asked him to write a book about West Coast art. Robbins wanted to write a novel. When asked what the novel was about, Robbins, who had yet to write a word of it, replied, "Oh, it's about the discovery of the mummified body of Jesus Christ in the catacombs of the Vatican, its subsequent theft and reappearance in America in a roadside zoo." Such were the beginnings of *Another Roadside Attraction*.

The publication of *Jitterbug Perfume* marks a passage of sorts for Robbins. Ever since *Another Roadside Attraction*, his books have been published in simultaneous hardcover and oversized trade paperback editions, with an emphasis on paperbacks. This innovative procedure was deemed appropriate for an author whose appeal was reckoned to be greatest among young readers, who don't ordinarily fork over $16.95 for a book. But *Jitterbug*'s first printing will be exclusively hardcover. It's worth noting that Robbins's previous two books have been best sellers only as paperbacks.

Along with James Joyce, Henry Miller, Günter Grass, Claes Oldenburg, and George Herriman (the creator of *Krazy Kat*), Robbins lists among his influences the Coconut Monk, a Zen priest who buzzed around Saigon on a motorcycle during the Vietnam War. After presenting military officers with coconuts as emblems of peace, the Coconut Monk would say something completely eccentric and then disappear into the jungle, much as Robbins would if he weren't now trapped in his car with a reporter.

If the alligator mask were handy, he'd probably put it on again. Life is real, life is earnest, but it's once again time for goofiness. Years ago, when asked to state his ambitions on a standard college questionnaire, Robbins expressed a desire to write publicity for circuses.

"And that's really how I turned out, isn't it?" he asks. "A PR man for the circus of life. When a clown gets sick, sometimes I go in for him."

The Post-Modernist Outlaw Intellectual

Peter O. Whitmer/1984

From *Aquarius Revisited: Seven Who Created the Sixties Counterculture That Changed America* (New York: MacMillan, 1987), 235–49. Reprinted with the permission of Peter O. Whitmer.

. . . all a person can do with his life is to gather about him his integrity, his imagination and his individuality—and with these ever with him, out in front and sharp in focus, leap into the dance of experience.

"Be your own master!

"Be your own Jesus!

"Be your own flying saucer! Rescue yourself.

"Be your own valentine! Free the heart."

—Tom Robbins, *Even Cowgirls Get the Blues*

A long, thin strip of water separates the tiny town of La Conner, Washington, from the Swinomish Indian Reservation. It's as if some force larger than either was still enforcing a white-man/red-man standoff. On the reservation side, the darkness is almost total. The only lights are from a few fireworks stands, open long before and long after July Fourth. The feathery white noise of the wind through the cedars and the water through the channel is rudely spiked by the explosion of a Moon-and-Air Cracker and two Chinese Red Dragons. Then nature takes over again, and the Skagit Valley fog fuzzes up the row of lights from the bars and stores on First Street. The breeze off the Japan Current swirls and twists the sound of someone's huge wind chimes, and the sound bounces through the fog like some distant cosmic xylophone.

This place, with its nearly total isolation, is perfect for someone whose vocation requires spending quiet days at a desk. Distractions are at a minimum here.

La Conner is about as far from Hollywood as you can get. The closest touch of sun and swaying palms I found was in the men's room of the La Conner Tavern, where a dispensing machine advertised, "Silky Samoa—In Tropical Colors—the Condom with the Polynesian Touch."

Over at the pool table between the bar and jukebox, only a seven ball separated one of the locals from victory. As the seven ball disappeared into a corner pocket and the two began another game, I slid off my bar stool, walked around the pool table, and put three quarters into the music machine. Perversely, I plugged in the numbers to play Carly Simon's "Jesse" four times in a row, followed by "Mamas Don't Let Your Babies Grow Up to Be Cowboys," then "Jesse" one more time for the road. Not only do I like "Jesse," I like to see the reaction this repetition gets. It is a good finger on the pulse of a community.

The pool ace was, in many ways, a typical La Conner resident. He appeared to have just gotten out of his VW bus after the drive up from Haight-Ashbury. He pushed the cue stick with the expertise of someone whose avocation may earn him more money than his vocation.

"Yep, I musta set the land speed record, Seattle to Ketchum—fourteen hours—and it burned out me and my car. But my old lady slept like a redwood the whole damn way." He shot a puzzled glance at the jukebox behind him as "Jesse" caught its second wind.

Skinny as his cue stick, he had a ponytail down to the middle of his back, and red suspendered Levi's tucked into over-the-calf, yellow-striped athletic socks that disappeared inside a pair of well-worn logger's boots. He looked like an anorexic winger from the all-1960s Lumberjack Soccer Squad. His John Lennon rimless specs shot back twin glints from the pool-table lamp as he related his most recent plight. "I was supposed to go to Alaska, but the guy with the boat ran it up on the rocks, so he got fired. Shit-canned my job, so here I am. . . ." At "Jesse's" third appearance he hollered at the waitress, "This damned thing's stuck—it's driving me nuts," to which she paid no attention. I acted rather uninvolved and bought three chances to win fifty dollars on a punch board—a sort of honeycomb of fortune, where you use a tiny metal rod to push out a rolled-up piece of paper that holds your financial future. Each of mine turned up worthless.

The fourth round between "Jesse" and the pool player proved decisive, although those scoring the event might have given it a split decision. After becoming rigidly catatonic at the all-too familiar first notes, he took off after Carly Simon's voice. He attacked with the thick end of his pool cue and nearly knocked the juke out of the box before the waitress ran over, unplugged the machine, and bought the poor guy a beer to calm his "Jesse"-jangled nerves. No one else in the bar even seemed to notice. This was indeed a laid-back place.

The waitress fiddled with the back of the jukebox, plugged it in, and to the soothing three-four time, plunk-plunk-a-plunk of "Mamas Don't Let Your Babies Grow Up to Be Cowboys," the sapling-skinny version of Minnesota Fats began banging at balls again.

As the song wound down, I paid my bill, closed my notebook and headed out into the quiet, cool night, just as all hell broke loose. "Jesse" was back, but I was gone.

The next day, at Tom Robbins's suggestion, I somewhat hesitantly returned with him to the scene of the crime. The same waitress was back on duty, and I wondered if she had any idea. . . .

It is a rare clear day in La Conner; the sun has burned off the Skagit fog that hung so tightly last night and early this morning. It has gone quickly from a Pendleton-and-boots morning to a T-shirt-and-sandals afternoon, as Robbins and I sip beers out back of the tavern, on the waterway. He looks as I expected he would—a slightly older and wiser version of the face on the back cover of *Still Life With Woodpecker*. The crow's-feet from the 1980 photo have deepened slightly. He has the hesitant smile of a self-proclaimed "recluse," a perpetually tousled head of once-red hair, and an outlaw twinkle in his eyes.

As the waitress approaches, he says, "I'd like a large order of French fries, with a side of mayo, extra ketchup, lots of tartar sauce, and a pocket map of Venezuela." It all comes out in a quiet molasses-slow monotone, as if he didn't want to let the sea gulls know food was coming.

The waitress fires back, never looking up from her pad, using the same laser-straight monotone, "Okay, but you know the map of Venezuela doesn't come with the fries. It's extra." She knows how to deal with the prattle that has sold millions of copies of paperbacks.

It takes a special environment to nurture Robbins's creativity. When he first stepped his tennis-shoed foot into La Conner, he immediately understood this was the place to set up practice.

His intuitive feel for the area, he quips, is partly because Jack Kerouac used to hitchhike through here. He did, too, in the summer of 1956, to and from an eight-week summer job as a fire-watcher in the Cascade Mountains. Robbins elaborates on his affinity for this part of the country in more realistic terms. "Rain is ideal for writers. It reduces temptation. During the rainy months you're forced to stay indoors. You turn inside. It's a cozy feeling, very comfortable and introspective. In life as in literature, I prefer wet to dry. And, of course, living out here in Monsoon Central, I can be as secluded as I need to be."

He sees life in this tiny fishing village as a necessity for maintaining a clear artistic view and a sense of purity in his work. "I think it's important to live far from the centers of ambition, to keep away from literary politics, and the sort of social contacts that can put the wrong emphasis on one's work."

He bought his recently renovated, century-old frame house on April Fool's Day 1970. "I always make important decisions on the first of April," he explains. "That way, if anything gets screwed up, I have something to blame it on."

> Jesus:Hey dad.
> God:Yes, son?
> Jesus:Western Civilization followed me home this morning. Can I keep it?
> God:Certainly not boy. And put it down this minute. You don't know where it's been.
> —Tom Robbins, *Another Roadside Attraction*

"I get depressed talking about myself, and believe me, I don't get depressed easily," Robbins admits as we discuss the origins of his spirituality. "When I wrote the last sentence in *Woodpecker*, 'It's never too late to have a happy childhood,' some critics looked at that and saw an endorsement of frivolity, but that was not the intention. I think you can cut loose from the past. The past can be a prison. I view my books as cakes with files in them. You can eat the cake and lick the frosting, but inside there is a file that you can chop through the bars with, if you are so moved. I really believe we do not have to be weighed down by the past." But past influences spring eternal in his works. He grew up in North Carolina. His mother, who was a nurse, wrote children's stories for Southern Baptist magazines. His father moved up the corporate ladder, becoming an executive with a regional power company. Robbins had a younger sister, who died in childhood; his mother prayed for twins and had them—two girls. "I believe in prayer," Tom says, matter-of-factly.

His family was steeped in religion. "Both my grandfathers were Southern Baptist ministers. One was ordained. The other was not, and he traveled back into the 'hollers' of Appalachia on a mule to preach. I've been accused of preaching, even before my first book. I say 'Okay, what's wrong with that? We have the epistolary novel, journalism as a novel, the diary as novel. What is wrong with the sermon as novel?' Whatever works, works. Instead of trying to cut that out of my work, I have decided to perfect it, refine it, but go ahead and preach and make it work in the context of the book.

"My characters suffer. They are killed. They die. They have all the griefs and sorrows that characters in so-called realistic novels have. But in the end, they insist on joy in spite of everything."

Robbins recalls that as a child, "Johnny Weissmuller—Tarzan—was my big hero. I sort of grew up going to the Southern Baptist Sunday school and felt that Jesus *should* be my hero. But, somehow, he never measured up to Tarzan. I would go to Sunday school every Sunday and really try to get excited about Jesus, but he didn't move me. The latest Tarzan film would come around and I was 'up' for months. So I dealt with that in my first book, *Another Roadside Attraction*. I actually had a meeting between Tarzan and Jesus, trying to work that out."

Poking fun at religion and man's mortality is a time-honored practice, yet few can carry it off with Robbins's incisiveness:

> Wiggs:One last thing about death.
> Pris:What's that?
> Wiggs:After you die, your hair and your nails continue to grow.
> Pris:I've heard that.
> Wiggs:Yes. But your phone calls taper off.
> —Tom Robbins, *Jitterbug Perfume*

For nine months of the year, Blowing Point,* North Carolina, was "like Dogpatch. It was Appalachia all the way—impoverished, ignorant, populated by men who beat their wives and drank too much—a rather *mean* place, abounding with natural beauty and colorful characters, but violent, snakebit and sorrowful all over."

During the summer months, however, the town of seven hundred people became a country resort for the wealthy, who came to take the mountain air. The streets were lined with Rolls-Royces; glamorous men and women played golf and tennis, and a theater played first-run films. Then after Labor Day, everything shut down again.

"The dichotomy between the rich, sophisticated scene and the hillbilly

---

* Blowing Point may be what locals call Blowing Rock, North Carolina.

scene affected me very much," Robbins says. "It showed me how the ordinary suddenly could be changed into the extraordinary. And back again. It toughened me to harsh realities while instilling in me the romantic idea of another life. And it left me with an affinity for both sides of the tracks."

The "other" side of the tracks was represented by a roadhouse just outside of town, called The Bark. There, hard drinking, cigar smoking, tattooed men, and their women, roared through the red clay parking lot on Harley-Davidsons. "At The Bark, folks drank beer and danced," Robbins remembers. "Can you appreciate the fact that among fundamentalist Southern Baptists, drinking and dancing were major sins? My mother taught a Baptist Sunday School class for people aged sixteen to twenty-three, and once a week, Wednesday night, this class would meet at our house. It was partly religious, party social, but they did a lot of gossiping, and the hottest items of gossip always involved The Bark. 'So-and-so was seen leaving The Bark Saturday night,' and so forth. Now I was a little kid—seven, eight, nine—while this was going on, but they made The Bark sound so attractive, so fascinating! I just loved eavesdropping on those shocked conversations about the evils of that roadhouse. All I wanted to do was grow up and go to The Bark, to drink beer, squeeze floozies, dance, get tattooed, smoke cigars, and ride a motorcycle."

Before he was old enough to sample the pleasures of The Bark, Robbins's family moved to Burnsville, North Carolina, where they lived on the edge of the campus of a vacant private school. Tom's introduction to magic—a theme that permeates his writings—came first with the overnight transformation of the vacant schoolyard into an oasis of flapping canvas tents, strange odors, weird animals, and exotic people: the Barnes and Beers Traveling Circus had slipped into Burnsville in the middle of the night.

"I was an eleven-year-old with an active imagination and went over right away to get a job so that I could get in free." He watered the llamas, set up the menagerie, and scraped moss off the back of a six-foot alligator. But something else really caught his attention: "I met Bobbie and just fell totally in love. She was the most exotic thing I had ever seen. She had waist-length, brilliantly blond hair. She wore black, patent-leather riding boots and riding britches. She had this pet black snake and scars on her arm where it had bitten her. I have always been a romantic, one of those people who believes that a woman in pink circus tights contains all of the secrets of the universe."

Whether it's Amanda setting up the flea circus in *Another Roadside Attraction*, Sissy Hankshaw thumbing rides on passing clouds in *Even Cowgirls Get the Blues*, Princess Leigh-Cheri contemplating "how to make love stay" in *Still Life With Woodpecker,* or *Jitterbug Perfume*'s Kudra mixing the potent potion of life, the theme of feminine insight to heavenly delight runs deep: Tom Robbins is a heroine addict.

Robbins's fascination with the circus put him in touch with something at the core of human existence. "The circus is a real metaphor for society at large. What appeals to me in particular is the wire-walkers. They are totally unnecessary. Society does not need aerialists in any literal sense. What role is fulfilled by a man risking his life walking on a wire? It is a Zen act not only to risk your life but to devote your life to these curious obsessions.

"Karl Wallenda, another of my heroes, once said, 'On the wire is living— everything else is only waiting.' During the time it happens, you are in contact in a primitive way with 'that which of which there is no whicher'—a God-force—the essence of the universe."

Somewhat irreverent as an adolescent, he was sent to a military school, then entered college at Washington and Lee University in Lexington, Virginia, as a sixteen-year-old. He pledged Pi Kappa Phi, wore a coat and tie to class, and worked as a cub sports reporter under T. K. Wolfe III. "Tom Wolfe was a senior when I was a freshman. He was the editor of the campus newspaper, the *Ring Tum Phi.* Ridiculous name. It was kind of a ridiculous school. I didn't last long.

"One of my friends was sitting at the fraternity housemother's table, and I tried hitting him with a pea. It went off to the side, hit her in the chest, and ran down her cleavage." Some of the fraternity brothers began berating Robbins, questioning his parentage among other things. "I just reached over, picked up some biscuits, and started lobbing them at her. Not to hurt her, but I sent this whole shower of biscuits. *That* was the end of my days there."

His next experiment landed him in the Air Force. He lasted two weeks in officer-candidate school then was assigned to study meteorology at the University of Illinois before being shipped off to teach in Korea. "Korean pilots had very little interest in meteorology. They would not circumnavigate storm systems. They would fly right into them—it was just their style. They were bored and I was bored, so we operated a black-market ring instead. Small stuff—cigarettes, cosmetics, and Colgate toothpaste—which I found out later were going into China. I had this fantasy that I was supplying Mao Zedong with his Colgate toothpaste."

Working shifts of four days on and four days off, Robbins would hitch rides on Air Force planes to Tokyo, where his interest in Eastern thought blossomed. He had enough time there to take a course in Japanese culture and aesthetics, an interest he would later pursue briefly at the University of Washington. The Orient was a heady experience for a twenty-year-old from the Carolina hills. "I became enamored with the romance of solitude. I love waking up in strange cities, where I know no one and don't know what the next move is going to be. I used to wander around Tokyo for hours and hours, knowing very little Japanese. All those strange sights and smells. . . ."

Even after winning the enlisted men's Scrabble championship, Robbins was still the only member of his outfit not to receive a reenlistment lecture. He came back to the States, got a degree in art at Richmond Professional Institute, and began work in the Richmond *Times-Dispatch.*

Given his interest in travel, he harbored thoughts of becoming foreign correspondent and ended up the international-news specialist on the copy desk. One of his other duties was to edit the syndicated Earl Wilson celebrity gossip column, pick out one of the people mentioned, and get his or her photo from the newspaper morgue. "One time without even thinking, I put in Louis Armstrong. 'Satchmo.' Well, they got letters! They suggested to me that I should not put a 'gentleman of color' in the column. Of course it really annoyed me. Some months later I was feeling ornery. The column mentioned Nat 'King' Cole, and I slapped ol' Nat in there." The managing editor warned him that a repeat performance would be his finale.

About two weeks later, Robbins sensed it was time for one of life's moments of decision. "It was one of those synchronistic things. On that particular day Earl Wilson mentioned Sammy Davis, Jr. He was one of the most hated black celebrities because he had married a white woman. So I put ol' Sammy in there and just walked out. I didn't give them a chance to fire me. I turned in my resignation."

The road headed west and slightly north—Seattle was as far as he could get from Richmond. Accepted at the Far East Institute of the University of Washington, Tom arrived early in 1962 and got a job at the *Seattle Times* to pay his tuition. This time around, his editing brought more positive attention; he wrote the headlines for the "Dear Abby" column, and nurtured an appreciation for her concise blend of wit and wisdom.

"She came by the *Seattle Times* and asked if she could meet the person who was writing her headlines. She was syndicated in about one hundred and fifty newspapers and none of them had headlines like the ones in Seattle. Someone had written in about Tarzan books being banned in California because Tarzan and Jane were not married. So my headline read, "Did Tarzan Live Too High in Tree?"

An opportunity arose to actually put his academic training to work when the *Seattle Times* art critic quit. Robbins felt the position was a chance for him to get into something where his "voice" might materialize. It worked for a while. He did some good work. He got a feel for the power of a critic and, predictably, tried to approach his role from "an educational standpoint. Not to try to punish people."

Then, on the way to becoming an art critic, lightning struck. Usually vague on dates, Tom remembers the day precisely: "July 19, 1963. I was given LSD from an enlightened physician in Seattle. I did not know a single other person who had had it. It was the most profound experience of my life, and it suddenly gave me a new culture. It was like being a Southern Baptist one day and a Russian Jew the next, so you don't relate to Southern Baptists anymore. I went looking for my people."*

He called in "well" one day and left for New York City, ostensibly to write a biography of painter Jackson Pollock (he actually did a lot of the research but never wrote the book).

"At that point in my life I had dabbled in the major world religions, the systems of philosophical liberation, a great deal of Zen and Taoism. But it was abstract. In one eight-hour session with LSD all this became totally real. My life was never the same after that."

In 1964, he lived two blocks from Allen Ginsberg in the East Village and, that fall, marched side by side with him in a LEMAR (Legalize Marijuana) demonstration. Robbins then went to hear a lecture by Timothy Leary at Cooper Union. The message that evening could be stated in one sentence: "You have to go out of your mind to use your head." The hall was packed, but Robbins got a seat close enough to see that the color-blind Leary was wearing red socks with his tweed suit. From that point on, Robbins wore red socks for years. (Later he began to wear mismatched socks, a personal eccentricity he uses as a constant reminder of the "clarity of vision" that can only come from swimming against the stream.) Being far too shy to approach Leary, Robbins recalls actually meeting him shortly after the lecture.

"I ran into Tim on the street after the talk he gave at Cooper Union. We were both at a vegetable stand, and I was buying Brussels sprouts. He said, 'How can you tell the good ones?' I told him, 'You pick the ones that are smiling.'"

* The date in question, which others have reported as July 16, 1963, is one Mr. Robbins is not exactly sure of. What is certain, though, is the transformative effect the event had on his outlook and thinking.

The 1960s, in New York City, later in San Francisco and then Seattle, were a potent time for Robbins. He is an artist irrevocably rooted in that decade, and he tracked the evolution of consciousness expansion like a dog lost and wandering in the forest, listening for his master's whistle.

"I followed it all, and in a certain sense I participated in it, right at a very core level, but I was never really a part of that scene. It was just not in my nature to be part of a scene."

The sun is dipping low across the waterway, and the evening chill begins to sink in. In this part of the country one changes clothing according to the time of day rather than the time of year. Robbins and I head out of the La Conner tavern and hitch a ride up the hill to his place. We had to catch his Seattle Seahawks drubbing the Minnesota Vikings.

As we approach the house, all that is visible is the fence. "The original house was built in 1873, the same year *your* Sigmund Freud"—and he turned to me as if to indicate some proprietary relationship—"dropped out of law school." (At the time I said nothing, but made a quick mental note. Later I verified the accuracy of his statement. Indeed, his research is inevitably thorough, if sometimes unorthodox. For *Another Roadside Attraction*, he read seventeen books on the life of Christ; for *Still Life With Woodpecker* he meditated for days on a pack of Camels.)

His literary successes have allowed Robbins to build some additions onto his house, though he admits, "It is built against all architectural concepts of open space. Its density—all these nooks and crannies—are just the way I write."

The humor evident in his books is here, too. In the glassed-in hot-tub area, as the steam dissipates, an eerie, etched UFO can be seen to materialize slowly from under the condensation. It's another reminder of his playfulness, like the framed *National Enquirer* pages here and there.

Sitting in his living room, Robbins talks about the long road back to the West Coast after his year in New York City. (Above him, Warhol's twin portraits of Mao look down sternly.) He spent a pivotal period in the San Francisco area—at Berkeley and in the Haight-Ashbury.

"In June 1966 I went to the Avalon Ballroom, and it occurred to me that things would never be the same. I really thought that we were in for a full renaissance. It was so mind-boggling. Cooper Union in New York was liberation on an intellectual level. But I walked into the Avalon Ballroom in San Francisco and there were people in costume and the first light show I had ever seen. There were children running around, rock bands playing, people dancing free-form, which was the beginning of dance for me. I had never really liked to dance before because I didn't like learning the steps. That night I started to dance. Children, dogs, everybody had a smile and a hug for everyone else. It was like Utopia. It was so totally different from any of my experiences in American culture. This was the *end* of the old world and the beginning of the new."

Back in Seattle, Robbins found an outlet in the underground newspaper *Helix*. By now the tides of change had washed all the way to Seattle. Robbins demonstrated the beginnings of his "voice" in the summer of 1967 in a review of a Doors concert:

> The Doors. Their style is early cunnilingual with overtones of the Massacre of the Innocents. An electrified sex slaughter. A musical bloodbath . . . . The Doors are carnivores in a land of musical vegetarians . . . . their talons, fangs, and folded wings are seldom out of view, but if they leave us crotch-raw and exhausted, at least they leave us aware of our aliveness. And of our destiny. The Doors scream into the darkened auditorium what all of us in the underground are whispering more softly in our hearts: we want the world and we want it . . . NOW!

He became a disc jockey for a radio show, *Rock and Roll for Big Boys and Girls*. (He politely refused a guitar audition by Charles Manson.) He began reviewing art for *Seattle Magazine*. Finally, in 1967, he was contacted by an editor from Doubleday. Like Dear Abby before him, the editor saw something unique in Tom's writing. He asked if Robbins wanted to write a book, which he did, but not about West Coast art, which the editor wanted. Initially both were disappointed, but then the editor asked what Robbins's book was about.

"I said, 'Oh, it's about the discovery of the mummified body of Jesus Christ in the catacombs of the Vatican, its subsequent theft and reappearance in America in a roadside zoo.'

"I'd had that particular idea kicking around in my head for six or seven years. Well, his eyes kind of lit up and he said, 'Tell me more.' I didn't know any more, so I started making it up then, to keep his interest. When he had finished his coffee, he asked when he could see it. I said it was in pretty rough form—I hadn't written a word. So I went home that day and told my girlfriend, 'I've got to start writing a novel.'"

The novel was begun in 1968, while Robbins was living in a three-dollar-a-night hotel on then-sleazy First Avenue. It became *Another Roadside Attraction*, the book *Rolling Stone* called "the quintessential '60s novel." A prodigious reader, Robbins cites as his literary influences Henry Miller, Jack Kerouac, and Nelson Algren. "I have always admired them tremendously, yet in my finally realized style I don't think they had much to do with it. Many books about the 1960s failed because they used old novelistic techniques. I went from the inside out and tried to *evoke* the experience of the 1960s. The whole book is structured psychedelically. It doesn't move from minor climax to minor climax up a slowly inclining plane to a major climax. It actually develops in the way that a drug experience would. There are a lot of flashes of illumination strung together like beads. Some illuminate the plot, others merely illuminate the reader."

The idea behind the book had been in Robbins's mind since childhood. He was intrigued by the extent to which Western civilization—from its cultural myths to individual behavior—was predicated on the divinity of Christ. "So I wondered, what would happen if we were to learn conclusively that Christ was not divine? What would this say about Western civilization, about the future of Western civilization? Could we continue to lead moral and ethical lives if Christ was proved to have died and stayed dead?"

Robbins had never made a serious attempt to write fiction before he began his first book. "I'd been writing stories off and on since I was five years old, but nothing I wanted to show anyone, and I'd never begun a novel or anything like that. I concentrated on non-fiction. I was waiting to find my voice. Once I found it, I was off and running."

Robbins is quick to add an important point concerning the relation between the psychedelic experience and his unusual writing style. "Drugs did not make me more creative. I don't think they gave me any talent I didn't already have. What they did was free me to make connections that one doesn't normally make. A more multidimensional relation to reality."

When *Another Roadside Attraction* was finished, Robbins felt he *had* found his voice. Unfortunately, few readers found his *book*—at first. "I was making one and a half cents a copy, and at that price you have to sell a lot of books to make any money. I had a bad contract because I was an unknown first novelist and didn't have an agent."

Like his characters, always insisting on joy, he pushed himself into a second novel. When *Even Cowgirls Get the Blues* was published in 1976, its instant popularity pulled sales of his first book in its wake; there are now over two million copies of *Another Roadside Attraction* in print. It became an underground classic, passed conspiratorially from hand to hand to hand, like a never-ending joint of the best grass. Critics were puzzled; most reviews were negative.

Typically, Robbins answers with a story. "*Another Roadside Attraction* was the Hells Angels' all-time favorite book. Also, did you know that Elvis Presley was reading *Another Roadside Attraction* the night he died? True. A copy of it was lying beside him on the bathroom floor. With the Hell's Angels and Elvis on your side, who the hell needs the *New York Review of Books*?"

From his study of Jackson Pollock, Robbins emerged with a perspective on creativity that, once understood, illuminates his writing, as well as the ongoing lack of respect afforded him by most reviewers. "I consider Jackson Pollock a realistic painter and Andrew Wyeth an abstract painter," he says. "Wyeth's paintings are two-dimensional reductions of the three-dimensional world. Thus, they're abstracted from the external world. They are pictures *of* things. Pollock's paintings don't refer to things, they *are* things: independent, intrinsic, internal, holistic, *real*. Now, in a sense, books are abstractions in that they refer to countless things outside of themselves. In my books, when I interrupt the narrative flow and call attention to the book itself, it's not cuteness or self-consciousness but an attempt to make the novel less abstract, more of a real thing":

> This sentence has a crush on Norman Mailer. This sentence is a wino and doesn't care who knows it. *Like many italic sentences, this one has Mafia connections.* This sentence is a double Cancer with Pisces rising. This sentence lost its mind searching for the perfect paragraph. This sentence leaks. This sentence doesn't *look* Jewish . . . This sentence has accepted Jesus Christ as its personal savior. This sentence once spit in a book reviewer's eye. This sentence can do the funky chicken. This sentence is called "Speedo" but its real name is Mr. Earl. This sentence may be pregnant, it missed its period This sentence went to jail with Clifford Irving. This sentence went to Woodstock. And this little sentence went wee wee wee all the way home. This sentence is proud to be a part of the team here at Even Cowgirls Get the Blues. This sentence is rather confounded by the whole damn thing.
> —Tom Robbins, *Even Cowgirls Get the Blues*

Robbins's irreverence is also carefully crafted, and here he makes an "important" distinction. "Important humor is liberating and maybe even transformative. Important humor is also always inappropriate—if a joke is appropriate, you can rest assured it is unimportant. But a joke in the *wrong* place at the *wrong* time can cause a leap in consciousness that is liberating to the human spirit.

"Have you ever noticed that nothing upsets an intellectual as much as discovering that a plumber is enjoying the same book he is? The literati are too insecure to ever admit to liking a book that isn't inaccessible or esoteric."

After his third book, *Still Life With Woodpecker*, Robbins's success was assured. Ironically, it also reintroduced him to the man with whom he had once discussed Brussels sprouts. Robbins was in the parking lot behind Papa Bach's, a Santa Monica paperback bookstore, autographing copies of his new book for a long line of fans. It was night, and searchlights were set up in typical L A. fashion to hype the event. A rock band played as Robbins talked to the people coming to have their books signed. Behind a cyclone fence at the edge of the parking lot some Chicanos took note of this strange spectacle.

"Pretty soon," Robbins remembers, "there were fifteen or twenty Mexicans standing against the fence, drinking beer, watching this whole scene, trying to figure out if I was some renegade pope. It really did look religious the way the people had to kneel before me at this little low table. Every once in a while I would look over and kind of bless them. About halfway through I looked over and standing against the fence was Tim Leary."

The two have remained close friends ever since. In *Jitterbug Perfume*, the character Dr. Wiggs Dannyboy, the defrocked Irish ex-Harvard anthropologist, is partly modeled on Leary.

In Robbins's view, the 1960s were an aborted evolutionary leap. He disagrees with Leary regarding the democratization of consciousness-expanding chemicals. It should not have been so egalitarian, Robbins contends, but used, as Huxley suggested, only by an elite few, "an enlightened minority, like in the Eleusinian Mysteries in the Golden Age of Greece, where one was condemned to death if he revealed the secrets." He feels that the stream was further polluted at the source by sloganeering and extensive media coverage. A throng of mutant imitators was created, out just to be part of the party, rather than seeking enlightenment. In a recent letter, written to me on his Sidd Finch Fan Club stationery, he expanded on this theory:

> It boils down to this: what happened in the Sixties was only secondarily political. First and foremost it was a spiritual phenomenon.
> And I believe it proved my thesis that if we work on changing spiritually, philosophically, then the political changes will naturally and automatically follow. For centuries, we've been putting the cart before the horse.

The magic of the Sixties, the triumph of the Sixties, began to dissipate when we took our eyes off the spiritual ball and shifted our focus to the political fallout from our spiritual advances.

Next time, I want us to get it right.

Robbins's thoughts on any subject are never written in haste. He writes in longhand from 10:00 A.M. until 4:00 P.M. each day. The density of his work is a sign of his craftsmanlike approach: A half hour might be spent on a single sentence; two pages a day is his goal.

"My method of writing is to paint myself into corners," and then, he says, "see if I can reach into my pocket and find suction cups to put on the bottom of my feet and walk up the wall, across the ceiling, and out of the room. That is a terrifying way to work. I would not recommend it to anyone. It sort of keeps you on the edge of terror all the time, but for me that's salubrious. It adds something to the work."

He then scurries over to a pile of magazines in his living room, pulls out a copy of *Fiction International,* and reads me his most recent contribution. It is clearly the definitive statement of his attitude toward his craft.

"Some of these are long-winded," he says with disdain. "Mine is quite short. 'A writer's first obligation is not to the many-bellied beast, but to the many-tongued beast. Not to society but to language. Everyone has a stake in the husbandry of society, but language is the writer's special charge—and a grandiose animal it is, too! If it weren't for language, there wouldn't be society. Once writers have established their basic commitment to language and are taking the blue guitar-sized risk that that relationship demands, they are free to promote social betterment . . . but let me tell you this: Social action on a political, economic level is wee potatoes. Our great human adventure is evolution of consciousness. We are in this life to enlarge the soul and light up the brain. How many writers of fiction do you think are committed to that?'" He snaps the magazine down and looks at me with a challenging smile.

Mentioning a many-tongued beast was a piece of synchronous timing. Ka Ka Ka ZAP, Robbins's five-foot-long Sumatran thunder lizard, a souvenir of an Indonesian raft trip, enters the kitchen and begins eating with a horrendous crunching-belching-ripping sound. I turn toward the creature as it looks toward me, emitting a long, menacing hiss, eyes glowing like electric tangerine Life Savers.

"Why the three *Ka*s in her name?" I ask, disconcerted.

"Birth defect," Robbins says quietly. "She has an extra fork in her tongue and can't even hiss properly. I've heard better third-grade piccolo sections. But for God's sake, do not pity the poor bastard. With equipment like that, she is simply hell on flies."

"Don't you ever lock her out?"

"I'm just too nice a guy," he says sheepishly, tossing more chickens into the huge ceramic bowl in the corner.

I leave Tom Robbins feeding Ka Ka Ka ZAP. The Buick, at the end of a long and hazardous trip, now sounds like a McCormick reaper on a rocky field. Leaving La Conner, I cross the steel bridge to the reservation side, in search of something I had seen years ago as a child, driving through here to visit relatives in British Columbia. As a child it was a curiosity; as an adult it would hold deep significance.

For many years, there was a unique totem pole in front of the Swinomish tribal headquarters. Unique, in that very few people—except the Swinomish, and maybe Tom Robbins—understood and appreciated its profundity. A heraldic reminder of the clan's ancestry, carved with dignified restraint, it portrayed the guardian spirit figures of key importance to this coastal tribe's survival and it placed them in an order that reflected the biological food chain. Near the bottom were stylized ocean waves with a salmon curling above. Then came the beak of a fish hawk, then the great fanged bear. On top, complete with monocle and cigarette holder, was carved, with paramount reverence, the head of Franklin Delano Roosevelt.

Any understanding of Tom Robbins, and indeed, the entire decade that was the Sixties, must include a rather thorough amount of empathy for the magical and the mystic. In the heraldic, carved fir trunk, the power of the ocean at the base and the power of the president of the United States on top would have been joined, had Indians had the ability to carve "totem wheels" instead of totem poles. It is only to white man's separate reality that FDR seems more powerful than the ocean waves. In Tom Robbins's view the full circle of the world is seen from a different perspective, one that disdains the tyranny of power of anything except the power of the individual over himself.

Tom Robbins

Nicholas O'Connell/1986

From *At the Field's End: Interviews with 20 Pacific Northwest Writers* (Seattle: Madrona, 1987), 264–84. Reprinted with permission of Nicholas O'Connell.

In his novels *Another Roadside Attraction* (1971), *Even Cowgirls Get the Blues* (1976), *Still Life With Woodpecker* (1980), and *Jitterbug Perfume* (1984), Tom Robbins takes a deliberately subversive attitude toward Western civilization. While the bright surface of his prose enchants and enraptures, the philosophical underpinnings of his books call all kinds of attitudes and institutions into question. But whether he's castigating the Roman Catholic Church, poking fun at Ralph Nader worshippers, or satirizing dead-serious feminists, Robbins remains a critic in a clown costume, a modern-day court jester, a writer as much interested in entertaining and amusing his readers as in making a point.

Born in Blowing Rock, North Carolina, in 1936, Robbins was raised in small towns in Virginia. He studied journalism at Washington and Lee University, where he was expelled from a fraternity for tossing biscuits at the house mother. After spending some time in the Far East as an Air Force meteorologist, he enrolled at the Richmond Professional Institute, a school of art, drama and music from which he graduated in 1961. He worked as a copy editor at the Richmond *Times-Dispatch* before moving to Seattle, Washington, to attend graduate school in Far Eastern philosophy at the University of Washington. While in graduate school he began working as a feature editor and art critic at the *Seattle Times*. He left to work part-time for the Seattle *Post-Intelligencer*, and while there, began writing *Another Roadside Attraction*, the publication of which got his career as a novelist off the ground.

Robbins has been married twice, and has a teenage son, Fleetwood Star Robbins. He lives in La Conner, Washington, in a modest house on a quiet street. The interview took place there in the fall of 1986. Robbins is a low-key fellow with a soft Southern accent and modishly styled, graying brown hair.

64

Contrary to his public persona as an outrageous character with a roguish grin, Robbins in private is a quiet, introspective man who seems quite serious about his life and his work.

Nicholas O'Connell: There are several stories about how you got your first novel published. How did it actually happen?

Tom Robbins: Well, the true story involves the Order of the Golden Envelope, of which I'm a knight. You see, the post office is my favorite institution. With some people it's the church, with some it's the university, with me it's the post office. The mails have a lot of potential as an art form, correspondence artists can attest to that, plus there's a certain amount of wonderment in the whole postal process. Paper mail is doomed by computers, so let's enjoy it while we can. At any rate, ever since I was knee-high to a mail slot, I had believed that someday a letter would be delivered to my box that would change my life. Alter it forever. And in my fantasy, that letter had a light, a golden aura around it.

In 1966, while I was living over a machine shop in Ballard [neighborhood of Seattle], I went downstairs to the mailbox one day and pulled out a letter. I opened it and was nearly blinded by the golden light. It was from Luther Nichols, West Coast editor of Doubleday, saying that he was coming to Seattle and wanted to talk to me about writing a book. I thought, "This is it, the life-changing golden letter has arrived." I'd had books on my brain since I was a tot.

I met Luther in a coffee shop in the Benjamin Franklin Hotel, which now has been replaced by the Westin. It turned out that he wanted me to write an art book, a book about West Coast art. He'd been reading my art reviews.

I was disappointed. I told him I was really interested in writing a novel. Then he was disappointed. But I covered my disappointment and he covered his, and we continued to converse. He said, "Well, what's this novel about?"

And I said, "It's about the discovery of the mummified body of Christ in the catacombs under the Vatican and its subsequent theft and reappearance in America in a roadside zoo."

His interest picked up. He said, "Tell me more." Well, I didn't know any more. That was an idea that had been kicking around in my head for a few years, but I'd never done anything with it. But when he said, "Tell me more," I started improvising on that idea, plotting on the spot.

He said, "When can I have a look at the manuscript?"

I said, "Well, it's in pretty rough shape." I hadn't written a word, but I didn't want him to know that, so I said, "I'll try to clean it up and send it to you." I went home that day and told the girl I was living with, "I've got to write a novel."

I tried for a year to get something done on it, but I was so enmeshed in the Seattle art world that I couldn't find time to write.

Eventually I cut my ties and moved down to South Bend, Washington, into a storefront that was rented for eight dollars a month, not eighty dollars, but eight. That's where I began *Another Roadside Attraction*. I actually wrote all of it in South Bend, though not all of it in the storefront; we moved to a more legitimate house later on.

I worked weekends at the *P-I*, drove up from South Bend. The girl I was living with was a waitress in Raymond, and she brought home left-over shrimp and scallops and oysters from diners' plates; that's how we survived. Slops de la mer.

NO: That was for a year?

TR: Two years.

NO: Did you have anybody read it over as you were working on it?

TR: I wrote thirty pages and sent it to Luther Nichols. He liked it and he sent it on to Doubleday in New York. They said, "This is unusual. Can we see some more?" So I wrote seventy more pages.

The younger editors liked it, but the senior editors weren't too sure. Even the younger editors said, "Well, this is really interesting, really different, but we can't tell where it's going."

I thought, "I can understand that perfectly. I don't know where it's going either. If I knew where it was going, I probably wouldn't be writing it."

By this time, though, I was determined to finish it. It had become central to my life. I was going to finish that sucker, whether they bought it or not.

I was hoping to get an advance. After neither of the initial readings would they give me a dime, but by then I was committed to the book. I finished it in my own way and at my own pace, eating left-over shellfish, and I thought I'd try Doubleday one more time and if they weren't interested, the hell with them, I'd send it to somebody else.

This time, as I understand, there was a real battle over it between the senior editors and the younger editors. Doubleday began as a Roman Catholic publishing house, I wasn't aware of that, and some of the senior editors were of that persuasion. They battled about it and finally the younger editors won out. I got a $2,500 advance and went out immediately and bought a ticket to Japan. Converted it to yen and sin. The rest, as they say, is geology.

NO: Was the book autobiographical at all?

TR: Any work of art is to a certain extent a self-portrait. It wasn't what you would call an autobiographical novel per se, too much of it came strictly out of my imagination. Some of it came out of psychedelic drug experiences. A lot of it came out of what was going on in America in the late '60s.

NO: Were you attempting to make sense of the '60s?

TR: I was trying to re-create and evoke the true mood of the '60s. I didn't want to write a traditional novel. I didn't want to report. I didn't want to write *about* the '60s, I wanted to make the '60s happen on the page. I could see all around me people writing about the '60s, and even those who didn't miss the point completely, as many of them did, were never quite able to explain the '60s to someone who didn't participate in them, particularly someone who hadn't had what we called "The Experience"—the ingestion of lysergic acid diethylamide 25.

So I based the book on a psychedelic model to re-create through style, as much as content, the mood of the '60s. *Rolling Stone* called *Another Roadside Attraction* the quintessential novel of the '60s. I think that's because it looked at the '60s from the inside out; instead of trying to describe the era, it evoked it, in style as much as content.

NO: The narrator in that book is funny. He's always trying to sum up what's going on, just as an objective reporter would, but . . .

TR: Yeah, it keeps blowing up in his face, which was the whole point. He wanted to relate to it in traditional ways. If you're operating from a base camp of logic and rationality and good old-fashioned literary values, you just end up with the '50s in '60s drag. When in Oz, you have to use Ozmosis.

NO: When you were working on the book, did you try to write it straight first?

TR: No. I was trying to get over being straight. Actually, the straight and narrow path has never interested me very much. In fact, I've become convinced that if you find yourself on the straight and narrow path, you know that you're headed in the wrong direction.

NO: Is it harder to find another path?

TR: Certainly. That's why the traditional paths are so crowded. The wild and crooked paths, the left-handed paths, so-called, are not for the lazy and the faint of heart. You have to be willing to jettison a lot of intellectual and emotional baggage that has been piled on your luggage rack by people and institutions that, their claims to the contrary, do not have your best interests in mind. You have to have the nerve to cut free of 90 percent of what you've been taught by your family, your schools, your news media, and, especially, your government and your religion. The paths of ignorance and superstition

seem smooth and easy. The path of truth and liberty looks impossibly difficult. But it can be very exhilarating. So much so that the path itself becomes
the destination. You can't be overly concerned with where it's leading. Who
knows where it's leading?

NO: How did you find that path?

TR: Deep desire. Then hit and miss. Once you're on it for a while, even if
it's but for a few steps, your toes start to tingle in such a delightful way that
you're willing to take all sorts of risks to get back on. And even now I stray
off the path frequently. No one stays on the path all the time unless they're
enlightened, and even then I think there are times they wander off into the
brambles. I'm in the brambles right now or I wouldn't be talking like this.

NO: Are there certain books and traditions that help you stay on the path?

TR: Oh, yeah. It's a crazy old road, but there are plenty of signposts, if you
know how to interpret them. They are usually in a language you can't understand. An early signpost for me was a book called *Generation of Vipers*
by Philip Wylie, which I read when I was eighteen. It was the first thing I'd
ever encountered that really questioned all of the values I had been taught to
hold dear. It went over those values, not with a magnifying glass or a comb,
but with a chainsaw. It was a milestone in my life.

NO: When you were younger, were you at all rebellious?

TR: From birth. And I became more rebellious when the hot hormones of
adolescence began to spin off of my artery walls. I have always been in a
rebellious state. My goal is to be eternally subversive. But I think I'm falling
short.

NO: Is writing an acceptable adult way to be rebellious?

TR: Sure. All art is in a sense an act of rebellion, a protest, at any rate. The
Venus de Milo is a protest against every flat-chested woman in the world.
And the Belvedere Apollo is a protest against every pot-bellied man. Art
creates the world as it ought to be, and therefore is a protest against the
world as it is, although I find plenty in the world as it is to celebrate.

NO: What were you like as a young man?

TR: When, last year?

NO: No, more like a teenager.

TR: I was sensitive and shy, but covered it up by becoming the class clown. I
was such a mischief-maker that nobody noticed I was a bit of a loner. I was a
closet bookworm, a regular little intellectual, but I kept that side of me well
hidden. I'd even fail tests on purpose, writing bizarre, surreal answers to
questions that I could easily have answered. I gave myself a completely secret education. In the redneck, rural South, this deception was necessary.

At fifteen, I went out for basketball and played well. Wore a varsity letter, chased cheerleaders, had dates and rowdy friends. But I also maintained a secret life. I still do. Except the secrets have changed.

NO: Did you like growing up in the South?

TR: I liked it just fine. I didn't think much about it one way or another; it was like a bird being born in a particular forest. It wasn't until I was about eighteen and began to experience directly the non-Southern world that various aspects of the South began to oppress and offend me.

NO: To the extent that you wanted to move?

TR: First, I wanted to change the South. I tried that for a few years, involved in civil rights and all, and then bloody but unbowed, I decided I could make better use of my time simply to transport myself to a more liberated part of the world. St. Augustine said, "Repair it by flight."

I don't want to be in a position of denying my Southern heritage, though, because it has had a great deal to do with who I am, particularly as a writer. Many writers have come out of the South, and I think there are some good reasons for that. So it's probably quite fortunate for me that I was born there, although I've often felt that I was a bit like a Tibetan Jew born into an Anglo-Saxon Southern Baptist family.

NO: Why is the South such a fertile ground for writers?

TR: For one thing, the art of conversation is not dead there; people still converse with dignity and imagination. Cantankerous old men sit around in rocking chairs on front porches and gabble for hours. With style and grace and eccentricity. The eccentric is vital to art.

There remains in the South a trace of the only true aristocracy America ever knew, even among people who never were actually aristocratic. It left a splendid residue, so that even in the midst of all that redneckery and racism and insecurity about manhood and all the other things that make the South so frustrating, there is a regard for language and for stories and for eccentricity and for honor. I think there's a lot of honor-seeking in writing. A lot of writing is concerned with avenging injustices, or is a conscious effort to perform some large, honorable act.

There's a sense of honor in the South, despite the Ku Klux Klan and that whole underbelly, that doesn't exist anywhere else in North America. And there's also an elitist attitude there, and I think all great art, great thinking, comes out of an elitist situation. There's no such thing as great egalitarian art; democracy does not produce great literature. Barbara Rose said that when elitism began to become a dirty word in America, it sounded the death knell for any possibility of the development of a high culture here. She may be right. Of course, we may not need a high culture. Our low culture is pretty wonderful.

NO: Did the South retain a certain elitism?

TR: Yeah, and a lot of it is ugly and stupid but, nevertheless, good for fostering literature. The regard for the eccentric that is retained is even more important, however.

NO: Did you feel it was an honorable thing to be a writer?

TR: Well, I decided to become a writer at such an early age that the word "honorable" probably wasn't in my vocabulary. I was five years old when I made that choice. I didn't care if it was honorable or dishonorable. I did know that there was a certain magical quality about books. I liked the way books looked, I liked the way they felt, I liked the way they smelled, I liked their weight in my hands, and the quality of the paper. So in a sense I was in love with the book as an object.

And for better or for worse, the fairy that tapped me with a wand in my cradle gave me a strong, active imagination. Around the age of five or six, I began to see where the book-as-object could be a vehicle or vessel fueled by that imagination. There was some kind of intermingling of the book-as-object and my active imagination. Somewhere in that molecular bonding between the book and the imagination, I was programmed to be a writer.

NO: Did it take you a while to develop the writing style first seen in *Another Roadside Attraction*?

TR: I think I wrote that book when I was in my early thirties. I was just over thirty. One reason I never really tried to write fiction before was because I knew that I hadn't evolved my own voice, and I didn't want to sound like anyone else. I didn't feel particularly pressured about it. I wasn't in any hurry. I looked at the field of literature and realized that there are no child prodigies, with the possible exception of Rimbaud. Most writers develop late.

Sometime in my early thirties, I recognized that in my nonfiction writing I was acquiring a voice that was decidedly my own. It happened to have been influenced by, and to coincide with, the psychedelic revolution in the '60s. So the time was ripe to inflict it on the world.

NO: Did working for the newspapers help to refine your writing?

TR: Yes and no. It's possible to hone your skills while writing for a newspaper, but only if, one, you're willing to stand up to editors, and two, if you're disciplined enough to push yourself toward excellence. I saw a lot of fine talent wither and shrink in Seattle's newsrooms. Newspapers are fairly timid and they don't much cotton to adventurous writing, writing that's likely to offend their advertisers or stretch the minds of their subscribers.

Also, newspaper editors don't demand very much of you in terms of high intellectual or stylistic standards. Accuracy, clarity, and good old meat-and-potatoes mediocrity are enough for them. I only grew as a writer because I wasn't afraid to rock the boat, and because I was too committed to personal growth to allow myself to snuggle into a nice, safe, comfortable journalistic niche. You know, when I was at the *Times* and *P-I*, there wasn't an editor on either paper who'd so much as thumbed through McLuhan's *Understanding Media*. I found that appalling. Perhaps today the brass is a bit more in touch. But generally speaking, newspapermen and women are the salt of the earth: they don't come any better. Seattle is really lucky to have two pretty good dailies. Our sportswriters, in particular, are outstanding.

NO: When you decided to leave the South, why did you choose to move to Seattle?

TR: Intuition, probably. I operate a lot on intuition and don't know why I do half the things I do. Seattle has changed so much since I landed here, in some ways for the better, in a lot of ways for the worse. I'm thinking of gentrification, French flu, tour buses in the Public Market, that sort of stuff. It was a good choice, though. I was right out of art school and bursting with ideas. I was able to manifest many of them in Seattle. It would have been impossible in Richmond. In my early years here, I staged happenings and things that I never could have gotten away with in Virginia.

NO: What kind of happenings did you stage?

TR: They were art events, although they usually took place on a stage. Today they would be called performance art. I staged one in Kirkland that was called *Low-calorie Human Sacrifice to the Goddess Minnie Mouse.* It created somewhat of a scandal. I was arrested at the end of it, although not booked. That was fun.

I also did one down in Pioneer Square [Seattle] in an art gallery. That was called *Stronger Than Dirt.* It had a scandalous effect, too. Lloyd Cooney [television station president] did an outraged editorial about it on KIRO.

NO: After living in Virginia, did you find it hard to get used to the Seattle climate?

TR: The rain appealed to me, and still does. It's one of the reasons why I live here.

NO: Why do you find the rain appealing?

TR: It allows for prolonged periods of intimacy. It's cozy and reduces temptation. It keeps you inside where you can turn inward, rather than scattering yourself about the beach and the boulevards. And it makes the little mushrooms grow.

I think that there was a lot of rain in my heart before I moved here, so in a sense it was simply finding an external environment that ran parallel to my internal weather. And when I say it was raining in my heart, I don't mean that I was depressed, because I don't find rain the least bit depressing. It's romantic, basically, and I am essentially a romantic being.

NO: Why did you move to the Skagit Valley?

TR: It's unusual to find a small town—particularly a small rural community, a farming, fishing community—where you can be yourself to the fullest extent of yourself; normally you'd have to go to a large city to do that. But there was a kind of sophistication in La Conner, and a tolerance of eccentric dress and behavior that made this place especially appealing, in conjunction with its natural beauty, the peace and privacy it offered. And that was largely the work of Morris Graves. When he moved here in 1937, he was treated very badly, because he was different, because he was an artist, because he walked around with a rope holding his pants up, and had a beard. But Morris is a very powerful person, and a singularly charming man, and he was able to break the ice, to clear a path for everyone else. He got through to the people and made it easier on the rest of us.

NO: Why did you set *Another Roadside Attraction* in the Skagit Valley?

TR: It was an area that appealed to me, visually and psychologically. It was an area that had not been written about very much, and it had an enormous amount of natural charm and was unique—certainly unusual—in certain respects. It was a rich poetic vein to mine. And I knew it fairly well. I didn't write the book in the Skagit Valley, though. I wrote it down in South Bend, so I was far enough removed from it to write about it with a slightly different perspective than I would have had, had I been here in the middle of it. It actually allowed me to write about it in a fresher way.

NO: When you started writing about it, did the landscape impose its form on the writing?

TR: No. I suppose any poetic image, if it's good, will have been imposed upon to a certain extent by the object or place that's being described, but it wasn't the kind of book it was because of the Skagit Valley; it was the kind of book it was because of the landscape of my mind, which for several years had been tended by small green gardeners in Day-Glo robes.

NO: Did taking LSD change your way of looking at things?

TR: Definitely. It reinforced some things and threw others overboard. It gave me a lot more ease in moving between different levels of reality. It was a liberating experience.

NO: Is it something you can remember and draw from?

TR: I don't draw from a specific experience. The psychedelic experience was much like being handed a new kind of telescope or microscope through which I could look at the world for a few hours in a totally different way, seeing it for the first time without the filtered glasses on, the blinders of education and social conditioning. Maybe seeing it accurately for the first time, in all of its manifestations. And then somebody takes the instrument away. But even though you can't duplicate through your own eye what you saw through that micro-telescope, you can remember that there are other ways of seeing, other levels to see.

If you're looking at a daisy in a field, having observed a daisy through the magic acid lens, even though you're not seeing it now as you saw it then, you're still aware that the daisy possesses other dimensions and an identity as strong as your own. In a sense, it's the Zen concept of is-ness, daisy-ness, as well as an "erotics" of perception, to borrow a Susan Sontag phrase. There's the sensation that there are hidden energy forms beyond time and space which shape our time-space world. I can't talk about it without sounding demented or sophomoric or both. That's why I say it can't be reported, it can only be evoked, and even then inadequately.

NO: So taking LSD made a big difference to you and your writing?

TR: It was a watershed experience. I think psychedelic drugs, particularly natural plant drugs like mushrooms, are the most efficient way of expediting the evolution of consciousness. There's no other way that even comes close. And I think it's an enormous human tragedy that scientists and philosophers and artists haven't been allowed to make real use of those drugs, that the government finds them such a threat. The government has finally, twenty years after the '60s, succeeded in creating a climate of absolute anti-drug hysteria, which is sheer idiocy.

It's so stupid, so hypocritical, so wrong, so shameful. A million people a year, according to estimates from the United Nations, die around the world as a result of tobacco. Less than three hundred die from cocaine, yet the country's in an absolute hysterical frenzy over cocaine. Cocaine's not even a drop in the bucket. In my opinion, it's a bad drug not because it's dangerous physically, but because it makes people stupid, whereas psychedelics actually can enhance intelligence.

There's some real lunacy there, some real hypocrisy and muddled thinking. You'd have to be an idiot to get worked up about the evils of cocaine when there's so much death resulting from alcohol and tobacco. But on the other hand, it really isn't idiocy, because the totalitarians recognize unconsciously that drugs are agents of change, agents of decontrol, and the government doesn't want us to change, and it certainly doesn't want us to be decontrolled. It is in their interest to control us. Nice safe, Christian, family values are a wonderful way to sedate the population. Keep us docile, easy to manipulate.

The evolution of consciousness is not something the government favors, because ultimately it would transform the politico-economic system and cut into the profits of the people who are really behind the government, who really run this country and the other countries of the world.

So there is a solid, legitimate reason for this drug hysteria that probably really isn't known consciously to most of the people who are creating it. I think it's the most frightening thing to happen on this planet in a long, long time. It scares me more than the bomb.

It isn't even the drugs per se. I could go on at great length about the value that there is in psychedelic drugs, although not for everybody. As Hermann Hesse said in *Steppenwolf,* "The magic theater is not for everyone."

But say it's not drugs, say it's blue cheese; the fact that the government can get people so easily worked up over blue cheese, the fact that people will buy this propaganda, swallow it hook, line, and sinker, and get in a panic over something they know nothing about, is extremely frightening. It's the Hitler technique.

NO: Do you try to respond to issues like this in your writing?

TR: A lot of my life has been spent fighting the tyranny of the dull mind. Obviously, I try to do it in my work. I'm not going to go out and lead a pro-drug crusade. What I can do is to try to set an example. And to offer people the tools they might use to liberate themselves from totalitarian, anti-life control.

NO: You wouldn't want to go joining a political movement?

TR: Absolutely not. Political movements are trivial in my estimation, except in a very secondary way. If we want to change things, then *we* have to change. To change the world, you change yourself. It's as simple as that, and as difficult as that. Politics is not going to make anything any better. There are no practical solutions. Sooner or later, we have to have the guts to do the impractical things that are required to save the planet.

NO: And your job as a writer is to make an individual reader aware of the implications of some of these things?

TR: And entertain them at the same time. My job is to awaken in the reader his or her own sense of wonder. An entertaining wake-up call from the front desk.

NO: And this wake-up call should be funny?

TR: There's no wisdom without humor, I'll say that flatly. Wisdom does not exist without humor. Humor is both a form of wisdom and a means of survival. A lot of evolution, which seems to be the primary force in the organic universe, is a matter of game-playing. A lot of things are done in evolution just for the hell of it. If evolution were only concerned with survival of the fittest, we wouldn't even be around. The world would be exclusively populated with cockroaches and ants; they're much better at survival than we are.

Evolution is constantly playing games, experimenting, inventing, innovating, trying new things, seeing if they work—"Let's put horns on this jackrabbit, see what happens. Well, it didn't work but it made a cute postcard." So to be playful is not to be frivolous; it is, ultimately, to be realistic, to be in tune with the universe, to be an agent of evolution.

One of the problems with playfulness for a writer is that there's a thin line between playfulness and cuteness. But that's a risk I have to take. Any artist who isn't taking risks is a mediocre artist. The best artists are willing to risk something, and that is part of my risk; I risk being cute. But I think I stay on the playful side of the line enough, so that it's a risk worth taking.

And to be playful at a highly conscious level is a very desirable thing. I'm not particularly interested in the tradition of Western literature. I'm interested in the tradition of word as celebration, metaphor as magic, language as an agent of liberation, and narrative as cosmic connection. That tradition is much older than Western literature. That's the old storyteller-as-enchanter, as spellbinder and counselor, around the campfire.

NO: Is that one of the reasons you chose to tell a fractured fairy tale in *Still Life With Woodpecker*?

TR: Fairy tales are the most profound literature that we have ever developed. Many of them are thousands of years old, and they were honed and refined over tens of thousands of tellings until they speak directly to the psyche. They resonate there, if they're told in their pure form. The Walt Disney version or the nice safe liberal versions where nobody really gets hurt totally pervert them; you lose everything, you lose all that's valuable in them. But a true fairy tale is a remarkable piece of verbal science.

NO: By using a fairy tale in the *Woodpecker* book you seemed to be getting at what people want out of romantic relationships: a kind of love which is like a fairy tale.

TR: No. A fairy tale is not a pretty, idealistic deception. In the original fairy tales you got a strong dose of reality. On a psychological level, at any rate. There was Prince Charming, there was also the witch, and both of these were aspects of your own personality. When they said there was a witch, they didn't mean that there was some evil old woman who lived in a cabin in the woods; that witch was part of you, or part of your mother, or sister.

NO: So the original versions of the fairy tales were quite instructive?

TR: The earliest Dr. Ruth; the fairy tales were absolutely teeming with sexual instruction. They were told to prepare children for life, to teach children about growing up, about their sexuality, romance and marriage, and all the things that children in a peasant environment would have needed to know about their own psychological life. Psychologically, they're incredibly complex and deep.

NO: So you found them useful?

TR: I found that one useful ["The Frog Prince"], considering what I wanted to deal with in that book: romantic love and objecthood. I wanted to write about inanimate objects in a way they had never been written about before. There have been some good books in which inanimate objects played a large role, but invariably as a symbol. They were dealt with symbolically, like the pistol in James Jones's great little novella [*The Pistol*], or the overcoat in Gogol.

But I wanted to write about an object in a non-symbolic way, where the secret life of the object itself, the energy of the inanimate object itself, was as real as a character in the book, as a human being.

NO: In a fairy tale, are all the objects charged with a certain supernatural energy?

TR: They have meaning, largely symbolic. I chose a fairy tale where an object was a symbol, but I also chose another object, a Camel pack. The golden ball remained a symbol. It symbolizes unity.

When we were children, people would say, "Look at that kid. He's a ball of energy." And while they might think that they were using a mere figure of speech, when we're young our energy is very contained, we *are* like balls. The older we get, the more dispersed it becomes; we lose that union with the universe.

That's what the golden ball represented. When the little girl lost her golden ball, that was her loss of innocence, her loss of universal unity. Of course, she wanted it back, but it was very difficult to get back.

I dealt with it on that level, but the Camel pack I chose to deal with non-symbolically, as a real object standing only for itself. Even though it was rich in association and meaning, and engendered games and riddles and puns, it nevertheless had a life of its own.

NO: Why did you choose the pack of Camel cigarettes?

TR: I wanted to use something human-made. I didn't want a seashell or a pine cone, something from nature. I wanted it to be something that had been shaped by a human hand, I wanted it to be something that was in common usage, that you'd be likely to see anywhere, in anyone's home or car. So I thought, "Something from the supermarket would be just right."

I'm really attracted to package design, cans and labels. It occurred to me that the Camel pack had the most potential because of all the lore that accompanies it, all the games and riddles and things that had been invented by sailors and convicts, men who are alone with objects. The design, of course, is quite appealing; maybe the most successful package design of all time, plus it had all these other psychological and aesthetic associations. The Camel pack was a very rich subject. I collected a lot of stories about it and only used a few of them, one-tenth of what was available.

NO: Did you try to see the whole universe in that one object?

TR: Yeah, Blake's idea of seeing the universe in a grain of sand, the macrocosm in the microcosm. I actually shut myself up in a room for three days with nothing but a pack of Camels.

NO: Just like Princess Leigh-Cheri in the book?

TR: Yes, although I only did it for three days. But I got the essence of it. I just meditated on it for three days.

NO: That must have been a strange experience.

TR: Strange experiences can be the best experiences.

NO: A pack of cigarettes is normally something we take for granted. Were you trying to reanimate the object?

TR: Quite the contrary. I wanted to explore and to celebrate the inanimate. My goal was the opposite of anthropomorphism. There may be a million stories in the Naked City, but there are a trillion dramas unfolding every fraction of a second on the subatomic level. Even on the molecular level, there are amazing bonding romances going on. Who knows what secrets an object really holds? I guess I was trying to say that we should *not* take them for granted. In the socialist countries that I've visited, there was a severe shortage of interesting objects, and I keenly felt their absence. Bare shelves signify more than one kind of deprivation. They must emaciate the imagination.

There's a method of looking at the world, maybe we could call it "poetic awareness." That sounds pretentious, but it's just a way of training yourself to be constantly aware of the vitality and connectedness of the things around you. You automatically begin to register the vectors or association between unlikely objects and images and events. You spot a can of Red Devil lye in the supermarket, for example, and you're instantly reminded of thirteenth-century Christianity. Then and there, you could compose an essay on the relationship. Cross-reference to the max. It's an interesting exercise in mental aliveness. The world becomes one big poem. Or one big parlor game.

NO: You seem to do that a lot in your writing.

TR: Well, it's my way of defining reality. Or *not* defining reality.

NO: How about cartooning? Do your books owe something to cartooning?

TR: Hardly a thing. That's a fake notion that's been perpetuated by the press. Cartoons, more specifically comic strips, are an integral part of American popular culture. Now popular culture possesses a tremendous energy, vitality, and humor that can be tapped by the serious artist and put to higher purposes. I certainly do that, and I'm amazed that so few serious writers have harnessed the power of pop culture to illuminate their fiction. Maybe they're afraid of being considered lightweight or frivolous by the academic dullards. In any case, pop culture, comic strips included, has great potential as literary fuel. You have to keep in mind, though, that it's only the fuel, not the vehicle, itself. I learned a lot about structure from George Herriman, creator of "Krazy Kat," as did Philip Guston, the late painter. But Herriman was a structural genius and most cartoonists are not.

In fiction, the bottom line is language, and my language owes no more to cartoons than does the language of Henry James. True enough, I don't paint deep, detailed psychological portraits. But that doesn't mean my characters are cartoons. What it means is that I find that sort of writing boring, boring to do and, increasingly for me, boring to read, although there are writers who've done it exceedingly well. I employ a different dynamic, one that in the interest of freshness and swing—"It don't mean a thing if it ain't got that swing"—requires the reader to fill in some of the blanks, some of the notes. It is more accurate to compare it with jazz than cartooning.

NO: The surface of your prose is like a package design—bright, shiny and alive—but there always seems to be something going on underneath.

TR: Well, I hope that's true. That's part of my approach. I've described my books in the past as being cakes with files baked in them. That's kind of an obsolete image, but years ago in movies and in comic strips, prisoners would receive a cake from a friend and there would be a file hidden in the middle and they would file their way out of jail. I try to create something that's beautiful to look at and delicious to the taste, and yet in the middle there's this hard, sharp instrument that you can use to saw through the bars and liberate yourself, if you so desire. It's not imperative. You can just eat the cake and throw the file away if you want, but the file is there; it is always there in anything I write.

NO: Is it important for you to have an audience, or would you write the books anyway?

TR: I certainly wouldn't write as much.

NO: When you're writing are you aware, like a circus performer, that an audience is there?

TR: No, and I don't think Karl Wallenda would have thought about the audience very much when he was up on the wire. You're too busy trying to stay on the wire. I think about the wire and how I'm going to get from this side of Niagara Falls to the other without falling off. You don't think of the people down below until you're safe and sound on the other side.

Nowadays, I write under contract. I thought that might be a problem, knowing that I had a deadline and all that, but I don't think about that, either. When I go in to write, I forget everything else. I don't feel any pressure from the publishers, not that they put any on me. And I feel no pressure of trying to please an audience. It's just between me and the page. I'm lucky that way.

NO: Do you feel that your reputation is always on the line when you do a book?

TR: I don't give a rat hair about my reputation.

NO: But you were talking about writing being a high wire act?

TR: I was probably just being fanciful. I'm a long-time admirer of aerial acts, and I'm capable of fancy. No, the problem with reputation is that it's bound up with egoism. And the ego is the source of most of humanity's unhappiness. Hell is a solidified ego, heaven is a dissolved ego. Simple as that. The reason so many writers are depressed and dismal is that they tend to have large, stiff egos. Look at Saul Bellow. Now, he has a great reputation. He's rich and famous, he's won a Nobel prize, critics everywhere wash his feet with their slobber. But Saul Bellow is one miserable old hound dog. And he's merely one example. If you think a grand reputation will bring you joy, think again.

To return to the original analogy, the real joys and thrills and fulfillment in writing don't come from audience or critical response, they come from working high up on the wire, alone, without a net. But I really should apologize to Karl Wallenda's ghost for that presumptuous analogy.

NO: Does it scare you to work up on that wire?

TR: Always. That's good, because if it isn't scaring you, you have to figure that you're becoming a formula writer. If you're not scared, then you're too comfortable, too smug. There's something missing when you're not scared. Terror is very inspiring.

NO: Scared of what?

TR: Of falling off the wire, writing a stilted paragraph or a stupid book, or at least one that doesn't work for me. The ones that work for me, other people might consider stupid, so that's neither here nor there. You can write bad books and still have a good reputation. If I do something that I'm not proud of, then that's what I have to deal with, that's the fall that'll break my bones. I'm making it sound more dramatic than it really is.

NO: Do you try to write back to the people who write to you about your books?

TR: I get an awful lot of truly wonderful fan mail, and I don't think it's because my audience is so huge, it's because we have a special relationship, my readers and I. Thus, they write. Someone who likes my books is more apt to write me a letter than, say, someone who likes John Updike is apt to write him. I answer as many as I can, but too often people expect me to be their pen pal.

NO: Do you like the solitude of being a writer?

TR: A writer has got to like solitude. It's a solitary and lonely business. A lot of talented people have failed as writers because they couldn't stand being alone.

NO: Do you work every day?

TR: Five days a week.

NO: Early morning?

TR: It's not healthy to get up too early. [Laughs] I work from ten to three, approximately. That's the time I'm at my desk with implement in hand. Actually, I'm working almost all the time. When I'm in bed at night waiting to go to sleep, I'm working. When I'm walking the fields I'm working, when I'm playing volleyball or honky-tonking, I'm working; it's always on my mind.

NO: So every part of your being goes into a book?

TR: Dream and imagination, wit and sexuality, insight and intuition, *weltschmerz* and wang-dang-doodle. You stir in every spice on your shelf, although, ideally, in amounts and combinations that won't spoil the stew. But you've got to hold some stuff back for yourself and your loved ones. I, for one, refuse to use up my life in literature.

NO: Is it fun to sit down at the writing desk? Do you feel you're discovering things?

TR: Well, it's definitely a journey, an odyssey. It's fun and it's edifying and it's laboriously hard work and it's terrifying and it's very, very mysterious.

The truth is, I don't know how to talk about writing. Authors such as William Gass and Stanley Elkin speak so beautifully about the act of writing, in all of its various ramifications. But you ask me to describe the writing process, all I can think to say is that it's like a cross between flying to the moon and taking a shower in a motel.

NO: Are there a lot more books you want to do?

TR: To paraphrase every football coach in the country, I just take 'em one book at a time.

Joy in Spite of Everything:
An Interview with Tom Robbins

Bill Strickland/1987

This interview was originally published in two parts in *Writer's Digest*: February 1988, 30–33, 69, and March 1988, 32–36. Reprinted with the permission of Bill Strickland. Condensed and edited by Tom Robbins, 2009, with the approval of Bill Strickland.

"What are you looking for in a typewriter?" A salesman asks the Tom Robbins narrator in the prologue to *Still Life With Woodpecker*.

"Something more than words," Robbins as narrator replies. "Crystals. I want to send my readers armloads of crystals, some of which are the colors of orchids and peonies, some of which pick up radio signals from a secret city that is half Paris and half Coney Island."

Now, a flesh-and-blood Robbins is sitting relaxed, responding in the slow, measured drawl befitting his Southern upbringing, to questions about the vivid colors of his personal literary palette and the odd signals picked up by the mind behind *Another Roadside Attraction, Even Cowgirls Get the Blues, Jitterbug Perfume*, and the aforementioned *Still Life With Woodpecker*, novels which although off-beat, have sold many hundreds of thousands of copies. Before we get very far, however, we have to pause and deal with the motorcycles.

There are more than seventy toy motorcycles (Robbins quit riding bikes after a few too many close calls, but he still loves the image) in his writing room, and the problem, which he's just noticed, is that they've recently been rearranged by his housekeeper.

"This won't do!" he exclaims, shaking his head. With his hands he describes zigzags, tangents, and lopsided circles. "They were going off in various different directions, and now they all face the same way. Look at that. They're straight."

His reaction to this obvious affront could very well serve as a metaphor for the Tom Robbins approach to writing: go off in unexpected directions, swerve, pop wheelies, run red lights, always avoid the straight and narrow, and never allow a cop or a housekeeper (a reviewer or an editor?) to cramp your style. It's also indicative of how serious and dedicated he is in his approach to his craft, how very orderly is his ostensible disorder.

When the toys have been appropriately, creatively scrambled, we commence again.

Writer's Digest: When people think of Tom Robbins, they often think of figures of speech, of metaphors and similes. How do you create images?

Tom Robbins: Well, they're never, ever arbitrary, I can tell you that much. I suppose my method is a combination of intense concentration and freewheeling imagination. I'll simply stare at an object or mentally picture a person, place, or thing, and expound on it and extrapolate from it. Spin it in a lapidary. Sooner or later, unlikely yet pertinent associations and connections will reveal themselves. The purpose, of course, is to illuminate the image, to enliven it, to cause it to pop up like Jack-in-the-box in the reader's mind—and maybe stick there. With any luck it might both surprise and delight the reader and provide him or her with a fresh and heretofore unimagined understanding of something that normally would be taken for granted.

WD: But "the sun is an orange" doesn't get it. You'd elaborate on that.

Robbins: Right, that's way too predictable, too ordinary, too forgettable. To write, "the sun came up like an orange" has no visual resonance. But if you say, "the sun came up like a big bald head," as Laurie Anderson once did, then you've reached down inside the sentence and pulled out something evocative. You've jiggled the cortex.

Aldous Huxley pointed out that "fire escapes don't urinate" is a self-evident truth that the reader can pass right over with a shrug; but if you say instead, "black ladders lack bladders," then something intriguing and even memorable may come into focus in the lens of the mind.

WD: The purpose is . . . ?

Robbins: To both enhance the narrative—to enliven and deepen the story—and in rare cases, to provoke a little leap of consciousness, to light up a sentence, a phrase, in such a way that there's a little flash, a brief momentary glimpse of the unseen world. When properly executed, it won't in the least interfere with the plot, yet it calls attention to something beyond the plot, beyond *all* plots; something cosmic, we may be forced to call it.

Mysticism is such a loaded and suspect word, but, hey, there are forces, dimensions in life that even a marginally evolved person can sense though never fully identify or comprehend. You know what I'm talking about? Something above the sky and behind the rain. And when we suddenly interface with it, well, there's a rush, a small epiphany, a bolt of inexplicable recognition and exhilaration. More often than not, that hidden door in consciousness is thrown open by language, although the pictorial and musical arts can certainly jimmy the lock as well.

We're treated to those unexpected cosmic zingers from time to time in Kafka and Hesse and in F. Scott Fitzgerald. There are a surprising number of them in Norman Mailer, although they're totally absent in Hemingway. They occur more often in poems than in novels, naturally. A particular image, skillfully illuminated, will not only freeze the moment, eternalize it, but provide a launch pad, a springboard to a higher level of awareness.

WD: How do you decide when and where to use metaphoric imagery?

Robbins: It's usually decided *for* me. By the flow of language and ideas, the engagement with the page, the intense concentration on the material. Sometimes a character will demand it. Only a very few images generate a cosmic connection, of course. Occasionally, I'll select an image for no other reason than the entertainment factor or, more frequently, to improve the rhythm of a sentence. People read with their ears as well as their eyes, you know. Cadence is as important in writing as in music. "The sun came up like a big bald head" has a beat, a rhythm. "The sun is an orange" does not.

WD: Rhythm aside, how do you know if the picture you're evoking is too ridiculous to be accepted.

Robbins: Accepted by *whom*? Somebody's Aunt Minnie? In the first place, that problem would only arise for writers and readers of imaginative fiction, fiction that's stylistically adventurous, that stretches the senses. I mean, it isn't going to be a risk in Erle Stanley Gardner, is it? And in any case, to scorn the ridiculous is to scorn much of life itself.

In the end, whatever works, works—and a writer who can't tell if it works should probably abandon imaginative fiction and start cranking out lawyer novels. Better yet, he or she should consider giving up literature altogether and enroll in a good law school. As for readers, I'm unconcerned. My readership does not generally include the dull of mind or the stiff of wit.

I don't believe there're any rules in fiction that with the proper verve and under the right conditions cannot be broken. For example, I hear tell that in creative-writing classes they warn you against preaching. Generally speaking, that's pretty sound advice. But what if a writer can make preaching *work*? In *Jitterbug Perfume*, as a sort of challenge, I elected to deliver a couple of sermons. And why not? I'll go out on a limb and contend that the way they were crafted they enhanced the reading experience, enriched rather than distracted from the narrative.

WD: Some critics also say your characters aren't believable, that they exist only as tools for your philosophy and your humor.

Robbins: Yeah, they would say that, wouldn't they; having spent a lot of time and money learning all about proper characterization in graduate school—from some pedagogue who previously learned all about it in another grad school from some earlier pedagogue, now deceased, who learned . . . ad infinitum. They'd be astonished if they knew how many people identify with my characters, emulate them, name their children after them, write letters to them in care of me, etcetera.

True, I don't always develop characters in the conventional way. I'll paint a few strokes here, a stroke or two there, so that a portrait is gradually revealed over time. And I'll usually refrain from painting a complete, detailed physical rendering of the character. I'll allow readers some leeway in forming their own picture. For example, in *Even Cowgirls Get the Blues* I employed a variety of different and sometimes contradictory metaphors and similes in reference to Sissy Hankshaw's thumbs; comparing them in one scene to bananas, in another to eggplants or even baseball bats. The reader is invited to become involved. His or her own imagination—a precious commodity these days—is actively engaged.

It appears that some of my betters also have snorted that my protagonists are "larger than life." Well, in the sense that Falstaff in *Henry V*, or the King and the Duke in *Huckleberry Finn*, or McMurphy in *One Flew Over the Cuckoos Nest*; or, on the female side, say, Auntie Mame or Pippi Longstocking are larger than life, I suppose that's correct. But there exist, in fact, real people in life who appear to loom larger than life. I've enjoyed the privilege of knowing some of them personally. They interest me.

WD: Would you say that *you* are larger than life?

Robbins: Me? No, but I'm larger than a breadbox. (*Laughs*) Look, I'm just another glad fool on the left-handed path, following the Charmer's pipes through the lotus fields of longing and the honeycomb of language. Looking for . . . ? I don't know. The adjective in the lotus. The jewel in the inkwell. A blue dolphin leaping from a sink of dirty dishes.

WD: Is all that an aspect of your avowed creed, "Joy in spite of everything"?

Robbins: Did I avow that? Well, if it is, indeed, my creed, please let me assure you that it has very little with to do with mindless optimism or positive thinking. Positive thinking is all too often merely delusional. No, insisting on joy in spite of the rampant and ceaseless abuses of our pretty screwed-up world is, in reality, a cry of defiance. A battle cry. Sometimes it's despair refusing to take itself seriously. It's the triumph of love and laughter over misfortune and repression.

WD: Does that explain your tendency to make jokes?

Robbins: What jokes? In my first novel I was attempting to paste together a collage of American culture at that juncture of our history. Jokes were a part of that cultural detritus, so I naturally enough pasted some into the collage. (*Shrugs*) Haven't done that since. Humorous observations and comic scenes, yeah, but they shouldn't be confused with jokes.

Anyway, just for drill, let's consider what are arguably the absolute greatest novels in western history: *Ulysses, Don Quixote, Alice in Wonderland, Gulliver's Travels, Gargantua,* and *Huckleberry Finn.* All six of those classics have a strong comic dimension. Right? Even more recent masterpieces such as *Catch 22* and *The Horse's Mouth* and *Fear and Loathing in Las Vegas* and *The Ginger Man* and Saul Bellow's one and only great book, *Henderson the Rain King,* are also seriously funny. I rest my case.

WD: You're a successful author; do you have any advice for aspiring writers?

Robbins: Not a lot. Write—and read—everyday without fail. Challenge every single sentence: challenge it for lucidity, accuracy, originality, and rhythm. Never be afraid to make a fool of yourself. Stop worrying about getting published and concentrate on getting better. Don't mistake that which is dark for that which is deep. And always bear in mind that the only rule is whatever works, works.

And Tom Robbins might add, as smiling he looks around the room, never allow a well-meaning dullard to monkey with your motorcycles.

Tom Robbins:
Mr. Green Tea Ice Cream

Inga Muscio/1993

From *The Stranger* (Seattle, Washington), May 16, 1993. Reprinted with the permission of Inga Muscio.

As a local Seattle writer, there are certain people I feel compelled to yap with. In the arena of white men reside three: Martin Selig (our Donald Trump), Tom Robbins, and Jesse Bernstein. So far, Mr. Selig has chosen to avoid me like the plague, though I am making some headway with Mr. Bernstein. Mr. Robbins, on the other hand, needed little prompting. In fact, all that was required to gain an audience with him was a short note, reading, "If you will let me interview you for *The Stranger*, I will buy you an ice cream cone." To which he readily replied acquiescence.

We met at "the snout of the pig" in the Market and he led me to a Chinese restaurant where he assured me, we would find "the best ice cream in town." The waitress came to our table.

Waitress: (Brightly) Hello! Can I take your order?
TR: Ice cream. A lot of it.
W: That's all? How much is a lot?
TR: Yes, that's all. Two large bowls.
W: We don't have large.
TR: Well, give us a lot.
W: How much? (laughing) Ten orders? I think we might be out.
TR: You can't be out. It's *very* important!

The waitress left, Mr. Robbins seemed distressed. He muttered, "They can't be out" a few more times. Presently the waitress returned.
W: We have some.

TR: Oh, thank god. Two large ones please.

That settled, we began the interview.

IM: When did you start writing?

TR: When I was five. Well, I couldn't actually write when I was five. I'd dictate to my mother. Sometimes she'd change what I'd say—you know, to make it sound clearer—and I could always tell when she was doing that. I'd get very angry at her until she changed it back the way I said it. My mother died recently—she kept a Snow White and the Seven Dwarves scrapbook for me, only instead of pictures, it was full of the first stories I wrote—but during the feeding frenzy after she died, it disappeared.

IM: Feeding frenzy?

TR: You know, when they come in and fight over every stick of furniture. (musing) The last time I saw it (the scrapbook) was ten or fifteen years ago. I leafed through it and saw the first story I ever wrote, about a cow that was marooned on a tropical island, kind of like a Gary Larson cartoon. To survive, the cow taught itself to eat sand, to derive nutrients from the sand.

IM: Have you ever been mad at the universe?

TR: (Holds face in hands. Grimaces. Sighs, looks to ceiling.) Um. No, I only get mad at the inhabitants of the universe. I think the universe is operating with perfection. Human beings are the monkey wrench in the machinery of the universe.

IM: Why?

TR: 'Cause they don't realize that they're perfect, so they behave imperfectly. And also because there's too many of us. That's the big problem right now. There's too many people. For that, we can blame religion. Religion is destroying the world. It's the single most dangerous force in the universe. (Looking thoughtfully at interviewer.) Have you ever had green tea ice cream before?

IM: Uh, no.

TR: I bet they don't have any but I made it sound so important that they sent out for some.

(Just as this sentence leaves his mouth, our waitress comes with two oval plates heaped with pale green ice cream, candied nuts, oranges, and a lemon slice. The interview is brought to a temporary impasse, as we pork down like crazed fools. When the ice cream's gone he reaches for a cookie to learn his fortune.)

IM: What's your fortune cookie say?

TR: "You have given some thought to a different lifestyle." It's true. I've been thinking about becoming a beatnik again.

IM: As opposed to what?

TR: Mmm . . . as opposed to a surrealist. Next time, I want to be a rich beatnik. When I was a beatnik before, I was poor, if that's not an oxymoron. I think a rich beatnik is a bohemian. Maybe that's my new lifestyle, a romantic bohemian. I think I'm in my Leonard Cohen phase.

IM: What's that mean?

TR: Well, he, uh, he meditates during the day in Armani suits, $2,000 suits. Then in the evening, he goes to cafes and flirts with beautiful women. You know who Leonard Cohen is, don't you?

IM: Uh, it certainly sounds familiar.

TR: He's a songwriter. A wonderful poet too.

IM: He's still alive, right?

TR: Oh yeah, hotter than ever.

IM: You ever met him?

TR: No. I've never had any desire to meet him. If we were together, he'd get all the attention.

IM: How do you define religion?

TR: Religion is umm . . . a widespread, inappropriate response to the mystery of being.

IM: What do you think is a more appropriate response?

TR: Spirituality.

IM: How do you define that?

TR: (Laughs) A widespread appropriate response to the mystery of being. No. Spirituality is just a connection to the mystery of being, a conscious strengthening of the connections to the mystery of being. A conscious attempt to enlarge the soul, whereas organized religion shrinks the soul. Washes the soul in harsh detergent and hot water, then throws it in the dryer at the highest temperature. The soul goes in quite large and comes out shrunken. Religion is spirituality for people who lack courage and imagination. I'm just making all this stuff up. That doesn't mean it's not true, but don't call me tomorrow and ask me what I said, 'cause I won't remember. (Staring at fortune cookie again.) That's a good fortune. I think I'll keep it. It's a good idea. I've thought about getting rid of all my possessions and moving into a beatnik hotel.

IM: How do you imagine you affect the world?

TR: Very little, more than most, but still very little. I can give you some concrete examples, though. Ad agencies have been stealing lines from my books for ads. I get a lot of mail. I get a lot of letters from people who say my books have affected their lives. That's satisfying. It's not why I write, but it's nice to hear that I might be helping people over the rough spots. I don't think that's my mission, but it's a nice fringe benefit.

IM: Do the characters in your books ever become archetypes of people you later come across?

TR: Not just characters, but whole events. Life imitates Art. It started in my very first book. A character kidnaps a baboon from the Woodland Park Zoo. Three weeks after the book was published, someone stole a baboon from the Woodland Park Zoo. At first, I thought it was one of my friends pulling a prank. The police found the guy, but it was a complete stranger, who'd never read the book (*Another Roadside Attraction*). A more recent example, in my last book, an Arab and a Jew open a restaurant together and it's bombed, um, because, for political reasons. I went to Jerusalem and found out that an Arab and a Jew *had* opened a restaurant. It had been bombed three times. Also, the last book predicted the Gulf War and that the Super Bowl would occur during it. In the book I'm working on now, the Stock Market crashed. So if you know anyone with stock, tell 'em to pull out now. It's scary. You have to be careful about what you write.

IM: You went to Jerusalem after *Skinny Legs and All* was published?

TR: No, it was sometime in the process of writing, but it was long after I'd completed the idea about the restaurant.

IM: How does it feel writing about something like the stock market crashing, when your frame of reference in this area tells you that it just might?

TR: Well, it makes me feel like I should take my retirement funds out of the stock market.

IM: When things in your books later come true, do you think you are the one making it happen or do you think you're just some weird mouthpiece for destiny?

TR: I'm never thinking about it consciously when I'm writing, I just come to the intuition.

IM: You smoke?

TR: Only cigars. I have this old antique fan that I set up so that it blows all the smoke away from me, so I don't get any secondhand smoke. The people I was hanging out with who got me into cigars all smoked expensive ones, so all the ones I like are expensive.

IM: Like how much?

TR: Four bucks. I actually got some Havanas recently, they go for sixteen bucks apiece. But a cigar will last me a week. There's a big ritual involved with lighting a cigar, that's why I think I like it so much, that ritual. It takes five matches—wood matches. The first four are to get it nice and hot, the flame never touches the tip. Then with the fifth, the cigar just explodes to life.

IM: You drink coffee?

TR: No. I've drunk coffee four times in my life and I remember each one vividly, I don't like any hot drinks.

IM: What do you like?

TR: Cold, carbonated beverages.

IM: Do you know what carbonation does? Like why it gives you that rush?

TR: (Taps temple) It creates intelligence.

IM: Who's your best friend?

TR: Um . . . I got a couple. A man and a woman. The man is a character in a French film called *Diva*. He lives in a big loft in Paris. In the middle of the floor is a bathtub. He sits in the bathtub all day, smoking cigars and looking at the wave machine. Have you seen those? It's like a plastic tank with blue water in it. It goes (sweeps hand to and fro) up and down.

IM: Why's he your best friend?

TR: Well, because I admire him so much. I know if I were in trouble, he'd come help me. In the movie, when one of his friends is in trouble, he'll get out of the bathtub and help them. He exerts the absolute minimum amount of effort, but he always helps his friends. Then he goes back to the bathtub. The loft is empty, by the way, except for the bathtub and the wave machine. But he has a beautiful car.

IM: And the woman?

TR: Well, her name's Alexa d'Avalon. She's not in a movie. She lives right down the street, as a matter of fact. She reads Tarot cards. A very gifted psychic.

IM: Will she mind if her name's in the paper?

TR: (Shakes his head no) Not as long as I'm expressing admiration. Her name, it looks like it'd be in a French movie, huh?

IM: Yeah, I thought she'd be a character from a book or something.

TR: Yeah. (Contemplates ceiling again. Sighs.) I live in a French movie with Japanese subtitles.

Tom Robbins's Book of Bozo

Jessica Maxwell/1995

From *Esquire*, January 1995, 18. Reprinted with the permission of Jessica Maxwell.

Tom Robbins's new novel, *Half Asleep in Frog Pajamas* (Bantam Books), immediately leaped onto the *New York Times* best-seller list. We caught up with him beside a Florida lagoon, wide awake in no pajamas, and asked him to explain his most amphibious novel to date.

Q: In establishing your theory that man is in essence an amphibian . . .
A: It's more than a theory. Think of the human fetus. Think of the primordial soup.
Q: . . . you write about an aquatic African tribe called the Bozo. Tom, are you making that up?
A: Having spent a week with them in Mali, I can assure you Bozos are real, we aren't them, and they aren't on this bus. Bozos travel by canoe, in fact, and their cosmology revolves around a legendary close encounter with amphibious humanoids from outer space. Supposedly, we earthlings are linked to those alien frogmen in numerous significant ways. The evidence is more convincing than the uninformed might imagine.
Q: So you actually ran with the Bozo . . .
A: Swam with them. Drank millet beer with them. It was too damn hot to run.
Q: . . . and bought into their religion?
A: Not exactly, although it makes at least as much sense as Christianity. On the most simplistic level, it's rather like Jesus with flippers.
Q: What led you to the Bozo in the first place?
A: When I read in a scientific journal that a couple of Malinese tribes have had for five thousand years detailed astronomical knowledge of a star system invisible to the naked eye, I realized there was a rip in the fabric of con-

sensual reality that begged to be explored. The Dogon have far more refined astro-aquatic rituals, but I favored the Bozo because I loved their name.

Q: You don't look quite so favorably on some of the Wall Street characters who actually dominate this novel.

A: Well, Jessica, there are Bozos and then there are bozos.

Tom Robbins: an outrageous writer in a politically correct era

Michael Sims/2000

From *BookPage*, May 2000, 5. Reprinted with the permission of Lynn Green, editor.

Tom Robbins believes in truth in advertising. His novels lure the adventurous and warn the timid with outrageous titles, which accurately predict outrageousness within. *Even Cowgirls Get the Blues, Still Life With Woodpecker, Half Asleep in Frog Pajamas, Skinny Legs and All*—these are not your usual well-behaved titles of popular novels. You won't see Robbins calling his books *The Firm* or *The Notebook*.

But for sheer mouthful of chewy syllables, you can't beat the title of Robbins's latest novel—*Fierce Invalids Home From Hot Climates*. It doesn't exactly roll off the tongue; however, it's more appealing than the rejected working title, "Syrup of Wahoo." In a recent interview, Robbins explained that he changed the first title because he didn't like the misleading connotations of sweetness ("while the book is upbeat and exuberant, it decidedly is not sweet") and because he kept having to explain to Generation X friends that "wahoo" was a cry of exhilaration that did not require "a dot and a com" after it.

Robbins says he took the title from his own translation of a line from a Rimbaud poem. "While it has quite literal significance within the context of my plot," he adds, "it has wider meanings, as well. All of us who've managed to survive intense love affairs, political confrontations, or periods of personal debauchery might be said to be fierce invalids home from hot climates."

Fierce Invalids, Robbins explains, was inspired "by an entry from Bruce Chatwin's journal, by a CIA agent I met in Southeast Asia, by the mystery surrounding the lost prophecy of the Virgin of Fatima, by the increasing evidence that the interplay of opposites is the engine that runs the universe, and by embroidered memories of old *Terry and the Pirates* comic books."

Why so long since his last book? "Hey, it's only been five and a half years. And I have no idea where they went. I've been writing, yes; and building a house and traveling and generally following the Charmer's pipes down oblique paths of mysticism and eroticism. Certainly, I'd like to write faster, but whenever I've tried it, the language has suffered. I tend to sift my mental lexicon for the fresher, more unexpected word the way an old prospector pans for the bigger, more valuable nugget. That takes time."

Robbins's many fans won't mind the wait. *Fierce Invalids Home From Hot Climates* is everything they've come to expect—humor, sex, adventure, ferocious rants about society and religion, characters who swear on the Bible and *Finnegan's Wake*, asides on everything from etymology to violence, and a disregard for anybody else's definition of good taste. Switters, the protagonist, is a gun-toting pacifist anarchist who works for the government. In other words, by embodying contradictions, he is in the tradition of such Robbins heroes as the Woodpecker and Sissy Hankshaw.

Robbins says he never goes back and reads his novels once they've been published. "I'm saving that experience, and any selection of favorites that might ensue, for my golden years. Provided my golden years aren't here already." He does, however, have favorite characters. "I suppose I'll always be in love with Amanda, the uninhibited young nature goddess from *Another Roadside Attraction*. Although I disguised her as a child of the '60s, she danced directly out of the collective unconscious, did not pass Go, did not give a damn for any stinking $200. At the moment, however, I'd have to say that I'm most particularly fond of Switters, the rascally protagonist of *Fierce Invalids*."

Not surprisingly, Robbins is impatient with political correctness in the arts, especially the variety that expects writers to stay in their own yards and not trespass upon the sacred turf of some other group. "What novelists do— what screenwriters and playwrights do—is get inside other people's heads and look out. The ability to do that convincingly, no matter whose head is so entered, is what separates the real writer from the polemist, the philistine, and the poseur. To say that artists should be limited to portraying their 'own kind' is to say that Shakespeare erred in giving us Lady Macbeth, that Anne Rice's books ought to have been composed by two-hundred-year-old male vampires, or that *Bambi* should have been written by a deer. Show me, for example, the Japanese woman who's written a more accurate life of the geisha than Arthur Golden and I might be tempted to buy into such a politically correct, asinine notion."

Like many creative children, Robbins seems to have turned to art partially as self-defense against his upbringing. "The family in which I was reared," he remembers, "was kind of a Southern Baptist version of *The Simpsons*—except that my father never would have eaten pie off of the floor, and I played the part of both Bart and Lisa. Which is to say, I was, on the one hand, a rambunctious little troublemaker, and on the other, a highly sensitive, creative, artistic type." Apparently the combination hasn't faded, because Robbins adds, "That dichotomy of personality can sometimes confound me even today."

However, Robbins credits his background with feeding his yearning for life and art. "Growing up in the mysterious old mountains of North Carolina (there was a Blair witch project behind every ridge), I was fed a fair amount of superstitious brain poison and homogenized ignorant pap." His parents, although not well-educated, were avid readers, and they inspired young Tom to read "numberless books." At school he was known as a basketball player and class clown; he kept his intellectual side secret. "What my background lacked in sophistication, it made up for in natural beauty, colorful language, and ample incentive to overlay numbing Sunday School ennui with dreamy longings for a romantic elsewhere. It gave me an appetite." Despite his anarchic sensibilities, Tom Robbins says that he maintains a regular writing schedule, because "sitting around waiting for inspiration is for amateurs." He's at his desk every morning at ten o'clock, whether, as he puts it, the muse shows up or not. Not surprisingly, Robbins offers no magic formula for the aspiring novelist. "Writing is an enterprise that demands unabated discipline and concentration—but, by God, it sure beats working."

The Green Man

Gregory Daurer/2000

From *High Times*, June 2000, 66–70. Reprinted with the permission of Mary McEvoy, publisher.

Welcome home, Tom Robbins: The bestselling—and beloved—author returns to the pages of *High Times*. In 1976, we proudly excerpted Robbins's wildly popular countercultural novel *Even Cowgirls Get the Blues* and published his article about *amanita muscaria* ("The Toadstool That Conquered the Universe"). In addition to *Cowgirls* (made into a 1993 film starring Uma Thurman), Robbins's books include *Another Roadside Attraction, Still Life With Woodpecker, Jitterbug Perfume, Skinny Legs and All, Half Asleep in Frog Pajamas*, and the just-released *Fierce Invalids Home From Hot Climates* (Bantam). The sixty-four-year-old Robbins's whimsical, mystical novels are like psychedelics: You never know where they're going to take your head, but you're always in store for an outrageous voyage.

HIGH TIMES: Looking back at your early life, what spurred your gift for storytelling?
Tom Robbins: I'm descended from a long line of preachers and policemen. Now, it's common knowledge that cops are congenital liars, and evangelists spend their lives telling fantastic tales in such a way as to convince otherwise rational people that they're factual. So, I guess I come by my narrative inclinations naturally. Moreover, I grew up in the rural South, where, although television has been steadily destroying it, there has always existed a love of colorful verbiage. My father was a hillbilly raconteur. My mother dabbled in prose and was an avid reader. By the age of five, I was so smitten with the magic of words that I'd already made up my mind to be a writer. A good little boy gone bad.
HT: Your novels bubble with humorous one-liners—twists of the language that double as punch lines. Do you think of those wisecracks as you research

a subject and then include them later at appropriate spots in your story? Or are they thought of spur-of-the-moment as you sit with a chapter in progress and try to finish it?

TR: Usually, my witticisms are composed on the spot. They're simply intrinsic; an inseparable, integral, organic part of my writing process—doubtlessly because humor is an inseparable, integral part of my philosophical worldview. The comic sensibility is vastly, almost tragically, underrated by Western intellectuals. Humor can be a doorway into the deepest reality, and wit and playfulness are a desperately serious transcendence of evil. My comic sense, although deliberately Americanized, is, in its intent, much closer to the crazy wisdom of Zen monks and the goofy genius of Taoist masters than it is to, say, the satirical gibes on *Saturday Night Live*. It has both a literary and a metaphysical function.

HT: All of your previous books have featured female protagonists, such as the hitchhiking Sissy Hankshaw in *Even Cowgirls Get the Blues* and the stock-trading Gwendolyn Mati in *Half Asleep in Frog Pajamas*. To what do you attribute your empathy for female characters?

TR: In general, I've found female protagonists more intriguing to work with than males. I cherish women and have always preferred their company, reveling in their perfumes, their contours, their finer-grained sensibilities, lunar intuitions, nurturing instincts, and relatively unfettered emotions—although I'm certainly not unaware that there are plenty of neurotic, uptight, stupid women in the world.

The female characters in my books tend to be independent, frisky, spunky, witty, emotionally strong, erotically daring, spiritually oriented, and intellectually generous; in short, the kind of women I admire in real life. Even Gwendolyn Mati has many of those qualities, although she also happens to be greedy, dishonest, and a bit of a manipulative bitch. I enjoyed Gwen's company despite her faults. It takes me thirty-six to forty-two months to complete a novel. If you're going to be shut up in a room with someone every day for more than three years, it might as well be someone whose company you enjoy.

My new book, *Fierce Invalids Home From Hot Climates*, is the first in which the narrative voice is thoroughly masculine—and let me tell you, writing from a male perspective really changed the energy of the enterprise. And a few of my personal traits did, indeed, rub off on the main character.

HT: Which ones?

TR: I probably ought to cop the Fifth Amendment on that. Do I have time to call my lawyer? Never mind, she's probably in bed with a judge. Here's one example: I gave my protagonist the same birthday as my own, July 22, the cusp between Cancer and Leo, which means that he's pulled in opposite directions by the sun and the moon, resulting in a personality that is torn between the hermit's cave and center stage, one minute wanting to cavort in the limelight and the next, wanting to crawl under the bed with a box of donuts.

HT: What subjects do you tackle in *Fierce Invalids*?

TR: This book was inspired by an entry from Bruce Chatwin's journal, by a CIA agent I met in Southeast Asia, by the mystery surrounding the lost prophecy of the Virgin of Fatima, by the increasing evidence that the interplay of opposites is the engine that runs the universe, and by old *Terry and the Pirates* comic books. It's about outwitting the corporate state, about having your cake and eating it, too; about the taboo against the natural sexuality of adolescent girls, about the contradictory nature of reality, and the possibility of finding both meaning and fun in a corrupt, sometimes dangerous world. My editors claim that *Fierce Invalids* is smart, funny, and inspiring, but also rather gnarly. I wouldn't know. I'm still too close to it to talk about it with even a rat poot of reliability.

HT: There may be some readers who aren't familiar with Bruce Chatwin.

TR: Before his early death from a mysterious illness about ten years ago, Bruce Chatwin was a brilliant, eccentric, larger-than-life Englishman who carried the craft of travel writing to a whole new level, due to his restless and reckless spirit and his provocative anthropological theorizing. Check him out.

HT: The belief in the Goddess—or a universal, feminine principle—is a recurring theme in your novels. Why?

TR: What really interests me about the Goddess is the fact that while she was beloved and honored by our ancestors, was the central spiritual archetype and prevailing deity all over the globe for thousands of years, she has been so successfully eradicated by revisionist patriarchal spin doctors that most modern Christians, Moslems, and Jews are totally ignorant of her massive and dominant historical presence. If someone or something of that enormous scope can be so thoroughly concealed from the masses, it can't help but call into question everything we've been taught by our various institutions. The subversion and repression of the Goddess is the Big Lie of the past two millennia—and as the dumbing down of America gains momentum, the duplicity is strengthening its grip. The good news is that a significant minority has recently become informed about the Goddess, and that has both revealed the essential spiritual foundation of feminism and inspired a growing distrust of traditional dogma and the meatballs who've propagated it.

HT: What do you recall about *High Times* during its earliest era?

TR: A lot of jelly has run through the donut since 1976, but here's how I seem to remember it: I'd written an article for *Rolling Stone* in which I speculated (this was years before Terence McKenna) that psychoactive fungi might have been the root source of all religious feeling in the human animal. The editors at *Rolling Stone* turned chicken and refused to run the piece. Shortly thereafter, I received a letter from *High Times*, which had just excerpted *Cowgirls*, soliciting a submission. *High Times*, of course, has never lacked for courage and it was pleased to publish "The Toadstool That Conquered the Universe."

I regret to report that my *High Times* essay was marred by a bit of misinformation. I wrote that because the *amanita muscaria* mushroom produces a state of grandiose drunkenness, because it swells the ego rather than dissolving it, it couldn't be considered a true psychedelic. Well, when consumed raw, that's entirely correct. What I was later to discover, however, is that if the *muscaria* is cooked (toasted, preferably), those rowdy alkaloids that once made Vikings go berserk are destroyed, while the more contemplative ones that remain after heating do provide a legitimate psychedelic experience. *Muscaria*'s a tricky sacrament, though (mistakes can occur in identification, organic dosages are difficult to gauge), and it should be harvested and ingested only with extreme caution.

HT: You were recently at a conference in Hawaii (the All Chemical Arts Conference) dedicated to the influence psychedelic drugs play on creativity. What were your remarks on the subject?

TR: One of the points I made in my lengthy lecture in Hawaii was that, as near as I can tell, the tiny gurus who reside in certain botanical compounds are not in the business of manufacturing human creativity. They don't sell imagination by the pound, or even the microgram. What they are capable of doing, however, is reinforcing, encouraging, and expanding that innate imagination that still manages to survive in a consumer society whose institutions, academic and otherwise, seem determined to suffocate it with polyester pillows from Wal-Mart.

I emphasized that the impact of psychedelics upon my own sensibility was to dissolve a lot of culturally conditioned rigidity. Old barriers, often rooted in ignorance and superstition, just melted away. I learned that one might move about freely from one level of existence to another. The borderlines between reality and fantasy, dream and wakefulness, animate and inanimate, even life and death, were no longer quite as fixed. The ancient Asian concept of interpenetration of realities was made physically manifest—and this served to massage the stiffness out of my literary aesthetic.

HT: What effect do you think the medical-marijuana law, which passed by ballot initiative in 1998, has had on the state of Washington?

TR: So far, the impact hasn't been very dramatic, but I would surmise—and hope—that the suffering of some individual patients has been alleviated. Of course, the multibillion-dollar antidrug industry, the Mafia, and Clinton's tight-jawed cowboys are doing everything they can to thwart the implementation of this civilized and humane law.

HT: Why, in your opinion, is fiction still an important art form?

TR: Much more than an entertaining set of exaggerated facts, fiction is a metaphoric method of describing, dramatizing, and condensing historical events, personal actions, psychological states, and the symbolic knowledge encoded within the collective unconscious; things, events, and conditions that are otherwise too diffuse and/or complex to be completely digested or appreciated by the prevailing culture. The human race has always defined itself through narration. That isn't going to change just because we've gone electronic. What *is* changing is that now we're allowing corporations to tell our stories for us. And as I write in my new novel, the message of the corporate story is always the same: "To be special, you must conform; to be valid, you must consume." Real fiction will prevail, however, because at its best it's an enchantment that refreshes the wasteland of the mind.

HT: How does it feel to be named one of "The 100 Best Writers of the 20th Century" (for combining "lust, religion, politics, and out-of-the-ordinary characters for an entertaining read") by *Writer's Digest* magazine?

TR: Well, if you can't be selected as *People* magazine's "Sexiest Man Alive," I suppose you would find being named one of "The 100 Best Writers of the 20th Century" an agreeable alternative. And I do. I'm sincerely flattered, but I know that if you allow yourself to puff up over your accolades, you pay with your soul.

HT: How do you spend your time when you're not writing?

TR: I'm glad you asked, because I do have an exciting new hobby. I've begun to practice the art of folding cold cuts. That's right. I take slices of ham, bologna, German salami, and olive loaf, and fold them into little animals. Little Black Forest animals. This morning, I fashioned all the characters from *Bambi* out of a roll of headcheese. Unfortunately, I ate them at lunch. It made me feel like a forest fire.

HT: You've identified three themes in all of your work: liberation, transformation, and celebration. How have these themes played out in your own life?

TR: Personally, I've undergone so many changes—some for the better, some for the worse—since being born into a strict Southern Baptist family in Appalachia that the faculty of MIT couldn't list them all on a supercomputer. Both liberation and transformation are ongoing tasks, they ebb and flow within the wobbly matrix of a never-ending process. Art is a part of the process, and psychedelics have a big role, as do reading, contemplation, meditation, yoga, imagination, and, perhaps most importantly, humor. And they're all cross-pollinators. Acts of liberation can be transformative, acts of transformation can be liberating. So much of it boils down to a matter of attitude.

As for celebration, if the need should come upon me spontaneously, I'm apt to bound off the sofa and dance around the room with greater abandon and at a greater length than might be deemed either cool or prudent. If it's a planned celebration, it usually involves a quantity of champagne. It should be stressed, however, that "celebration" is not necessarily a synonym for "partying." For me, to celebrate means to pay tribute to someone or something, ideally in language that's as eloquent, innovative and exuberant as my inadequate self can manage.

HT: What would you advise young people to do to improve their lives and the life of the planet?

TR: The goal of this generation's pioneers should be to restrict procreation and limit consumption. They should also take every opportunity to make themselves happy, realizing that the key to self-generated happiness (the only reliable kind) is the refusal to take oneself too seriously. I've got huge faith in them. The kids are all right.

Afterword

Tom Robbins agreed to be interviewed—in his own fashion.

Insisting that he's more articulate on paper than he is in person, Robbins proposed writing out—rather than verbalizing—his answers to our questions. Still, he welcomed a visit from *High Times* to his "sodden clam-chawed outpost" north of Seattle in order to flesh out his persona.

My first view of Robbins is literally downcast: He's lying on his back on his living-room floor with his hands on his chest as he converses in his folksy and mellifluous voice with his assistant, Barbara, and wife, Alexa. Had he been enjoying a meditative, guided relaxation? Or is he returning from a mind-blowing ayahuasca adventure? Actually, he'd injured his back in a freak accident and had been applying cold compresses. "So far, I've been unable to convince anyone that my tripping over a vacuum-cleaner cord was simply a practice session for a low-wire act," he quips.

The interior of Robbins's home is a visual feast. A trio of Andy Warhol soup cans hang in his living room; other walls are dedicated to accomplished painters from the region he's lived in for thirty years, Washington's Skagit River Valley. His writing desk sits in the same room as his collection of antique toy motorcycles; one almost imagines him going "Vroom! Vroom!" as he pens his latest novel by hand.

It's also the same room in which the FBI interviewed him a few years back. It seems Robbins was on the Unabomber suspect list because of similarities between Theodore Kaczyinski's then-anonymous manifesto and Robbins's 1980 book *Still Life With Woodpecker*. Although *Still Life*'s plot involves a romantic, anarchistic bomber named Bernard Mickey Wrangle (a.k.a. the "Woodpecker"), Robbins decries violence and insists he's not technophobic. "It wasn't really all that pleasant to think that someone could think that you're blowing up other human beings," he says. Robbins gives the FBI extra credit, though, for their smarts in the choice of agents they sent: two attractive, young women (they'd obviously gauged how to crack his nut from reading his books).

Though Robbins covets his privacy, he occasionally puts himself in the spotlight for a good cause, such as when he recently joined other celebrities (Woody Harrelson, Susan Sarandon, Richard Pryor) protesting the federal government's policies on medical marijuana. These days, Robbins explains, "I have a very high-pitched nervous system and a real low threshold for drugs. Three aspirin will knock me out. Anyone wants to date-rape me, all it takes is three aspirin: I'm yours."

Prior to his photo being taken, Robbins proves a stickler for detail: as a stylistic matter, he insists on donning sunglasses, just as he appears on his latest book cover. Afterwards, he promptly takes them off again—in waggish, Tom Robbins fashion, of course.

An Interview with Tom Robbins

Russell Reising/2001

Originally published in *Contemporary Literature* 42.3 (Fall 2001): 463–84. © 2001 by the Board of Regents of the University of Wisconsin System. Reprinted by the permission of the University of Wisconsin Press.

It was a dreary, Poe-esque Sunday. Clouds hung over northern Washington State like a lone gunman leaning out of the Texas Book Depository on this, the thirty-sixth anniversary of the gunning down of J.F.K. and of the death of Aldous Huxley. It was a day when the international situation was desperate, as usual. The only welcoming committee that greeted me upon entering Mr. Robbins's Neighborhood was a large, professional-looking, but obviously jury-rigged sign reading, Welcome to Washington State's Most Unscrupulous and Overpriced Town, a sign I later learned was erected by some malcontent who feels he had the throw rug pulled out from under his dream of an oversized antique mall in this Northwest dreamscape by local planning commissioners. Tom Robbins, unscrupulous? Overpriced? Impossible. And you know what, I was right.

After Tom greeted me in his Jimmy Swaggart Bible College sweats, we exchanged the top secret, Kosher Bandaloop, divulge-this-and-I'll-have-to-kill-you handshake and settled in for an autumnal afternoon's chat. But not before Tom spread a lavish and bracing platter of salmon dip (made by his father-in-law, and not only botulin-free but delicious), crackers, and radishes before us. I passed on an Egyptian beer that Tom defined as the worst in the world and snapped up a Snapple. While he handled a phone call, I got a chance to nose around a bit, losing myself for a while in the Andy Warhol soup cans, Chairman Maos, and Lynda Barry blowups gracing every wall. I must say that it warmed my heart to find side 2 of John Lennon's *Imagine*, with its inside-half-of-the-apple looking up at me, on the turntable. Not the side with "Imagine," mind you, but gems like "Give Me Some Truth," "Oh

Yoko!" "Oh My Love," "How Do You Sleep?" and other tunes that proved John maintained his edge even as he pursued his utopian yearnings.

I had come to interview Tom for a book I'm writing on LSD and Anglo-American culture. I had thought of introducing *AcidSpeak*, much like Ishmael introduces *Moby-Dick*, with an "Extracts" section in which I would include gems of psychedelic wisdom garnered in a series of interviews I would conduct with everyone from LSD celebrities to ordinary folk about the impact psychedelics had on their lives and thoughts. Hoping to provide a basis for my own analysis in this tribal archive, I believed my perspectives would be deepened, challenged, qualified, and otherwise communalized by the inclusion of the ideas of many like-minded psychedelic voyagers.

It was for that reason I ventured to northern Washington to meet with the premier psychedelic practitioner of the art of fiction. While much of our early exchanges spiraled around the double helices of our shared psychedelic pasts, Tom and I agreed that his work and theories as a fiction writer provided a valuable meeting ground for many of our shared interests. This interview extracts the literary segments of our talk that day, some of it still spinning around questions of psychedelic imagination and questing, but much of it equally of interest to anyone concerned with the state of contemporary fiction.

Since leaving his work as a newspaper copy editor and art critic to write *Another Roadside Attraction* (1971), Tom Robbins has been a powerful and generative force in and conundrum for the professional and academic literary establishment. Tom's most recent work, *Fierce Invalids Home From Hot Climates*, published in May 2000, is his seventh work of long fiction. *Even Cowgirls Get the Blues* (1976), *Still Life With Woodpecker* (1980), *Jitterbug Perfume* (1984), *Skinny Legs and All* (1990), and *Half Asleep in Frog Pajamas* (1995) round out the list of Tom's published novels to date.

Tongue-in-cheek, Robbins introduced himself at the September 1999 All Chemical Arts Conference on psychoactive creativity in Kona, Hawaii, as an artist who "writes trashy novels about profound subjects." He went on to say that in his mind's ear, he fancies himself sounding rather like Sir Laurence Olivier, but that when he hears himself on tape, he realizes that the voice is closer to that of Daniel Boone: "a voice marinated in moonshine whiskey, sulphur, deer musk, and lard." He claimed he speaks "the way a can of cheap dog food would speak if a can of cheap dog food could speak" but is proud, nonetheless, that he hasn't "suddenly developed an overnight British accent like Madonna and John Irving." When someone from the audience asked how he got started as a writer, Tom wove an elaborate story about how, after he saved a lovely young woman named Debbie Sue from drowning in a secret lake underneath Graceland, the grateful Memphis belle had a dwarf in a bright green suit deliver to Tom's motel room a stack of brown paper packages, each one of which proved to contain a manuscript that Tom dutifully opens and sends off to his publisher at regular five-year intervals. He's a passionately serious writer who refuses to fall into the trap of taking himself too seriously.

In fact, Robbins tweaks and confounds many of the notions that abound in contemporary literary circles. Amazingly, his writing is simultaneously ironic and heartfelt. It has a kind of innocence while never shying away from the vividly erotic. Straining at the limits of metaphor and simile, pumping up plots to within a half-breath of exploding, Robbins hurtles himself over the top and outside the envelope, scandalizing hidebound traditionalists while thrilling millions of readers worldwide (his books have been translated into sixteen languages, and he receives an average of ten fan letters a week).

The subject of surprisingly little academic attention, Tom Robbins's work engages us where it might be said to count, by provoking his readers to consider possibilities outside of their conventional frames of reference, challenging us to interface with paradox and mystery, and to project ourselves beyond the bleakness of what he calls "Killer B" culture (brutal and bland), with its repressing and withering effects on the human spirit.

Thus whether it's a highly principled mad bomber on Hawaiian holiday in *Still Life With Woodpecker*, a hitchhiking beauty with enormous thumbs, surfing the mysteries of time and sexuality in *Even Cowgirls Get the Blues*, a Greek chorus of inanimate objects exposing the mythological roots of the Arab-Israeli conflict in *Skinny Legs and All*, a pair of transhistorical, immortalist archetypes on a quest for the ultimate aroma in *Jitterbug Perfume*, a prissy stockbroker turned inside out by the combined genius of the faculty of the University of Timbuktu in *Half Asleep in Frog Pajamas*, or a mummified body of Jesus Christ turning up in a roadside zoo in *Another Roadside Attraction*, Tom Robbins's ideas, characters, and literary style titillate, inform, delight, and shock his readers into expanding their vision, even as he ratchets up appreciation of the English language with that lyrical voodoo that he do so well.

Q. Since I came here to talk about LSD, can I start by asking you what effects, negative or positive, your experience with psychedelics may have had on your life and work?

A. Well, hmmm. Negative? I don't know if there *were* any negative effects—unless you count the time I nearly drowned in a cup of hot chocolate. I became mesmerized by the bubbles on top of the cocoa; you know, their architectural structure and the chromatic spectrum that was reflected in them, and my face just kept inching closer and closer into what looked like some miniature, sunlit, Buckminster Fuller futuristic city, until eventually my nose and mouth were down in the liquid chocolate, breathing it. My girlfriend dragged me out and almost had to give me CPR.

Q. In *Moby-Dick*, Ishmael talks about how divine it might be to drown in a whale's head full of sperm. You came close. A cup of hot cocoa might be our modern version of a head full of sperm.

A. Thanks, pal, you just put me off cocoa forever. Look, if there's any significance to that little episode, I guess it's the fact that LSD can stretch an imbiber's attention span to unbelievable lengths—it's the opposite of booze—and that can be a valuable asset for a nonformulaic writer like me. For example, I never work from an outline. I develop each multilayered plot sentence by individual sentence, maintaining control over the many disparate elements but also allowing the flow of the thing, the adventure of it, to surprise me and draw me along. To accomplish that seamlessly and with any degree of artistry requires intense focus and an enormous amount of concentration. Maybe my training from the acid genie helped me to tighten the screws of my focus. Or maybe not.

Q. Sounds like acid might have both liberated you and taught you discipline.

A. Quite likely. It certainly made me a lot less rigid intellectually, emotionally, and I guess I could say spiritually. Certain boundaries and barriers just seemed to dissolve. The differences between so-called reality and so-called fantasy, between wakefulness and dreaming, between animate and inanimate, between the world of the living and the world of the dead were no longer so distinct. I think that acid might have increased the range of my mobility and awakened my appreciation of the tricky balance of opposites. I could move back and forth between conflicting states of mind with much greater ease.

You see, I happen to think there can be a fairly thin line between the silly and the profound, between nonsensical playfulness and the most serious and intense creative work, and it occurred to me that that borderline—that frontier—is the single most risky, revolutionary, and potentially significant place upon which artists and philosophers can station themselves. I'm astounded, actually, that more writers aren't pitching their tents on that frontier. Anyway, I'd have to venture that because of LSD, I've not only been able to discern that boundary line, but to straddle it more easily than most. Or maybe not.

Q. There's a great recent and unfortunately overlooked Jim Jarmusch film that negotiates these lines in an inspired way—*Dead Man*, with Johnny Depp playing an Old West character named William Blake. It's a truly psychedelic film. Did you happen to see that?

A. I did, and your assessment is entirely correct. It's a ninety-minute mind-stretching audiovisual poem! *Dead Man* and Alan Rudolph's innovative adaptation of *Breakfast of Champions* are both maligned cinematic masterpieces. It's a sad, sorry comment on the state of American film criticism when stunningly original movies like *Dead Man* and *Breakfast of Champions* are savaged or ignored.

Q. Originality is frequently punished. Are there other reasons for this critical blindness?

A. You know, there are certain films—and *Dead Man* and *Breakfast of Champions* are perfect examples—that have the capacity to hypnotize a viewer, almost from the opening credits. Well, it's an accepted fact that rigid, smug, arrogant, insecure people make poor subjects for hypnosis. I think you can see what I'm driving at here.

Q. How about literary critics? In the same cement boat?

A. That's another story. Right now, I want to make a couple of things very clear. First, my life doesn't revolve, nor has it ever revolved, around psychedelics. They enhanced my life—psychedelics can enhance the life of any intelligent, courageous person, and they might even represent our last great hope for planetary survival—but they didn't *replace* my life or become its central focus. Second, it shouldn't be implied that the acid elves sell talent by the pound—or the microgram. The psychedelic drug doesn't exist that can make a creative genius out of a hack or turn a neurotic weenie into a happy, fully conscious human being. You have to bring something to the table. And be willing to risk your belief systems. Some people want to go to Heaven without dying.

Q. Amen. Now, getting back to critics . . .

A. The truth is, despite what some people may wish to believe, I've received scores—no, *hundreds*—of favorable reviews. I don't read them, I haven't read a review of one of my books since 1977, but my agent and my editor tell me about them. And I see the blurbs. So I have no complaints. Of course, some of the big establishment critics do everything they can to discredit me, but what else can you expect from men who wear bow ties to work every day? I feel no ill will toward them, because they really can't help it.

Q. Are you saying, "Forgive them, for they know not what they do?"

A. In a sense, yeah. You see, the underpinnings of my literary aesthetic are not anchored in Western tradition, and that's the only tradition they recognize and understand. They're hemmed in by the narrowness of their experience. There's nothing in their cultural background to prepare them to recognize, let alone embrace, the universe's predilection for paradox and novelty. They have no concept of ego dissolution; romancing the Tao is not part of their repertoire; the flux and elasticity and transmutability of reality escape them, and nonspecific ecstasy is a suspect, if not alien, state to them. Even more problematic for them is, well, I suppose what you'd have to call the *playfulness* in my work.

Q. They miss its underlying seriousness.

A. Wit and playfulness aren't only serious, they're a form of wisdom and a means of psychic survival. A comic sensibility can open secret doors that are closed to the sober and the prudent. I'll go so far as to say that a seriously playful attitude represents humanity's most effective transcendence of evil. It's certainly transcendent of bourgeois banality.

I've had the good fortune to meet several truly wise people in my lifetime, most of them Asian, and the one thing they all had in common was an almost childlike playfulness. They weren't giddy little do-gooders, you understand; they'd cut a phony into chopped liver without a second's hesitation. They were tough customers, but they were lighthearted about it. Well, if you're an Ivy League bow tie–sattva from the *New York Times*, you're unable to distinguish what is lighthearted from what is merely lightweight. As they say in the Orient, "To the unenlightened, the God-laugh will always seem frivolous."

Q. Yes, but your novels aren't set in Asia. You don't write about Zen priests or—

A. Or Sufi masters or yogis or mutant ninja sushi chefs. No, no way. It's my *attitude*, my *approach* to writing that's been formed to a certain extent by Zen koans and Sufi stories and tantric systems of liberation, and, especially, the Tibetan concept of "crazy wisdom." But, you see, I've covertly integrated that approach into a brash and breezy, thoroughly American narrative. That's what confuses *Time* magazine.

Q. But a person doesn't need to be familiar with Tibetan tricksterism to enjoy your writing.

A. No, not to enjoy it, but if someone's gonna *analyze* it or *interpret* it or *criticize* it in any meaningful, scholarly way, they're gonna have to have more than a passing familiarity with those wisdom systems that not only have contributed to my philosophical stance but that I incorporate within the plexus of a lively, I guess you could say post-postmodernist narrative. And the critic should have some understanding of Greek mythology as well.

Q. Really? I mean, your plots do have a mythic dimension.

A. Again, it's a matter of an *approach* to material. Although Pan makes a cameo appearance in a couple of my novels, I don't have a rat poot of interest in retelling the old myths. Believe me, I don't want to reset the Theseus and Phaedra story in contemporary Detroit. That kind of thing is way too easy; it's been done six hundred times already. But let's take a look, let's list the literary characteristics of Greek myths. They were painted in broad strokes without a lot of physical or psychological detail. They emphasize ceremony and mischief. They feature larger-than-life protagonists, fantastic and absurd situations, abundant and often kinky eroticism, lyrical language bejeweled with vivid metaphors, and, frequently, inanimate objects and animals playing roles that are as significant as those of the human characters. Well, to one degree or another, all those qualities are characteristic of my own writing as well. I point this out for the benefit of those who're inclined to see Homer of Springfield in my work instead of Homer of Smyrna.

Q. Speaking of *The Simpsons*, I suspect you might have been a lot like Bart as a boy.

A. Weren't you? Actually, I was as much like Lisa as Bart. Sure, on the one hand, I definitely was a rebellious little troublemaker, but on the other, I was sensitive and studious and very creative. Frankly, I don't know that I've ever outgrown that dichotomy. Have another radish.

Q. *Merci.* Twice in the past few minutes, you've mentioned inanimate objects. In *Still Life* and *Skinny Legs*, objects have quite a dramatic presence. It's much less obvious in your other novels, but do you think that what you've called "objecthood" is a theme in everything you write?

A. Well, hmmm, no, I don't think that the inanimate, or for that matter our anthropocentrically (did I say that right?) chauvinistic sense of superiority to it, is a *theme* in anything I write. I do go to fairly great lengths to *acknowledge* objecthood. After all, our environment is largely comprised of "things"; they're a major part of the content of human intelligence. Language itself may well have developed as a means of describing or differentiating between inanimate objects. So I try to pay them their due. In many objects—and I mean household products and supermarket icons just as much as precious objets d'art—it's possible to hear the whisper of the infinite. My wish is to amplify that whisper until it's audible to the reader.

Q. There's not a lot of precedent for that in literature.

A. You're right. Whenever serious writers have put an inanimate object on center stage, it's almost always been to play a symbolic role. I'm thinking of Gogol's overcoat, or the handgun in that brilliant James Jones novella *The Pistol.* But I want to move beyond symbolism. I want to honor the object innately and intrinsically as a thing of consequence in its own right.

Q. How do you accomplish that? Through metaphor?

A. Largely, yes. Surrounding objects with words that intensify and illuminate them. But also through the roles I assign them in the narrative; you know, roles that give them a kind of, I guess you'd have to say *magical* quality. Magic realism? Look, all realism is magic realism if recorded with sufficient poetic fervor. The social realism that Tom Wolfe is so puffed up about is merely one layer of a many-layered cake. Most of the action in the universe is occurring at speeds too fast or too slow for human senses to register it, and most of the matter in the universe is in amounts too large or too small to be perceived by us. What Wolfe and all the other champions of naturalism would have us accept as ultimate reality is actually the behavior patterns of a swarm of fruit flies on one rotting peach in an orchard with a thousand varieties of strange fruit, stretching beyond every visible horizon. Granted, those fruit flies are pretty damn fascinating, but why the reluctance to so much as nod at the limitless orchard around them? That is, if you want to call yourself a realist.

Q. Do you call yourself a realist?

A. I don't know. Fellini said, "The visionary is the only true realist." Beyond that, depending on which scientist you listen to, our bodies are made up of anywhere from 70 percent to 85 percent water. We're more water than we are anything else, and we're also fundamentally amphibious, in our biological history as well as in the womb. So, OK, how many writers can you name who take our essentially aquatic nature into the tiniest consideration in their novels? I can only name two. James Joyce and your humble provider of radishes. *Finnegans Wake* has so many references to water you practically have to wear a wetsuit to read it. I do a riff on the man-water interface in every one of my books, and I really dive into it in *Frog Pajamas.* Does that make me more of a realist than those authors who choose to focus on cancer and bad marriages? Probably—or maybe I'm just damp behind the ears.

Q. A condition that we could cure with a dry martini, not that these radishes aren't ravishing, mind you. Right now, though, I want to get back to your similes and metaphors. They're clever, surprising, and very original; they'd be unthinkable before you wrote them or I read them, and they seem to be doing some kind of profound work.

A. I'm sincerely happy to hear you say that. If my metaphoric phrases were sloppy or irrelevant or hidebound or cute, I'd be willing to admit that they might be some kind of stylistic gimmick. But I work harder and longer than you'd ever guess to ensure that my figures of speech are not only fresh, imaginative, and unexpected, but that they're *pertinent*—that they deepen the reader's subliminal understanding of the person, place, or thing that's being described. That's what it's all about. Metaphoric language can be employed to heat up a scene, to heighten it, to lift it out of the mundane mire of mere fictional reportage—to eternalize it, if you will.

Q. And if I won't?

A. It's one thing to tell a good story; it's another to try to tell it in words that delight and excite the psyche.

Q. Pynchon's *Mason & Dixon* comes to mind.

A. My God, yes! *Mason & Dixon* knocked my socks off—and I was barefoot at the time. Basically, it's an account of the professional problems of a couple of eighteenth-century surveyors. Yet Pynchon turns it into something thrilling and glorious by dint of his language—and countless acts of stylistic daredevilry. Mark Twain said the difference between the perfect word and a word that's merely adequate is the difference between lightning and a lightning bug. Pynchon generates one lightning flash after another. Same thing is true of Shakespeare. If it weren't for his electrifying language, Shakespeare would be just another pretty plagiarist.

Q. Although neither Pynchon nor Willy the Shake has quite your flair for simile. I'm thinking of when, for example, you say in *Cowgirls* that the Countess's dentures "worked over his ivory cigarette holder like a chiropractor realigning the spine of a Chihuahua." Or that he had a smile "like the first scratch on a new car." Or you say in *Roadside*, when Amanda doesn't wash after sex, that "she smelled like the leftovers from an Eskimo picnic." Or, in *Fierce Invalids*, a November day in Seattle is said to have a grayish glow "that might have been filtered through frozen squid bladders, a kind of sunlight substitute synthesized by Norwegian chemists." I could go on and on and on. Now, I'm aware that you can no more explain where these flights of fancy come from than John Coltrane could have detailed the origins of his riffs. But can you say something about the process involved?

A. Well, I can tell you that I definitely don't keep a simile bank—you know, a notebook in which I jot down any little piece of wordplay that happens to occur to me at odd moments, hoping to put it to future use. And I don't pause at a particular juncture in the narrative and say, "Right about here we ought to have us a show-stopping metaphor." I doubt that any writer does that. For me, similes and metaphors simply arise as a natural, integral part of an ongoing organic process. For example, if my protagonist is gazing up at a tropical night sky, and I want to give the reader a sense of what the character is seeing and/or feeling, and to convey that in a way that gets the reader's attention and perhaps even awakens in the reader a personal sense of wonder, while at the same time affording me some compositional pleasure—the pleasure of sporting with language—I'll close my eyes and picture the scene, concentrate on that sidereal sky, and after a while—it could be ten seconds, it could be ten minutes—I'll come up with something such as, "The stars were as big and bright as brass doorknobs, and so numerous they jostled one another for twinkle space." And go on in that manner for as long as it works or seems effective.

Q. "For as long as it works." That seems important.

A. Yeah, that's the bottom line. There's really only one rule in fiction: whatever works, works. In a university course, the writing teacher will chisel dictums in stone, such as "Show, don't tell." Generally speaking, that's probably a pretty good rule. However, if you can tell and make telling *work*, then there's absolutely no reason to restrict yourself to showing. That's self-imposed tyranny. The rub is, you've got to know when it's working and when it isn't, and a lot of would-be novelists lack that ability. How do you know? You just *know*, damn it! And if you lack the gift to instinctively and intuitively know, maybe you should consider going into law instead. We can always use more attorneys.

Q. I think that the aspect of your process that you've just described often results in what I call "surreal escalation." For example, the passage in *Woodpecker* about the prolific growth of blackberries in the Pacific Northwest. It begins rather factually, routinely, and builds: you crank it and crank it until toward the end of the paragraph, you're describing blackberry vines pushing up through solid concrete, forcing their way into polite society, entwining the legs of virgins, trying to loop themselves over passing clouds—

A. Stop me before I kill again!

Q. This exuberant escalation and the way that it invokes the life force, the *chi* that percolates in human and nonhuman alike, well, I'm not sure that it, or somewhat similar passages in Haruki Murakami's novels, could have been written by somebody who hadn't taken psychedelics.

A. Impossible to determine, in my case, at least. I mean, I was versed in surrealist poetry and Henry Miller and the 'pataphysics' of Alfred Jarry well before I ever shoved my little canoe out onto the vast, savage, iridescent ocean of psychedelia. I've gone to what some people might consider fairly extreme lengths to, well, *connect* with a subject—or an object—but none of those exercises had any direct relation to psychedelics. When I was occupied with *Woodpecker*, I at one point locked myself up for three days in a room that was completely empty except for a pack of Camel cigarettes. My paramour handed me a sandwich through a heavily draped window several times a day, and the rest of the seventy-two hours I forced myself to concentrate solely on the Camel pack, meditating on it, walking around it, tossing it in the air, sleeping with it on my chest. Mostly just staring at it. It wasn't sensory deprivation, either. More than any other mass-produced consumer good, the Camel pack is loaded with imagery. It's rich. For generations, sailors and convicts—men alone with time on their hands—have made up puzzles and riddles and jokes about the Camel design. Sure, many of them were as crude as they were clever, but they provide evidence that even a commonplace package off a supermarket shelf can be a point of departure for a mental adventure—and in a more evolved mind, an aesthetic and even spiritual adventure.

My exercise was a teeny bit unorthodox, I suppose, but when I got around to writing about the lovesick Leigh-Cheri being sequestered in that attic with only her own unopened pack of Camels for company, I knew what I was talking about. That doesn't mean I necessarily subscribe to that other ubiquitous ironclad rule of creative writing departments: "Write what you know." A more enlightened suggestion might be, "Write anything you can successfully imagine." The ideal situation would be to acquire some firsthand experiential knowledge and then stir it up in your cerebral Cuisinart with generous glugs of unfettered imagination. Which is what I attempted with the Camel pack.

Q. Do you smoke?

A. Only when my hair's on fire. No, but by the third day I was almost ready to eat those cigarettes.

Q. Your studious Camel scrutiny causes me to wonder how you prepared for your notorious girl-love scenes.

A. You mean, did I lock myself in an empty room with a couple of lesbians? Not exactly. However, in the early seventies, I lived with a darling young coed who happened to be actively bisexual, and it was her practice to pick up girls on campus and at concerts and bring them home for both of us to share. So I've done some firsthand research in the field of girl-love, up close and personal. But we needn't discuss that any further.

Q. Oh, fine! You pique my curiosity and then stonewall me. But I so want to talk some more about women. Your books are popular with both sexes, of course, but female readers seem to identify with your female characters and to fall in love with your male characters.

A. Makes me sound like a romance novelist. Fabio Rosemary Robbins. Well, if what you say is true, it's probably because the women in my books tend to be smart and frisky and independent, just like the women I admire in real life; and my men tend to be fun. I don't know if you've noticed this, but women like men with robust emotions—and men who can make them laugh. Frankly, I don't waste a lot of ink on miserable victims or soulless cynics or self-involved neurotics, and I avoid both writing and reading those dreary little dramas of domestic discord that are so cherished in certain lofty circles, not to mention Oprahland.

Q. Yes, but some of your characters do suffer, and some even die. And they often do reflect important social issues. *Cowgirls*, in fact, has been called the only significant feminist novel ever written by a man, if I'm not mistaken. Its characters, like the primary characters in all of your books, are not finely drawn psychological portraits, but more on the order of the figures in legends and epic tales. And I'd venture that that deep archetypal resonance accounts for much of their appeal. But why, exactly, with the exception of the rascally Switters in *Fierce Invalids*, have your main protagonists always been women?

A. I can't answer you *exactly.* The amount of time I've spent analyzing my motives is approximately equivalent to the amount of time it takes a neutrino to pass through a slice of Swiss cheese. I mean, I just do what I do and hope that God doesn't punish me too harshly for it. I may have a couple of explanations, however.

First, I've generally speaking had a lifelong preference for the company of women. Now, it takes me thirty-six to forty-two months to complete a novel. If you were going to be living in your head day and night for over three years with someone, wouldn't you want it to be someone whose company you enjoy? More importantly, perhaps, I strive to avoid the autobiographical in my books, but when I'm focusing on a male protagonist, no matter who he is or what he does in life, it's very hard to keep my own personality, my proclivities, my beliefs from manifesting themselves in his thinking and behavior. By adopting a feminine voice or spotlighting a female protagonist,

I can step outside of myself a little further. It affords me greater freedom and a certain distance from the material; it grants me a degree of objectivity. Also, it allows my anima to surface, which ends up softening the tone of my contempt for corporate America and the looters and polluters it nurtures. Does that make sense?

Q. I'll buy it. But you can't convince me that there isn't a modicum of sexual titillation involved. Your female characters are spunky and courageous, often with strong spiritual undertones, but they're simultaneously very physical. Aside from Jeanette Winterson, no author has ever written such graphic and poetic adorations of that organ that your courtly CIA defector Audubon Poe, in *Fierce Invalids*, refers to as "a woman's treasure." Although they're on a higher level, your paeans to the vagina remind me of Larry Flynt. I heard Flynt say in an interview, "This is where we all come from and where we all want to return, so I'm going to show it to you as clearly as I can." Is that a fair comparison?

A. Flynt probably didn't realize it, but he was propagating an essentially tantric idea. One of the major differences between us, though, is that I want to present the vagina in a way that reinforces rather than dispels its mystery. Uh, let me violate my principles here and lapse into autobiography for a moment.

When I was growing up, my father moved us a lot, usually from one small southern town to another. And for some reason, we always seemed to land next door to a family with little girls. These female playmates taught me plenty, especially in the realm of sensitivity, a realm no southern male child would dare visit in the company of his daddy, his uncles, his brothers, or his peers. Anyway, we moved to Burnsville, North Carolina, when I was eight, and the family next door to us was named Angel, and they had two daughters. Angel girls. I'm not making this up. Barbara Angel was ten and the most sophisticated female I'd ever met, and Helen Angel was seven. There was an older brother, Jack, who'd survived polio, and the father had built Jack a steel aboveground swimming tank so that he could exercise his withered legs. Well, one summer afternoon while I was taking Jack's waters, I turned to see Helen squatting on the rim of the tank. She was in a short cotton dress and was wearing no underpants. You get the picture? It was totally innocent, but there she was, there *it* was, not twenty inches from the tip of my nose. The pretty little treasure. The vertical smile. The mollusk pried open by an undine's salty thumb. Raw and moist and fresh and sweet and crimped and apertural; unobscured as yet by a single hair; as pink as one of these radishes and more mysterious than the Appalachian forests by moonlight. I was absolutely mesmerized.

Before long, Barbara tapped Helen on the shoulder to alert her to her indiscretion, and the way that Barbara acted so protective and Helen became so embarrassed, well, it just magnified my fascination. This secret enfolded flesh flower that had suddenly bloomed before my eyes was not merely mysterious, it was forbidden. Forbidden! A taboo, and therefore sacred. The next time I eyeballed one of those tidewater orchids, both it and I were more fully developed, but the experience was no less vivid and no less unforgettable. And why would we, any of us, want to forget our introductory encounters with nature's most supercharged attractants? It isn't that often in the modern, civilized world that something has the power to galvanize and enrapture us on such a primal level.

Q. I cannot disagree. I cannot disagree. And you're correct to keep it in the forefront of your literary consciousness. But as a man who often speaks in a feminine voice, what's your reaction to those today who submit that white people can't write intimately about blacks, or that a male European writer shouldn't even attempt to project himself into the life of, say, a Filipino grandmother?

A. My reaction? I nod and grin. Because it serves to further remind me that the dumbing-down of America has by no means been limited to the rubes on the right. Such notions are as dull-witted as they are politically and egocentrically motivated. Look, what novelists do—what screenwriters and playwrights do—is get inside other people's heads and look out. The ability to do that convincingly, no matter whose head is so entered, is what separates the real writer from the polemicist and the poseur. To proclaim otherwise is to suggest that *Bambi* should have been written by a deer.

Q. Well, they'd argue that since deer can't write—

A. Hey! Most human beings can't write, either! And I'd argue that a good black writer can write about white culture far more compellingly than a bad white writer. And vice versa, naturally. Background don't mean a thing if you ain't got that swing.

Q. Who has "that swing" for you? Who's doing important stuff these days? I don't know of anyone who's doing anything remotely like what you're doing, not even Murakami. I still go back to William Kotzwinkle's brilliant work from thirty years ago, but even his farthest-out narratives pull up short of yours in terms of sheer rhetorical exuberance. Besides Pynchon, who do you read?

A. I don't know about *important*, but there's no shortage of *interesting* stuff. Every time I pass a bookstore I want to fall to my knees and give thanks that I wasn't born before the invention of the printing press. Or, for that matter, before the duck press and the full-court press, being a devotee of Chinese food and basketball. Reading happens to be one of the supreme earthly pleasures, and my taste is pretty eclectic, although in general I prefer the daring to the cautious, the poetic to the prosaic, the imaginative to the literal, the upbeat to the morose, the quirky to the predictable, the comic to the sober, and the erotic to the chaste. I've already made it clear how weary I am of fiction about bad marriages, dysfunctional families, and unhappy childhoods—but, you know, *The Antelope Wife* by Louise Erdrich deals with all of those wretched subjects, and it's flat-out terrific. *The God of Small Things* by Arundhati Roy is in the very same boat. So I guess it depends on who's doing it and whether or not it's done with verve and humor and a generous spirit. On the whole, though, all these depressing novels about all these depressing situations just end up creating more depression in the world. Everybody knows the cookies are burning. How about a book now and then that turns off the fucking oven? Life imitates art. But then, what else *would* it imitate?

Q. So, then, let me rephrase my previous question. Are there contemporary writers who rescue the cookies for you? Talk to me about them.

A. Dead men don't write novels—as far as we know, at any rate—so I guess a guy who bought the ranch around 1981 couldn't properly be called "contemporary," but nevertheless, I'd like to toot a few toots on the long golden trumpet on behalf of Nelson Algren.

Q. Toot away. Algren's one of those who've managed to slip through my net.

A. A pity, because when he was at the top of his game, Nelson Algren could write circles—and rectangles and polyhedrons—around Hemingway and Fitzgerald, both. He's been largely forgotten, except by Lou Reed, who's been shamelessly borrowing from him for years. I've been reading *A Walk on the Wild Side* recently, and if *Mason & Dixon* blew my socks off, *Wild Side* is blowing off my feet. Blowing off my legs. Turning me into a damn paraplegic. Algren's wittier than Oscar Wilde, in a seamy, street-smart, oddball sort of way, and his choice of words is all lightning and no bugs. Every lyrical sentence has that tough, broken-down, holy radiance of Allen Ginsberg's *Sunflower Sutra*. But funny! He's Gorky with a sense of humor, Mark Twain with an erection, and Voltaire with a cheap gin hangover. It's a disgrace Algren isn't taught in the universities. Also, those other underrated genius outsiders, Henry Miller and Nathanael West. And Richard Brautigan, for that matter. *Trout Fishing in America* is the most original novel ever written, more radically innovative even than *Tristram Shandy*. No plot, no characters to speak of, no conflict or crises or coming-of-age, each chapter an extended, surrealistic haiku, yet as hard to lay down as a John le Carré. And less whimsical and more sardonic than some folks realize. Young people really respond to this stuff. If you want to get a student excited about reading, just turn him or her on to Brautigan.

Q. I do, I do! Have you ever considered teaching?

A. Yeah. For about as long as it takes a stewed prune to pass through a diarrheic squirrel monkey. Now, please, I don't say that out of any disrespect for the teaching profession. I value it sincerely and highly. It's just that I wasn't born in the right frame of mind to take orders from administrators.

Q. Boy, have I been down that highway to hell. But getting back to contemporary authors . . .

A. Well, Gabriel García Márquez and Günter Grass are the grand masters, no doubt about it. But García Márquez is himself apparently dying, and Grass has apparently run out of gas. Who'll replace them? Louis de Bernières is a likely candidate—he has the juice and the heart, if not quite the imagination—but there's another young British writer who takes more risks and whom I find more exciting: Tibor Fischer. Fischer's *The Thought Gang* is a philosophical pinball machine that eats rubber quarters and pays off on tilts. Wonderful! As is Nancy Lemann's *Lives of the Saints*, not to be confused with that earlier book of extreme Catholic behavior; and then there's *Mumbo Jumbo* by Ishmael Reed. Andrei Codrescu is making some brilliantly crazy sense. Neal Stephenson, Steve Erickson, Jim Harrison. "My Three Sons," if you will. But it's meaningless to make lists, and anyway, I always forget and leave some of my favorite people off. What I'd really like to do is bring out the solid gold horn again and toot it for the most powerful piece of fiction I've encountered in many a moon.

Q. I can hardly wait.

A. It's a short story, actually, and I don't normally care for the form. The short story, being stuck somewhere between the anecdote and the opus, has drawbacks similar to those that sailors find in a mermaid: you know, too much fish to eat, not enough woman to love. Anyway, this one is called "Sweetheart of the Song Tra Bong," and it's in the Vietnam War collection *The Things They Carried*, by Tim O'Brien. Man, what a jolt! It's spooky as hell and chilling, but it left me feeling absolutely exhilarated—left me so intoxicated I had to go out and walk around the block. And then read it again.

There's a darkness in it that goes beyond good and evil, the kind of romantic, transcendent darkness that lies at the core of magic and facilitates a genuine cosmic connection.

Q. I agree with you about short stories. I love huge novels and Emily Dickinson lyrics. Anything in between seems somehow evasive. But you're saying this story transcends both its form and its darkness and succeeds in rescuing the cookies?

A. To a large extent, it does bring home the cookies, and from a very unexpected direction. But let me qualify that. If "rescuing the cookies" can be taken as a half-assed metaphorical reference to a literature that has the ability to elevate consciousness, to dare us to participate in something beyond the realm of normal expectation, to wake us up, to pull the rug out from under our belief systems yet end up making us feel better than ever about being alive, then "Sweetheart of the Song Tra Bong" only partially succeeds. It stands out because most other works of fiction—contemporary, modern, postmodern, or classical—don't succeed in that area at all. And maybe that's OK. It probably isn't the job of fiction to enlighten us in that way. Maybe that should be left to philosophers and gurus, or to such mind-stretching nonfictional tomes as Fritjof Capra's *The Tao of Physics* and Terence McKenna's *The Archaic Revival.* Fiction has other missions, other functions, other chores. Still, in my heart of hearts, I can't help but feel that it isn't enough for novelists to describe misery. We ought to offer ways, however subtle or oblique, to defeat misery or transform it. I'm afraid I'm in total agreement with Kafka when he said, "A novel should be an ax for the frozen sea around us."

Q. Wow! OK. Holding that in mind, I submit that your novels, in the way that they flow yet elect to go against the flow; the way they *ebb* and flow, between seriousness and playfulness, between the profane and the divine; the way they seem to struggle to recover something that's lost, whether it's innocence or freedom or pre-Christian vitality; the way they mock what you've called "the tyranny of the dull mind"; the way you put the "fun" back in "profundity"—with all those things, you're obviously chopping holes in the ice that surrounds us with the best of them.

A. I get in a few licks, I suppose, with a monkey wrench as well as an ax. But chopping up the frozen sea is certainly not on my mind when I sit down to write.

Q. But subconsciously, at least, you must entertain some such far-reaching goal or goals.

A. Not while the pen's in my hand. Then, it's just me, the ink, and the wood pulp. Later, if you held a gun to my head and forced me to state some ultimate purpose, what I'd probably stammer is that I'd like to twine images and ideas into big subversive pretzels of life, death, and goofiness, on the chance that they might help keep the world lively and give it the flexibility to endure.

That about sums it up. Oh, I'm sure there must be other levels of ambition involved, but as I've confessed, I've always shunned self-analysis, and I don't think I'll start now. At this juncture in my life, due to chronic, debilitating, poisonous eyestrain headaches, I am facing the possibility that I may be physically unable to ever write another book. It doesn't matter. For decades, I've been fortunate enough to spend my days and nights doing precisely what I love best, with complete artistic freedom, and to have been nicely compensated for it. I don't want to sound like some low-rent Lou Gehrig, but I consider myself an extremely lucky guy. I'm grateful.

Q: And proud, too, I would hope.

A: Once in a while, maybe. I'm proud that I've never pledged allegiance to a flag, been a contestant on a TV game show, or worn an item of clothing designed by Tommy Hilfiger. As for writing . . . I've seldom been entirely satisfied with the work I've produced. However, a few years ago I received a letter from a stranger, a woman in the scientific field, and she said, "Your books make me think, they make me laugh, they make me horny, and they make me aware of the wonder of everything in life." And I thought, hey, that's pretty great. That's perfect, in fact. You can't ask any more from a novel than that.

It Takes a Villa

J. Rentilly/2003

From *Pages Magazine*, May/June 2003, 54–56. Reprinted with the permission of J. Rentilly.

When a novel's first pages feature a badger-like creature skydiving into Japan, indulging his taste for homemade beer, dispensing Taoist mantra in English, and seducing pretty young things, the world sits up and listens. Or it should, anyway. Especially when the author is Tom Robbins, the Washington-based author well known for his intoxicating, counterculture literary mix of smiles, similes, and subversion in books like *Even Cowgirls Get the Blues, Jitterbug Perfume,* and *Skinny Legs and All.*

In *Villa Incognito* (Bantam), the latest and perhaps greatest book from Robbins, the author weaves a tangled, glistening narrative web that involves Japanese folklore, the circus, three American soldiers gone voluntarily MIA after the Vietnam War, modern man's propensity for living in disguise (even from himself), and the September 11 terrorist attacks. The result is phantasmagorical, richly layered, utterly hilarious, and unexpectedly poignant.

For too many years, it's been too simple for critics and the hard of heart to dismiss Robbins as a cult writer, merely a fabulist, a trafficker in images and wordplay that are only fanciful, boisterous, and unapologetically bold, a narrative crackpot all too eager to put Groucho glasses and clown wigs on his characters and plot. To go that route is to miss the very essence of Robbins. These are books, for all their splendiferous chicanery and merry mischief, that are about the Universe's Very Big Things as much as any book by any great writer ever could be: terrorism, feminism, materialism, politics, metaphysics, God, death, love, and all that jazz. Robbins courts, romances, and makes utterly delightful a universe full of wonder, danger, and paradox—one much like our own, but in which a can of beans and a painted stick can drive a narrative, where emotionally complex set pieces occur physically inside a pack of cigarettes, where beets are the leaping-off point for grand poetic rhapsody, where ninjas guard the dead body of Jesus Christ, where anything can happen at any time.

In *Still Life With Woodpecker*, Robbins writes, "Poets remember our dreams. Outlaws act them out." Pick up any of his eight novels and you will likely be convinced that Tom Robbins is one of the last men alive to be a little bit of both.

JR: What would you like a reader to take from *Villa Incognito*, and from your books in general?

TR: I've often professed that we're in this life to enlarge our souls, light up our brain, and liberate our spirits. This isn't necessarily a duty imposed on us by a higher power, but rather a recognition that we human beings are something more than walking seed packages and ambulatory egg cartons conniving to earn some future, highly nebulous reward. If my novels can lead a reader to encounter the . . . well, let's call it "the life force," in an exhilarating yet thoughtful way—wit and playfulness are integral parts of this process—then I'll feel that I've won a cigar, although my primary objective always and forever is to verbally fresco the page.

As for *Villa Incognito* specifically, I suspect that different readers will take different things from it: it's rather fully packed. One of its many themes is identity and how easily we can be stunted and imprisoned by false notions of who we really are, misconceptions that often are imposed upon us by our various institutions. Who among us is such a dullard that he or she has never secretly yearned to disappear, only to turn up later in another place—free!—as somebody else? I'd hope that *Villa Incognito* would encourage readers to enlarge their vision of themselves, extending it in unpredictable directions, while managing to thoroughly enjoy themselves in the process.

JR: As you've said, "joy in spite of everything." How might one begin to see things in this fashion (aside from reading one of your books)?

TR: It appears that over the years, the phrase *joy in spite of everything* has become my quasi-motto. Essentially, the phrase amounts to a kind of defiant attitude, a refusal to be depressed by events over which one has no control. It reflects a belief that life is too short to be wasted in the anger or bitterness that easily could be generated by reaction to the era or area into which one happens, entirely by circumstance, to have landed. We must acknowledge the injustice and suffering that abounds in the world and do everything we can to alleviate it, yet in the same instant insist on having one hell of a good time.

A few individuals seem to possess an innate ability to be simultaneously caring and carefree, but most of us have to work at it. It takes practice. In the beginning, it requires an almost hourly attitude adjustment, but one does get better at it. In the "crazy wisdom" philosophies of Asia, it's traditional to enjoy life as curious cosmic theater, a grand show fraught with paradox and delicious absurdities. In fear-based, narrow-minded, hierarchical Western cultures, however, such wisdom is usually mistaken for frivolity.

JR: In *Another Roadside Attraction*, you wrote that "the artist's job keeps getting bigger and bigger." What do you know about that statement now that you didn't know thirty years ago when you wrote it?

TR: Not much, actually. If one continues to evolve, as a human being and an artist, then one's vision is always escalating. So, no matter how technically proficient one becomes, one's technique never quite catches up. And should a writer's technique succeed in catching up to his or her vision, then it's all over, baby. From that point on, he or she will have become a formulaic, unexciting hack.

I might add that as the world grows smaller, the artist's job—if, indeed, an artist can be said to *have* a job—does grow proportionally larger. One's audience is global now, with all the diversity, complexity, and sheer danger implicit in the situation.

JR: Were the rules of art redefined after 9/11?

TR: No, not at all. The purpose of art—if, indeed, art can be said to *have* a purpose—is to provide what life does not. Art has no greater enemy than those artists who allow their art to become usurped by, or subservient to, sociopolitical agendas. Anyway, art doesn't have any rules. That's what's so liberating about it; that's what allows it to lift us out of mundane contexts. Art has demands, extremely rigorous demands, but the only "rule" as such is that whatever works, works.

JR: Yet 9/11 seems to have taken a bite out of you. Tell me what role 9/11 played in *Villa Incognito*. Was it always a part of the story or was it integrated as you created?

TR: In my last novel, *Fierce Invalids Home From Hot Climates*, a character comments that "terrorism is the only logical response to America's foreign policy." So, the death planes didn't surprise me. I happen to have been in the air on the morning of September 11, flying out of New Orleans. When the pilot announced that we couldn't be assigned a gate in Atlanta due to "an aircraft accident in New York," I instantly turned to my paramour and said, "Terrorists!" Just blurted it out. Our foreign policy made such an attack inevitable, and that may have been its most tragic aspect: it was entirely preventable—not by better intelligence gathering but by a more honorable, less arrogant American role in world affairs.

Anyway, I began writing *Villa Incognito* months before 9/11, but the recognition that such an event was highly likely may well have informed the text on some subliminal, indirect level. Since part of the novel was unfolding in real time, I suppose, then, that it was only natural that when the attack actually occurred, it had to make itself manifest. It just integrated itself seamlessly into the narrative, although it is far from the most significant element of the story.

JR: In *Villa Incognito*, you write, we are "chimps with bulldozers, monkeys with bombs." What hope is there for us anyhow?

TR: Good question. Maybe there is no hope—and maybe that's okay. Alan Watts, one of our era's most profound philosophers, once said. "When you become truly convinced that the human condition is hopeless, you start to enter the Zen state." In the Zen state, hope, with its implications of fear and desire, is just so much unnecessary baggage. On the other hand, for those not in the Zen state, the very admission that we are chimps and monkeys—that we're primates, animals not that far removed emotionally and physically from baboons—well, that acceptance itself could be a hopeful and helpful act. Our planetary survival may well depend on a reconnection with the ancient animal aspects of our being. We're going to go into an increasingly technologized future hand in hand with nature or we're not going into the future at all. At least, not with our souls intact. Our connection to our animal past is one of the themes of *Villa Incognito*.

JR: Your recent books have dealt with crashing stock markets, terrorism, certain Middle East shenanigans, and so forth before they occurred in real life, and you've been dead-on every time. So, where does one *get* a crystal ball like that?

TR: Everybody has one. It's right between their ears. The trick is to keep it clean, not allow it to become fogged over. And, of course, our advertising, entertainment, and news media—not to mention religious and governmental institutions—are large fog machines.

JR: Many people believe that the joy and joviality of your books, particularly the early ones, come from your experimentation with drugs. Tell me what role drugs have played in your creative life, both in the past and in the present. What does a drug like LSD offer the creative artist?

TR: Frankly, I don't know that I'm all that jovial. What I am is playful, but playful in the very serious sense that the best Zen, Taoist, Sufi, and Tantric masters have been playful. I think that what I may represent is an Americanized, individualized version of that old crazy-wisdom philosophy, the anti-doctrine that walks a slender wire, like the circus wire in *Villa Incognito*, between the towers of the holy and the hills of the fool.

Now, the contribution of psychedelic drugs to this anti-belief system is impossible to determine. Long before I took my first revelatory acid trip, I'd already been exposed to Zen and Surrealism and theoretical physics. More-over, I'd displayed a comic, mischievous temperament since early child-hood. I suppose that what LSD did was to validate, in amazingly graphic and concrete terms, my growing suspicion that life is some kind of scary but beautiful joke.

My psychedelic experiences also made it absolutely clear to me that every deer in the forest, every daisy in the yard, has an identity just as strong as my own. That knowledge changed my life in a way that I wish every anthropo-centric Christian and nature-hating cynic could share.

If LSD offers any specific value to writers—and no drug is ever going to transform an untalented hack into a literary genius—it may be in its power to loosen one up, to leave one less rigid both intellectually and emotionally, so that one's imagination might move more easily from one level of exis-tence to another. Most of our so-called realists deal with a pathetically nar-row spectrum of multidimensional reality. Now, many of them expound on that spectrum quite brilliantly, but in the end, life is a banquet and they're choosing to only write about the mashed potatoes.

JR: Speaking of banquets, you've written about love as a kind of moveable feast. I want to pose a question that you yourself have asked: How does one make love stay? You've been married several times. How does one keep mar-riage, for example, from becoming routine, a parody of itself?

TR: I'll claim that I've been divorced several times, married only once. In any case, love can never be *made* to stay. When we attempt to force love to be anything but its unpredictable, unfathomable self, the results are usually disastrous. The best we can do is to create conditions under which love has been shown to flourish. This is accomplished by refraining from clinging to love too tightly, by giving it breathing room, and by developing and expand-ing the personal consciousness that one can bring to a relationship. Many people are looking for someone to complete them. That's a fatal mistake, be-cause only *you* can complete you. When you become a whole, emotionally healthy, independent, secure individual; when you learn how lo live alone and relish it, that's when you'll attract a like-minded mate, someone of sub-stance and potential durability, not to mention delight. Cupid has an aver-sion to overly needy people. They make the little fellow gag.

JR: You've also demonstrated a certain fascination, particularly in *Villa Incognito*, with masks and disguises. Is it more or less difficult to induce love to stay when one is always in disguise?

TR: Well, in achieving a long-lasting relationship, the crucial thing is to break the projection. In other words, to cease projecting onto the object of your affection the image of who you think that person is or who you desperately would like them to be, and start seeing them—and totally accepting them—for who they really are. Every evolved person requires a private inner life, and we should never trust anybody who doesn't have secrets, but in a long-term relationship, the masks must be discarded. However, in the short-term—and under proper conditions, brief flings can be very sweet—going incognito has its rewards.

JR: You've managed to avoid divulging much information of a biographical nature. What about, for example, your activities as a black marketer in Korea? Is it true that for a year you supplied Mao Tze-tung with all his Colgate toothpaste?

TR: And his Marlboro cigarettes, as well. But there's nothing else I can say about that without compromising national security.

JR: Well, can you safely talk about your background as a performance artist?

TR: My contribution to that sorry medium has been greatly exaggerated. In Seattle in the '6os, I created a number of what were then dubbed "happenings." Performance art, so-called, is ridiculously easy, which is why so many supremely untalented people practice it. Toward the end of my most elaborate production, some upright citizen called the cops to have me arrested.

JR: Were you jailed?

TR: No. One of the cops turned out to be a guy who'd stopped me for speeding only a week before. At the time, I'd looked him in the eye and said, "Officer, I drive like I live: dangerously. You of all people should understand that. We're brothers in a fraternity of peril." Naturally, he'd let me off. When he saw who was responsible for the somewhat exuberant theatrical performance, he shook his head and let me go again.

JR: But at this same time, you were embarking upon a serious literary career. How did you begin writing fiction in the first place?

TR: I began before I was old enough to know any better. At age five, to be precise. My parents introduced me to books at an early age, and I fell totally in love with them; with the way they looked, the way they felt, the way they smelled. For my fifth birthday, I received a Snow White and the Seven Dwarfs scrapbook, but instead of pasting pictures in it, I filled it with stories. I couldn't actually write, of course, so I dictated them to my mother. I'm told that they exhibited signs of an alarming imagination.

JR: So you've almost always written?

TR: I have. It's a mysterious activity, writing fiction, and there's not much that can be said about it that isn't misleading. To try to explain the creation of a memorable paragraph—memorable for its poetry as well as its sense—is like trying to analyze that wolf howl that drifts down from the snowy hills on the outskirts of town.

Tom Robbins Incognito: Tracking the Pacific Northwest's Elusive Literary Outlaw

Christian Martin/2003

Originally appeared in the *Bellingham Weekly*, May 29–June 5, 2003, 7–8, 16; and reprinted as "Tom Robbins Incognito: Tracking the Pacific Northwest's Elusive Literary Outlaw," in *Moontrolling* 1 (2003): 1–9. Reprinted with the permission of Christian Martin.

I recently found a Tom Robbins passage that summarizes, for myself anyway, the underlying message the legendary Pacific Northwest author has been transmitting through his many novels over the past thirty years, the wisdom-medicine that he consistently administers to an ever-increasingly homogenous and obedient world: *"What matters* is that we enlarge our souls, light up our brains, and liberate our spirits. *What matters* is that we hop on a strange torpedo and ride it to wherever it's going, ride it with affection and humor and grace, because beyond affection, humor, and grace, all that remains is noise and sociology! *What matters* is that we never forget that the little paper match of one individual's spirit can outshine all the treasures of commerce, out-glint all the armaments of government, and out-sparkle the entire disco ball of history."

Of course, there's much more to Robbins than that. Since his first novel appeared in 1971, Robbins has served our culture as shaman, holy fool, romantic, high priest, teacher, trickster, and soul mechanic. He is, as an old business card he once gave me proclaims, simultaneously an Admirer of Clouds, a Part-time Buddha, and a Menace to Society. A book reviewer once opined that "Robbins needs to make up his mind whether he wants to be funny or serious." Robbins replied, "I'll make up my mind when God makes up his. If I have learned anything in my life, it is that there is no wisdom without playfulness."

With his new book, *Villa Incognito*, landing in bookstores across America this spring (as well as on to the *New York Times'* bestseller list), I thought it a brilliant idea to try and track down the Pacific Northwest's favorite literary outlaw for a chat.

It wasn't like I was on a treasure hunt without a map. Not only do I live just up the road from his home in the Skagit Valley, but Robbins's new novel was drawing him out of seclusion and on to the book tour circuit. Typically as secretive as the fabled Bigfoot, he was currently scheduled to speak in both Seattle and Bellingham, so my chances of finding him were quite excellent, nearly guaranteed. But I was looking for more than just getting my library of dog-eared Robbins books signed. I needed to be more than just a member of the audience. I needed an audience, my own, with Robbins.

La Conner

The heavens bow down low to the earth. Pregnant clouds roll off the Puget Sound, trailing dense curtains of rain behind them. An army of swollen raindrops fall recklessly against my windows. My windshield wipers can barely keep up.

I am crossing rivers and creeks and winding through farmlands on a two-lane highway. There is a quicker, simpler, more direct way to get to Tom Robbins's hometown of La Conner, but since the author's prose is anything but quick, simple, and direct, taking the backroads feels most appropriate. With the rumpled mass of the Chuckanut Mountains in my rear-view mirror, I zip across the Skagit Valley flats past the sleepy, cow-studded hamlets of Bow and Edison. I'm in the green land that Robbins celebrated in his first book, *Another Roadside Attraction*.

"It is a landscape in a minor key," as he described it. "A sketchy panorama where objects, both organic and inorganic, lack well-defined edges and tend to melt together in a silver-green blur . . . It is a poetic setting, one which suggests inner meaning and invisible connections. The effect is distinctly Chinese. A visitor experiences the feeling that he has been pulled into a Sung Dynasty painting, perhaps before the intense wisps of mineral pigment have dried upon the silk."

My first stop is the Calico Cupboard bakery. "Does Tom Robbins ever come in here for cinnamon rolls?" I ask the pretty bakery girl behind the counter.

She scrunches up her forehead. "Tom Robbins?"

Hmm. OK. That felt pretty silly. I walk on down the street and almost get hit by a beat-up Toyota Corolla festooned with Black Sabbath stickers pulling over to park.

"Sorry 'bout that, dude," the driver says.

"No problem. Hey, you live around here? Ever run into Tom Robbins?"

"Yeah, sure. He came into the restaurant where I was bartending all the time. He's a totally cool dude, really, really nice. But he dresses like a skater punk or something. Black studded belts and shit."

Maybe I'm on to something here. "What else?" I ask.

"Well, this restaurant is all fine dining and shit, real fancy. One night he comes in and orders up some dinner. He's just chilling out on his own, real quiet and well-behaved. He pays his bill and gets up to leave, but as he passes by the kitchen on his way out, he pushes open the kitchen door and yells at the top of his lungs, "That was the BEST FUCKING COD I've ever eaten!"

Unsure how to follow that tidbit up, I simply ask if he knows where I can find Robbins at this moment. He hesitates, then says, "We mostly let him have his space around here." I walk on.

I duck briefly into the Museum of Northwest Art, and then next door into the La Conner Brewing Company's pub for some lunch and a pint of IPA. I position myself at the curvaceous bar so as to have a view out the windows. The weather has turned mild, and tourist hordes have taken over First Street. Even though the annual tulip festival has come and gone for another year, flocks of visitors continue to migrate up and down the sidewalks, and occasionally out into traffic. Confused motorists search for parking, trying to avoid hitting the tourists.

What's the draw, I wonder? The Swinomish Slough that bisects Tom Robbins's hometown is muddy-brown, indifferent, and looks damn cold.

"Tugboat towns are a dime a dozen," La Conner's most famous denizen once told an interviewer. "That this was an intersection of art and fishing and farming is what's interesting and unusual and singular to this community." But the only hint I've seen that this berg was once, back in the Fifties, home to the world-renowned "Mystic Painters of the Northwest"—including Morris Graves, Guy Anderson, Mark Tobey, and Ken Callahan—was a lonely book of Graves's flower paintings for sale back in the art museum.

Nonetheless, Robbins declared himself "happy as a sugar bug on a rump roast" living in La Conner, so I settle up my tab to get on with my search. If I can get a move on, maybe I'll be able to ask him about his mysterious love of this place in person. The attractive waitress brings me change. "You ever pour beers for Tom Robbins?" I ask her.

She blushes, or beams, or a bit of both, and then waves her hand through the air. "He's always all over the place," she says. "Sometimes he comes in here, but usually he's down the street because they serve hard liquor down there. We only serve our beer here. But I haven't seen him for six months or so."

My hunt for Tom Robbins's hermitage is starting to bog down. The beer has made me sleepy, and nobody seems willing to spill the beans on his whereabouts. But there's one more place further on down the street for me to investigate, The Next Chapter bookstore, before I give up. Surely the bookworms, La Conner's literary folk, will understand my pilgrimage and help to warm my cold trail!

Upon entering, I cheerfully ask the proprietor where their "Tom Robbins section" might be. He ambles over to a shelf and points at a scant three titles. "Right here, sir!" he says. Sensing my disappointment, he wheels around and proudly shows off a feature display of *Villa Incognito*. "And right over there is his newest book!"

"Wow, cool!" I pick up the book, feigning interest. "So," I prod none-too-casually, "does Tom Robbins come in here often?"

The book man grins and says, "Well, I'm more likely to run into him over at the post office than here." But, just as soon as the words leave his mouth, he catches himself and a cold distance suddenly yawns between us. There is a long pause. "This town here is his little haven. He's really well-protected here."

The message is clear. Further questions pertaining to Tom Robbins aren't welcome.

I suddenly see the boorishness of my quest. What am I, a reporter for the *National Enquirer*? Here I am in Mr. Robbins's neighborhood, prying into his community of friends with my nosy questions. Do I think I'm just going to stroll through his garden gate and rap upon his front door? Then what? Robbins will just be lounging about with nothing better to do than to wait for some stranger to come by so that he can offer them soup and enlightenment? And what was I planning on saying then? "Hi Tom, remember me? We shared a booth in a Seattle bar about ten years ago. I love your work!" I feel like such an asshole.

As I walk back to my car to get myself back home where I belong, somebody sitting in their car up ahead is yelling something at me, something that sounds like "Hell-of-it! Hell-of-it!" I get closer and recognize the ex-bartender that I talked with earlier in the afternoon.

"Halibut! Halibut!" he yells.

"What?"

"It wasn't COD, it was the BEST FUCKING HALIBUT he'd ever had!"

The University of Washington

Kane Hall on the UW campus is filling up fast with people arriving for the scheduled Tom Robbins appearance: solitary students, hand-holding couples, teenagers, grandparents, yuppies, hippies, wild-hair coffee shop philosophers. I stroll in too, but with a secret certainty that I will be granted my personal audience after the evening's proceedings. As far as the quest goes, things are looking up.

By the time Robbins strolls out from behind the velvet curtain wearing dark shades and all black attire, the posh auditorium is full up, all 850-some seats. There is raucous applause as Robbins bellies up to the lectern; he returns the welcome with a small bow, hands pressed together at the chest like a Buddhist monk.

After some brief introductory remarks, he holds up a copy of *Villa Incognito* and introduces the audience to, as he puts it, "my latest affront to the literary sensibilities of the world." His voice, slipping into his native southern drawl every now and again, incants the mysterious world of a shape-shifting, sake-guzzling, farmgirl-loving, mythical Japanese badger-like creature named Tanuki. "It had been reported that Tanuki fell from the sky using his scrotum as a parachute," the tale begins. (A first sentence worthy of the esteemed company of other Robbins openers.)

Robbins reads for half-an-hour or so, including an illustrious passage on how the soul resembles a freight train. "Yes, a long, lonesome freight train rumbling from generation to generation on an eternally rainy morning: its boxcars are loaded with sighs and laughter, its hobos are angels, its engineer is the queen of spades—and the queen of spades is wild. Whoo-whoo! Hear that epiphanic whistle blow," Robbins exhorts in the voice of new character, Mars Stubblefield. The audience nods as if everybody understands. *Yes.* This is what we're here for. Feed us more.

"The train's destination is the godhead but it stops at the Big Bang, at the orgasm, and at that hole in the fence that the red fox sneaks through down behind the barn. It's simultaneously a local and an express, but it doesn't transport weaponry and it certainly ain't no milk run." Laughter and a smattering of applause, as if Robbins is a sax player who just blew an inspired solo, the one we came all this way to hear.

And still there's more, though it is clear that Robbins is winding this jam session up. "In the end, perhaps we should imagine a joke; a long joke that's being continually retold in an accent too thick and too strange to ever be completely understood. Life is that joke, my friends. The soul is its punch line."

A pregnant pause. "Let's not chisel that last remark in stone. Okay? It may be high wisdom, it could be pure bullshit. There's often a thin line."

Ta-da! There is great, adoring applause, though the author looks down at his feet and shuffles about, not entirely comfortable with the adulation.

Afterwards, a procession of some 850 fans stretches from Robbins's signing table on stage up the stairs to the nosebleed section of Kane Hall, across the back of the auditorium, and back down the stairs on the other side of the room, a giant spiral encircling the sunglasses-clad Skagit Valley scribe.

Obviously, I am not going to get the exclusive attention that I dream of here. Thinking swiftly, I jot down a note and bashfully pass it with my phone number to his wife, who is settling in the front row for a long wait.

The Phone Call

Sunday morning, I'm on my second or third cup of coffee, and listening to the musical patter of rain on the roof. I'm nearly hypnotized, until the phone breaks the spell.

"Christian, this is your long-lost childhood friend!"

I don't immediately respond.

"You remember, back from the pineapple plantation up in Nova Scotia!"

"Uh, yeah, who is this?" I sense a trickster.

"Hey, this is Tom Robbins. I'm calling you from Denver. My wife slipped your number into my briefcase and I found it this morning. I just read your letter, and think I can find some time to do something with your newspaper next week."

I jerk out of my drowsy state and begin taking notes immediately. The telephonic surprise awakens me more than all the caffeine in the world ever could.

The author has little time, perhaps little patience, for long-distance small talk. We immediately get down to the logistics of fitting an interview into his busy book tour schedule, and end up agreeing that within the week I'll fax him some questions to his home in La Conner. "That way I'll have some time to ponder my answers," he says. The mind of Tom Robbins pondering *my* questions? Sounds great to me. He rattles off the seven digits of his fax number.

"So," I say, jotting them down carefully, "this is *the* direct link to Tom Robbins, huh?"

"Yeah, well, the direct link to me, as well as to Villa de Jungle Girl. It's also the link to Jiffy Squid. And to the House of Thrills. It sometimes gets confusing with so many faxes coming in for us all."

"I understand."

"Yep. You know the nice thing about being schizophrenic, Christian? You're never alone."

The Interview

CHRISTIAN MARTIN: You're a hard man to track down, Mr. Robbins.

TOM ROBBINS: You gotta keep moving, otherwise you're a target. Just because I'm a cheap date doesn't mean I'm easy.

CM: Are you, like the theme of your new book, incognito? What's up with the dark sunglasses?

TR: Most of us wear masks, even when we look in the mirror. With a few of us it's deliberate, but for the majority it's because we don't really know who we are. Our various institutions and media are designed to prevent us from discovering our true selves—that all-important side of us that we seldom define as us, the side that has absolutely nothing to do with our name, address, or occupation.

As for the shades, I wear them to help melt the shadow between Our World and the Other World.

CM: With another tulip festival come and gone, how's life in La Conner these days? How's twenty-first-century Skagit Valley treating you?

TR: Like so many other lovely places, Skagit Valley has fallen victim to the hoax of "progress," to the insidious myth that growth is not only desirable but inevitable. Despite the cancer of development, however, it's still possible to live very well here, to find peace and privacy and friends, and to be inspired by those pockets of natural beauty to which the philistines are so insensitive.

CM: In accepting Bumbershoot's 1997 Golden Umbrella Award, you claimed that "in thirty-five years here I've seldom felt a (rain) drop I didn't like." Are you still as enamored with the drizzle and mist?

TR: I'm not John Denver. It's the clouds and the rain that make me happy.

I've always loved "bad" weather and always will. For a mystic or true romantic, there are few things more exhilarating than a stormy night or rainy morning. The polyester golfers and wrinkle freaks are welcome to their Arizona.

CM: So the Pacific Northwest remains a good place for you to work. When you get down to writing, which comes first for you: a main character, a plot, some idea to explore?

TR: At the risk of sounding corny, I'm obliged to report that creating fiction—especially imaginative fiction—is such a mysterious enterprise that there's very little that can be said about it that isn't misleading. It's extraordinarily complex, entangled and slippery. Generally, I suppose I'm led into beginning a novel by several unrelated ideas or issues that I've been itching to dramatize and explore. Then I hold auditions for characters. As for the plot (or plexus of plots), that develops over time once I've embarked upon what can only be described as a "journey," a voyage in the brain, an adventure on paper.

CM: I've heard you claim that you don't, except for words or a phrase here and there, do much rewriting on your books.

TR: There is, indeed, considerable reworking, but it's done slowly, sentence by sentence, word by word, as I go along. So even though I've only written one draft, there isn't a word in the novel that hasn't been examined and challenged about thirty times. It's probably a ridiculous way to write, but it suits me, even though it requires a concentration and intensity that would scare Tom Clancy out of his camouflage pajamas.

CM: Your last book, among other things, dealt with pedophilia and, er, creative intercourse with a nun. *Villa Incognito* opens up with scenes of interspecies sex in a monastery. Do you ever worry that one day you'll run out of taboos to break?

TR: As long as there are fearful, superstitious, ill-informed people in the world, there will be taboos. And as long as there are taboos, there'll be a need—in the interest of freedom and advancement—for mavericks who will risk publicly defying them. The central dynamic of history has never been the struggle between good and evil, but, rather, the struggle between ignorance and enlightenment. In my novels, however, many taboos are challenged besides the sexual ones you mentioned.

In that regard, it should be made clear that *Fierce Invalids Home From Hot Climates* deals not with "pedophilia" but with adolescent sexuality, which is a different matter entirely. Our culture sends young girls in particular extremely mixed messages about sex. On the one hand, youthful female sexuality is continually flaunted and exploited in every facet of our media, while, simultaneously, we're near hysterical in our denial of the powerful and natural pubescent sex drive. I was merely trying to cut through the hypocrisy. Moreover, this issue plays only a very small role in the book, and ultimately the protagonist has the moral strength to resist taking advantage of the carnal appetite that's flowering in the sixteen-year-old girl with whom he has fallen in love.

CM: Which readers do you hear the most from?

TR: Smart, open-minded readers with a sense of humor and an appreciation of language, readers who remain susceptible to wonder. These include people of all ages and from many walks of life. I get lots of letters from college girls, true enough, but also from college professors. And medical doctors and computer technicians.

CM: What do you enjoy doing that has nothing to do with writing?

TR: In one way or another, everything has some connection to writing. But for what it's worth, my non-literary enthusiasms include rivers and rain, meditation and wine, travel and women, wild nature and mythology, music and mayonnaise, cigars and circuses, basketball and psychedelics, French cinema and Japanese culture, all philosophical systems of liberation, modern art, ancient civilizations, and Krispy Kreme donuts—not to mention those things I can't discuss for reasons of national security.

CM: Speaking of which, you've been quite outspoken in your criticism of U.S. foreign policy and the current wave of ultra-patriotism. Why do novelists such as you, Kurt Vonnegut, Sherman Alexie, and Peter Mattheissen seem to get away with this criticism more so than do entertainers and political figures?

TR: Tragically, a nation that was created by intellectuals and visionaries has now been completely taken over by venal corporate gangsters, delusional Christian fruitcakes, and hopelessly shallow Texas shit-kickers. In such a dumbed-down environment, the cowboys in power probably don't feel that they need to pay much attention to the protests of the intellectual or artistic community. We're considered irrelevant. That's why when Jerry Falwell included me on the list of "traitors" he wants rounded up and shipped back to Guantanamo Bay, I was honored. Just put me in the same cellblock as the Dixie Chicks and I'll be happy to go.

Having said that, I must point out that I try to avoid the blatantly political both in my life and in my work. Instead, my approach is to encourage readers to embrace life, on the assumption that anyone who's saying "yes" to life will automatically say "no" to those forces and policies that destroy life, suppress it or reduce it to mere survival.

CM: How dangerous is the threat to independent thinking today?

TR: Worse than it's been in a long, long while. However, independent thinking has *always* courted danger because it's always bolstered enlightenment in its ongoing struggle with ignorance and dogma. It's a threat both to those who fear liberty and to those who profit financially from mindless obedience and herd control. Jesus, you may recall, was an independent thinker.

CM: Are there any escape routes left?

TR: Of course. *Villa Incognito*, for example, takes history, current events, and myth, braids them into a circus high wire, stretches that wire across the yawning abyss of consensual reality, and tempts us to walk across it if we dare. The wire leads inward. It's anchored in the soul, in full consciousness, in our ancient animal past. It connects us to the Mystery. It's the ultimate escape route. It's always been there. It can be obscured, but never destroyed.

Postscript: A Final Phone Call

"Hey Christian, this is Tom Robbins again. Say, when you're researching and writing your story, don't believe the stuff that's out there on the Internet. It's mostly a bunch a lies and crap."

"Yeah? Like what?"

"There's some site that claims I'm a masochist. Ha! It's so obvious that I'm a hedonist! I love pleasure!"

"Hedonist. Not a masochist. OK, got it."

"And then somebody else came up to me recently and said something like, 'I read you don't get out of bed until you hear the number 39.'"

"I hadn't found that in my research. That's a weird one."

"No kidding. Obviously, the number is really 23."

Even Tom Robbins Gets the Blues

Steve Bloom/2005

From *High Times*, November 2005, 64, 66. Reprinted with the permission of Mary McEvoy, publisher.

High Times: I heard your public-service announcement for the Marijuana Policy Project. How did that come about?

Tom Robbins: Since I'm a charter member of the MPP, and since I possess a doughnut crumb of fame, I suppose it wasn't surprising that I'd be asked to record a PSA that might at the very least call attention to the cruelty and inhumanity of the laws forbidding the medical use of marijuana.

HT: You talk about your mother having glaucoma and not having access to marijuana. Did she ever try it?

TR: My mother's conservative Virginia ophthalmologist opined that marijuana was the only treatment that might impede the progress of her glaucoma. I convinced her after considerable persuasion to give pot a try—but my father refused to allow it in the house because it was illegal, thereby condemning his wife to go painfully blind. He couldn't understand that unquestioning adherence to an oppressive law is also a form of blindness.

HT: Washington State, where you live, passed a medi-pot initiative in 1998. How's that going seven years later?

TR: The situation here is the same as in those other states that have approved medical marijuana: Terminally ill patients who use it, or physicians who recommend it, are in danger of being busted by the Feds. So much for Christian charity.

HT: What's your reaction to the Supreme Court's *Raich* decision?

TR: Considering that at least two of the justices are addicted to the deadly drug nicotine, the decision broadcast an aura of hypocrisy. On purely technical grounds, however, the court was probably correct in tossing the hot potato back to Congress. Of course, the Congressmen aren't likely to act with any enlightenment or compassion, despite the fact that 80 percent of their constituents favor prescribed marijuana for seriously ill patients. So much for democracy.

Conservatives contend that to sanction the medical use of pot would encourage children to smoke dope. That's like saying surgeons shouldn't be permitted to use scalpels because it would encourage kids to bring knives to school.

HT: How did your eye operation go? What was the problem? Are you okay?

TR: As a result of a sports injury, I've had scar tissue in my right eye for many years, and recently it had begun to harden and expand. I underwent surgery at the end of June, a procedure that so far seems to have left me seeing like a demi-Stevie Wonder—although I don't know if it's the Stevie half or the Wonder half. I'm praying to Voyeur, the Roman god of scrutiny, and St. Keyholeus, the patron saint of Peeping Toms, for the eventual return of binocular vision.

HT: In *Wild Ducks Flying Backward*, you write in a footnote about Hunter S. Thompson's passing: "Where are the men today whose lives are not beige, where are the writers whose styles are not grey?" With Hunter gone, that leaves you as one of the last great stylists of '60s and '70s counterculture lit. How does that make you feel?

TR: If true, then I feel like a canary with the mumps. It's bad form to use the words "I" and "great" in the same context, and, frankly, I'm not even sure what constitutes "counterculture lit." Does that refer only to fiction that has a subversive ant in its pants and an appetite for mind-altering hors d'oeuvre, or can the term apply to any writing that deliberately defies academic preconceptions and doesn't brisk down Commercial Street in genre shoes? While I'll never deny certain counterculture orientations, I'd like to believe that my books cannot be that easily categorized. For example, the two most "psychedelic" novels I've read in years are Manil Suri's *The Death of Vishnu* and Louise Erdrich's *The Last Report on the Miracles at Little No Horse*, neither of which makes any mention of drugs.

As for artful stylists, I suspect that there are some dazzling young prose wranglers lurking in the shrubbery, poised to seize the radioactive baton from the likes of Hunter and me. However, it's doubtful that they'll ride in on a horse named Blog. The Internet is invaluable as a source of information, but it doesn't lend itself to style.

HT: Can you share some thoughts about Hunter as a person and as a writer? Will we ever see the likes of another HST?

TR: While we were both born in the South under the sign of Cancer and shared the same editor for a while, Hunter and I were quite dissimilar. Hunter used substances to get gloriously, spectacularly fucked-up; whereas for me—though I've certainly spent many long hours playing with my toes, giggling like a monkey, and staring enraptured at spots on the wall—psychedelics were always part and parcel of a private vision quest. No matter how idiosyncratic and oblique, my life and work has had a mystical dimension, a level of consciousness in which Hunter had no interest.

Nevertheless, I was in frequent agreement with his social and political stance, and I was knocked goofy by his prose style. He seemed always to be on the verge of spinning out of control, a condition that in lesser writers is merely symptomatic of neurotic hysteria or inept craftsmanship, but which in Hunter's work was a consequence of the extreme to which he was pushing the verbal envelope. It was positively exhilarating!

HT: Another favorite of yours is Thomas Pynchon. You, Pynchon, and Thompson had an enormous impact on the counterculture generation. What do you feel you all had in common, and what differentiates your writing from theirs?

TR: If we three have anything in common, it's a passion for lively, picturesque language; a fascination with flamboyant characters (real or imagined); and an affection for unconventional ideas, ideas that sometimes can threaten the values—both literary and personal—of the critical establishment. Each of us is also a writer of serious comedy. Pynchon's humor is ominous and intellectual. Thompson's was savage and crazed. Mine has more of a rubber nose, I suppose, but that's not to say it has rubber teeth.

HT: Which other writers from your generation, living or not, should we remind *High Times* readers about?

TR: I've never been able to think of myself in generational terms. As someone who is nineteen one moment and sixty-nine the next, I guess I've resisted being defined in that way. Nelson Algren was born well before me, but anybody who hasn't read *A Walk on the Wild Side* has reason to run not walk to their nearest bookstore. Somewhat younger than me is Haruki Murakami, whose *The Wind-Up Bird Chronicles* is one intoxicating jug of surrealistic sake. As for writers closer to my own age, let's never lose touch with Allen Ginsberg's poetry, Richard Brautigan's funky vignettes, or the early novels of Ken Kesey, Ishmael Reed, Jim Harrison, and Thomas McGuane.

HT: I love your book titles. How do you come up with them?

TR: In imaginative fiction—an altogether mysterious enterprise—it can be difficult to pinpoint where the various elements come from. Titles such as *Even Cowgirls Get the Blues* and *Half Asleep in Frog Pajamas* were fished out of that slough at the bottom of the brainpan, the dark waters from which I spear most of my ideas and figures of speech. On the other hand, *Skinny Legs and All* was borrowed from a Joe Tex blues tune, and *Wild Ducks Flying Backward* is the name of a coital position described in an ancient Chinese sex manual.

HT: Can you elaborate more about "The Sixties," the chapter we're excerpting from *Wild Ducks*?

TR: Tight-assed old fearmongers and nearsighted young hipsters have been equally vocal in maligning the '60s, a historical period whose significance neither of them comprehend. In the interest of fairness and accuracy I came to the era's defense, although it was a risky proposition considering that there are lazy, dishonest critics who insist on relegating me to that bygone era—never mind that I'm not only not a "60s writer" today, I wasn't even one in the '60s. (I set two of my eight novels in the '60s, just as Hemingway set a few of his in the '30s.) In my remarks on the period, I was simply trying to correct some misconceptions, not gaze wistfully into a romanticized past.

HT: Could you have become the writer you are without the use of psychedelics?

TR: My early psychedelic experiences had a profound impact on me intellectually, emotionally, and spiritually, but since I began writing at age five, and because prior to my first trip I'd already been exposed to Surrealism, world mythology, modern art, theoretical physics, and Asian philosophy, it's impossible to gauge just how much LSD and psilocybin might have shaped my literary aesthetic. Certainly the sacraments left me more nimble-minded, more aware of the underlying fallacy of our dominant belief systems, better able to recognize the interpenetration of realities, and more comfortable about functioning outside the realm of normal expectations. Despite the fact that I often found them both deeply enlightening and marvelous fun, drugs never have been the axis around which my life has revolved.

HT: How do you feel about being excerpted in *High Times* nearly thirty years after we excerpted *Cowgirls*?

TR: The 1976 sampling in *High Times* was my first excerpt ever, and depending on the big dice that are always rolling, the *Wild Ducks* excerpt could be my last. I hope not—but if so, it would make for a perfect closure to what I've always regarded as more of *a careen* than a *career.* I'm grateful to *High Times*, its editors and its readers.

Barely Legal Grace

Connie Corzilius Spasser/2005

This brief interview by Connie Corzilius Spasser, entitled "Barely Legal Grace: Tom Robbins Talks About Crazy Wisdom, Miniskirts, and Two Guys from Bangalore" originally appeared in the *Reader's Choice Newsletter* (vol. 6, no. 1, Fall 2005), p. 1, in a slightly different format. Reprinted with the permission of the Follett Higher Education Group, Inc.

Q: One of the things that strikes me about your work—whether fiction or nonfiction—is that you love women. And not just in a "Me, Tarzan, You, Jane" sort of way, not just because you happen to be heterosexual. You exhibit an appreciation that seems to transcend the desirability—on the open market, shall we say—of any particular woman. You recognize the subtleties, the details that set her apart, and you acknowledge them. This is not typical, and it adds an irresistible charm to your already inventive and compelling writing.

Do you agree that your attitude toward women is extraordinary in its empathy, its sensual attentiveness, its appreciation of the Female? If so, why? Did you grow up with women?

A: When I was growing up, my family moved frequently, and we always seemed to land next door to a household with daughters. Those little girls taught me a lot. I found the feminine sensibility most enlightening, and as an adult I've continued to pay close attention to it. The future of the world may depend on it.

Q: *Wild Ducks Flying Backward* is a collection of short writings on a remarkable range of subjects. There are poems, paeans to other artists, activities, and icons (I especially loved "The Genius Waitress"), and answers to questions posed by magazine editors. I guess my question is: Do you write whatever occurs to you on any given day? Describe your writing habits a bit, if you would. How do you move from form to form, from forum to forum? If you knew you'd never again be published or have an audience, you'd still have to write, wouldn't you?

A: When it comes to fiction, you're correct: I write out of compulsion. It may sound corny, but each page of a novel-in-progress is a mysterious adventure that I embark upon armed only with imagination, education, and a sense of humor. I feel my way along a shadowy path of discovery. Conversely, almost every one of my nonfiction pieces was assigned by a magazine editor, and their composition was therefore much more deliberate—although I would hope, still lively and unpredictable.

Q: For better or worse, you're identified with a sort of sixties, free-love embrace of life. Is it, in fact, for better? Or do you find it annoying? How does it feel in a time when that attitude is so distant from prevailing morality and even vilified?

A: I operate out of an unorthodox but timeless philosophical stance that has nothing whatsoever to do with fluctuating mores. One simply cannot allow oneself to be victimized—or defined—by the age one happens to be born in. And those who would characterize sensual freedom and intellectual exuberance as some kind of retrograde "sixties thing" are merely revealing their cultural ignorance. If one is intent on assigning such qualities to a particular historical period, then why not, for example, *la belle époque* (Paris between 1885 and 1918)?

Q: What do you think about the writing and publishing scene today? Do you think the Internet—for example, e-zines—has helped or hurt literature?

A: Blogs and e-zines can be informative and fun, but to go to the Internet for *literature* is like going to McDonald's for Thanksgiving dinner.

Q: What are you working on now?

A: Believe it or not, I'm writing a children's book. I don't want to disclose the subject, but it's taboo to the extent that C. S. Lewis will surely be spinning at 78 RPM in his grave.

Q: Do you have any particularly vivid memories of bookstores from your past? What, if any, role did they play in your life early on?

A: I fell totally in love with books when I was five, so bookstores for me became combination cathedrals, amusement parks, and brothels. When, as a college student, I worked part-time in a bookshop in Richmond, Virginia, I felt like both a priest and a pimp. Talking to customers, I was in a state of barely legal grace.

Fame and Fortune: Tom Robbins

Jay MacDonald/2007

From Bankrate.com, July 21, 2007. Reprinted with the permission of Bankrate.com.

Long before *Another Roadside Attraction* and *Even Cowgirls Get the Blues* leavened the raw dough of '6os literature with the cosmic whimsy that allowed it to rise, Tom Robbins was living the freeform life of an East-meets-West Zen avatar/space cowboy.

Born the son of a power company executive in Blowing Rock, North Carolina, Robbins was a class clown and closet reader who molted as a teen from the straight life at roughly the same time kindred spirits Jack Kerouac and the Beats hit the road.

Robbins's search for self-discovery took a more circuitous route than Route 66, however, and included a three-year stint, from 1957 to 1959, in the Air Force as a meteorologist in Florida and South Korea. It was during his overseas tour that Robbins attended classes in Japanese culture and aesthetics in Tokyo that would significantly shape his unorthodox worldview.

Robbins spent the 1960s as a newspaper copy editor, columnist, and art critic, migrating from Richmond, Virginia, to New York's Greenwich Village to San Francisco and finally Seattle. Along the way, he took part in many of the "happenings" of the day, including lectures by Timothy Leary, a "legalize marijuana" rally with Allen Ginsberg, and a South American field trip with mythology professor Joseph Campbell.

It was in 1967, while writing a fevered midnight review of a Doors concert for Seattle's underground *Helix* newspaper, that Robbins happened upon his fictional "voice," that of a highly informed, unapologetically libidinous, free-associating enlightened soul who fully appreciates the cosmic joke of human existence.

At seventy, Robbins is as playful and engaging as ever. With eight novels and a new collection of short fiction and nonfiction, *Wild Ducks Flying Backward*, to appease his fans during the often-lengthy wait between

145

novels, he remains the turned-on, tuned-in, and drop-dead funny master prankster of his generation.

What would this intrepid inner-space explorer have to say on the topic of money? And what would he count as the biggest thrill of his life? Press on, gentle reader . . .

1. You're not typically thought of as a Southern writer, nor was Hunter Thompson, yet the two of you (arguably with an assist from another Southerner, Tom Wolfe) changed the American literary landscape. To what extent did your Southern upbringing influence your work?

A: The American South has, of course, a long and impressive literary tradition, but because I began dictating stories to my mother at age five, having already announced my intention to be a writer, I was probably much too young to have been influenced by that tradition in any conscious way. Maybe there's just something in the soil down there, in the lushness, the weather, or the Scotch-Irish gene pool. As I grew a bit older, my parents allowed me to roam freely in nature (we lived in the Appalachian mountains), to go to the movies and the library as often as I pleased, and to mingle with gypsies, moonshiners, religious snake-handlers, and old eccentric hillbilly gents, many of whom were colorful and hypnotic storytellers. My imagination was thus perpetually nourished.

Life in the South proceeds more leisurely than in the rest of the land, and that very languor may help keep imagination alive there. In a fast-paced, competitive environment where there's little time for daydreams, reflection, or language for language's sake, human imagination cannot thrive. Eventually, I was to find the South socially repressive, but not before it gave me an appetite for enchantment.

2: Your work is typically associated with the hippie movement of the late sixties and seventies, yet you were closer in age to the Beats, and were in fact on the road about the same time as Kerouac, Cassady, and Ginsberg. Were you aware of being on the cutting edge, surfing the zeitgeist, in the fifties? Were those enjoyable years or frustrating ones for you?

A: Some people do persist in associating me with the hippie Sixties, a misjudgment that both annoys and astonishes me. True, I did participate enthusiastically in the psychedelic revolution, and yes, I did write *Another Roadside Attraction*, which *Rolling Stone* deemed "the quintessential Sixties novel"—but that was nine books and nearly forty years ago. The protagonists of my subsequent novels have included CIA agents, stockbrokers, MIAs, and Japanese folk deities: characters who, though flamboyant and unconventional in their own right, obviously have nothing whatsoever to do with those love-fest summers of yore. My pigeonholers either haven't read my work or have pigeons roosting in their cerebral cavities.

Throughout most of the Fifties my homebase was Richmond, Virginia, and while Richmond entertained a large and active bohemian quarter (the fabled and much beloved by me Fan District), it was well off any major beatnik path. Even when I was on the road, I never had an opportunity to interact with the iconic Beats, not getting to know Allen Ginsberg until the winter of '64–'65. I sensed in the Fifties that America's square egg was starting to crack, but I don't believe it ever occurred to me that I might be somehow assisting in the cracking. It was a dichotomous decade, as auspicious as it was stifling. I found it both enjoyable *and* frustrating.

3: You're my first meteorologist. Where were you stationed, how did you adapt to Air Force life, and what effect, if any, did that four-year stint ultimately have on you?

A: I've always had a difficult time with authority, so you might guess that I was not well-suited to military discipline. However, I became quite skillful at the practice of passive resistance, managing to avoid serious trouble while having a pretty good time. I got to track hurricanes in Florida, teach weather observation to the South Korean air force (my students and I operated a black market ring on the side), and plot top-secret weather maps in a war room right out of *Dr. Strangelove*, three stories underground at SAC headquarters in Nebraska. I liked the camaraderie, and it is thanks to the U.S. Air Force that I was introduced to Japanese culture, in which I still have an interest that extends far beyond sushi.

4: You encountered LSD in the summer of 1963. What was your first trip like? Did it change the course of your life and work? How?

A: Frankly, the day I ingested 300 micrograms of pure Sandoz LSD was the most rewarding day of my life, the one day that I would not trade for any other. To try to explain why it was so transformative, so profound, would take pages—and even then would likely strike the uninitiated as flapdoodle.

I'll just say this: on that fateful day I experienced in a direct, first-hand, concrete, and thoroughly rational way that (1) time really is relative; (2) every daisy in the field has an identity just as strong as my own; and (3) what we smugly mistake for solid form in our "realistic" world is actually some strange fluid dance of molecular wonder. How could knowledge like that, lucidly demonstrated, fail to alter a person's life?

By the time I encountered LSD, I'd already been exposed to Surrealism, post-Einsteinian physics, and Asian philosophies, so the effect the experience had on my writing is difficult to gauge. Certainly, the psychedelic experience left me less rigid: emotionally, intellectually, and spiritually. This flexibility has reinforced my native propensity for detecting screwy humor and deep meaning—often simultaneously—in some rather unlikely sources. A professor at an Ohio university wrote that my books "put the fun back in profundity."

5: Was money a problem for you in the Sixties? Were you always able to stay ahead of the bills? How?

A: Money was scarce all right, but I just never considered its scarcity a problem. I contributed art reviews to various publications and worked weekends on the copy desk of a Seattle daily newspaper. That was usually enough to support a simple yet ecstatic lifestyle. While I was writing my first novel, my girlfriend was a waitress in a seafood restaurant. Every night she would bring home leftovers off of her customers' plates. We dined happily on slops de la mer.

6: The Doors piece in the *Helix* from 1967 really brought back the Seattle of my youth (Chrome Syrcus, PH Factor, The BFDs, Parkers, and of course the Fabulous Rainbow). How did you ultimately find your fiction voice?

A: As mentioned, I pledged myself to the muse at age five, but for decades I was hesitant to tackle a novel due to a perhaps delusional desire not to sound like any other novelist who'd ever lit up a page. I practiced journalism while waiting and hoping to develop a literary voice I might call my very own. Then, one July night, galvanized by a Doors concert, I staggered home and wrote a review that, although colored by Jim Morrison, sprang from a place inside me that I recognized was to be the wellspring of my personal literary style.

Not surprisingly, that style has evolved a great deal in the ensuing years, but I can occasionally still hear echoes of that Doors review in my more mature prose.

7: *Another Roadside Attraction* became an instant cult classic in 1971. Did it translate into any sort of financial security for you? Was there a revelatory moment when a check arrived or you signed a contract when you knew this was the path that you would walk in life?

A: My advance for *Roadside* was only $2,500, but I was elated to receive it and immediately jumped on a plane to Japan. By then, I'd already begun *Even Cowgirls Get the Blues* and part of my mission in Japan was to visit a remote wildlife preserve where I could get a close look at *tancho zuru*, a spe-

JAY MacDONALD / 2007 **149**

cies of cranes that closely resembles the elusive North American whooping cranes that were to figure prominently in that second novel.

Roadside, for all of its word-of-mouth popularity, didn't make any money for years and precious little even then. Bad contract. It wasn't until I scored an advance for the half-completed *Cowgirls* that I, having virtually abandoned journalism, could subsist without raiding produce fields by dark of night and relying on the kindness of waitresses.

8: Once your book career was established, how did you handle your finances? Do you have any interest in the money you've made, or do you prefer to have others handle it for you? Do you invest, and if so, in what?

A: In 1994, I published a novel, *Half Asleep in Frog Pajamas*, that one critic characterized as "Wall Street meets the X-Files." It deals with the essential aquatic nature of the human race, as well as with Timbuktu and some bizarre yet true astronomical mysteries, but it's set against a backdrop of the U.S. financial market. During the three years I worked on the book, I read the *Wall Street Journal* every day and did a fair amount of investing. Research.

Typically, I insisted on making my own investment decisions, which proved stupid and costly because once that novel was done, I'd go for weeks or even months without listening to a stock report or checking my portfolio. I couldn't bring myself to pay attention. There were just too many other things in life I found more interesting. For whatever reason, the itch to make money has never set me to scratching. I must be missing a gene or something.

Nowadays I have a smart broker, and what I don't spend on travel and debauchery (which, aside from donations to activist causes, is almost everything), she invests in bonds. Don't ask me which ones. I know I wouldn't own any Halliburton, but beyond that I haven't a clue.

9: What is the single best thing that success has brought you? What's the worst thing about it? Who gave you the best piece of advice about handling fortune or fame, and what was it?

A: Luckily, success didn't catch up with me until I was old enough, wise enough, not to take it seriously. Those who do take it seriously pay with their souls. I mean, it's imperative that one strive to perfect one's art, one's craft, but fame and fortune as ends in themselves can be narcissistic toxins injurious to one's psychic health. Readings in Zen, Sufism, Taoism, and Tantra, not to mention certain sound bites attributed to Jesus, doubtlessly helped guide me to those conclusions. A tiny bit I figured out on my own.

Having said that, I can't deny that success has its perks. It's afforded me greater mobility (hitchhiking and Greyhound buses hold a minimum of charm when one hits middle age); increased independence (it's been a long, long while since I've had to answer to the neurotic whims of a boss); and a generally more attractive standard of living (nostalgia notwithstanding, a plate of fresh belon oysters at Le Dôme in Paris is at least marginally more appealing than slops de la mer in a rundown rural love pad in Washington State).

Maybe the best perk, though, is the extraordinary people my literary success has permitted me to meet, some in person, many through the mail. The worst part is being physically unable to oblige those who express a desire to maintain a correspondence with me.

10: The MO that runs through all of your writing is the quest for higher consciousness. Have you achieved it, and if so, is it a happy place? What does it take to move readers toward expanding their consciousness in the current social and political climate?

A: A renowned Zen patriarch once wrote in his journal, "Now that I am enlightened, I am miserable as ever." No matter how high one gets, one cannot permanently escape the hassles and irritants of everyday living. The goal of enlightenment is not necessarily happiness or inner peace. The goal is to wake up. And waking up is harder than one might suppose, although it's as easy to come awake in a destructive era like ours as in eras of relative equanimity.

When one is fully awake, when one's consciousness is elevated, one views events from a wholly different perspective. Perspective is everything. When one can see existence as a grand and goofy and ephemeral show, a divine comedy in which even one's enemies play necessary roles, one can, for extended periods, float through life like a Ping-Pong ball in a mountain stream. The ball takes some sharp knocks, but it floats buoyantly, fearlessly on.

Maybe my novels possess the capacity to subversively activate a reader's sense of wonder and point him or her in the direction of an undammed stream. On the other hand, maybe they're little more than raffish entertainments. That's fine, too, provided every sentence has a taste for Dagwood sandwiches and is prepared to perform its own stunts.

11: Your biggest thrill, looking back?

A: It's been my good fortune to enjoy a flyspeck of international acclaim, to hang with some big-time artists and performers whose work I admire, to track orangutans in Sumatra, raft Africa's wildest rivers, et cetera, et cetera; but overall nothing has ever thrilled me more than watching a woman step out of her underpants.

Wisdom of the Rebels

Andrea Miller/2008

From the *Shambhala Sun*, July 2008, 72–77. Reprinted with the permission of Andrea Miller.

American novelist Tom Robbins has a well-deserved cult following, not just of gray-haired hippies but also fresh-faced students, back-packers in Banana Republics, and others. Take *Jitterbug Perfume*, the first book by Robbins that I was lucky enough to stumble across at the local library—how can one not be smitten by it? It's a book that begins with beets—"the most intense of vegetables"—and then dives into heady perfume, a good poke at a few of the world's major religions, and a host of zany characters, including a one-thousand-year-old janitor. Clearly Robbins owes some inspiration to psychedelics, but this wordslinger, as he calls himself, also owes something to Eastern philosophy. His heroes are the Zen rebels, Sufi saints, and wild yogis of the "crazy wisdom" tradition, as he interprets it. Like them, Tom Robbins cuts through self-serious, conventional mind with humor, insight, and a little bit of weirdness. I interviewed him by fax. —ANDREA MILLER

Andrea Miller: How would you define crazy wisdom?
Tom Robbins: The quick and easy answer is that crazy wisdom is the deliberate opposite of conventional wisdom. Like most quick and easy answers, however, that one isn't really satisfying.

For want of a precise definition, we might consider that crazy wisdom is a philosophical worldview that recommends swimming against the tide, cheerfully seizing the short end of the stick, embracing insecurity, honoring paradox, courting the unexpected, celebrating the unfamiliar, shunning each and every orthodoxy, volunteering for those tasks nobody else wants or dares to do, and perhaps above all else, breaking taboos in order to destroy their power. It's the wisdom of those who turn the tables on despair by lampooning it, and who neither seek authority nor submit to it.

What's the point of all this? To enlarge the soul, light up the brain, and liberate the spirit. Crazy wisdom is both transformative and transcendent.

AM: You seem to be particularly partial to Zen Buddhism. Is it Zen's version of crazy wisdom that appeals to you, or are there other elements that draw you to it?

TR: The branch of Zen Buddhism that has long interested me is Rinzai, the sect that eschews the mind-quieting practice of meditation in favor of the mind-blowing activity of wrestling with koans. Koans, of course, are those carefully crafted riddles that can never be solved by means of anything remotely resembling deductive logic.

On a purely intellectual level, attempting to solve koans is a perfect manifestation of crazy wisdom at work. It's important to emphasize, however, that, unlike Zen, crazy wisdom is not a practice, it's an *attitude* (an attitude I seem to have had since birth).

In general, I'm attracted to Zen's focus on absolute freedom and all-embracing oneness, its reverence for nature, and its respect for humor. When Zen or tantric masters visit North America, they're often astonished by how earnest, how overly serious, Westerners are about their spiritual practice. They'll go to a zendo in Minnesota, for example, and wonder aloud why nobody there is laughing. This led Chögyam Trungpa, in a lovely expression of crazy wisdom, to squirt righteously zealous meditators with a water pistol.

To be uptight about one's Zen practice, to become attached to it, is to miss the whole point of it; one might as well hook up with one of the fear-based, authoritarian, guilt-and-redemption religions.

AM: Can you give me some examples of crazy wisdom that interest you? I realize that you talked a lot about crazy wisdom in your *Harper's* essay "In Defiance of Gravity," but it would be nice to have more of a taste of what you mean.

TR: I'm a wordslinger not a scholar, I have a monkey mind not a monk mind, but I think you can trust me when I report that just as Zen evolved in China from a co-mingling of Buddhism and Taoism, there occurred in Tibet a dynamic meeting between Buddhism and Bön, the ancient Tibetan shamanic religion. The Buddhist masters who had infiltrated Tibet (around the eighth century) were eccentric *mahasiddhas* out of the tantric lineage in India, and the Bön shamans, having a natural affinity, took to their crazy-wisdom ways like Homer Simpson to donuts, maybe even improving (if "improving" is the right word) on their radical approach to ultimate awareness.

The Tibetan *siddhas* soon acquired a reputation as the wildest of spiritual outlaws. Siddhas slept naked in the snow, hung out in graveyards, nibbled on dung, drank wine from skulls, publicly engaged in kinky sex, and missed no opportunity to ridicule dogma. Believing in the possibility of instant karma, they employed shock tactics to jolt people into spontaneous enlightenment.

When a latter-day Japanese roshi would define buddhahood as "dried shit on a stick," or answer the question, "What do you do when you meet your master coming through the woods?" by advising, "Hit him over the head with a stick," you know they'd been infected with the virus of crazy wisdom.

Whether it sprang up independently in Persia and Turkey or was carried there by travelers along the Silk Road, I haven't a clue, but crazy wisdom permeates Sufism. One of my favorite Sufi stories concerns a man who, feeling in need of spiritual guidance, petitions for an audience with a renowned master. After a long wait, the request is granted, but the man is allowed to ask only one question. He asks, "What is God really like?"

The master answers, "God? God is a carrot. Ha ha ha ha ha!"

Feeling mocked and insulted, the man goes away in a snit. Later, suspecting that he must have misunderstood something, he requests a second interview, and after several years it, too, is granted. "What did you mean," the fellow asks, "when you said God is a carrot?"

The master looks at him in amazement. "A carrot?" he bellows. "God is not a carrot! God is a radish!" And again he laughs uproariously.

Turned away, the fellow broods over this outlandishness for many months. Then, one day, it dawns on him that the master was saying that God is beyond definition and can never be described, that anything we might say is God is automatically not God. At that moment, the man was powerfully awakened.

Examples of crazy wisdom also abound in the modern west, ranging from Joris Karl Huysmans sewing his eyelids shut because he believed that at age thirty, he'd already seen so much it would take him the rest of his life to process it all, to Muhammad Ali dancing in his undershorts at the Houston Induction Center after committing a felony by refusing to be conscripted into the army.

Unfortunately, however, crazy wisdom in the West is almost always devoid of a spiritual dimension.

AM: What influences or happenings in your life first prompted you to have a spiritual attitude?

TR: When I left home at age seventeen, I quit attending church because church had been providing me with nothing beyond an anesthetic numbing of the backside and the brain. By my mid-twenties, I'd completely rejected my Southern Baptist faith on the grounds that it was a bastion of fascist-tinged hypocrisy, based on misinterpretation of Levantine myth and watered-down compromises of the teachings of Jesus. Around that time, I began peeking into Asian systems of liberation, but it wasn't until my early thirties that I was literally propelled into the spiritual zone by the oceanic blast of psychedelic drugs.

Traditionalists won't like hearing this, but the fact is, tens of thousands of Westerners became receptive to and enamored of Buddhist and Hindu teachings as a direct result of LSD.

AM: Over time you have changed your mind about whether or not Americans can thoroughly and successfully adopt Asian philosophies such as Buddhism or Taoism. What is your opinion now?

TR: There are numerous paths to enlightenment. In Asia, the paths have been worn smooth by millions of experienced feet. The Western seeker, while he or she may have ready access to guides, maps, and road signs imported from Asia, must nevertheless stumble along overgrown, unfamiliar trails pitted with potholes and patrolled by our indigenous cultural wolves.

Americans may hold Buddhist ideals in our hearts and minds, but they're not yet in our genes. That takes time. Meanwhile, Asians are becoming increasingly Americanized. Who knows where this exchange will lead?

AM: In your first novel, *Another Roadside Attraction*, your character Marx Marvelous contemplates what religion would take Christianity's place if Christianity were suddenly to disappear. Can you describe the faith that you think might develop in such a situation?

TR: Suppose that from the environmentalist movement there should spring a revival of mystical nature worship, and suppose that this new nature religion should receive an infusion of crazy wisdom sufficient to keep it honest and amusing, free from any trace of dogma. Wouldn't that be the wildcat's meow?

AM: In real life, the religious right has gained a lot of power in the U.S. over the past number of years. What are your predictions regarding how this situation will develop in the years to come?

TR: There may seem to be a whiff of paranoid fantasy about it, but it's really not unreasonable to suggest that the Christian right presents by far the greatest threat to human existence in all of history.

I have a friend, a high-ranking officer in Naval Intelligence, who assures me that the U.S. intelligence services, military and civilian, are becoming packed with evangelical Christians. Congress and the White House are known to be heavily influenced by evangelicals, their doctrine, their votes, and their money. The danger they present is that they desperately want widespread war in the Middle East, they hunger for the fire and blood of Armageddon, thinking that it will force Jesus to come back and remove the "righteous" from this earthly existence that confuses and disgusts them.

U.S. foreign policy is now based on the apocalyptic Book of Revelation, which is to say, based on the ravings of a long-dead misogynistic madman. When he lived in Ephesus, the first thing the Apostle John saw every morning upon awakening was the gigantic statue of Artemis, with her multitude of naked breasts, and she made him crazy (though hardly wise). The Book of Revelation is the result. What sort of hallucinations do you think ol' John might have suffered had he run into Britney Spears?

As sentient beings, as a part of the One, the fundamentalist spawn of John deserve our compassion, but because they increasingly imperil all life on the planet, they must also be vigorously opposed.

AM: Your book *Still Life With Woodpecker* explores how to make love stay. How would you define love?

TR: Love is a carrot. No, no, it's a radish. Listen, better brains than mine have skidded off the road in pursuit of that elusive subject. I can say this much with confidence: genuine love, while it lasts, is a transformative emotional state that makes of the loved one an irreplaceable being. There's something magical, magnificent, and very sweet about that.

AM: *Still Life With Woodpecker* was published almost thirty years ago. Since writing it, have you learned anything new about how to make love stay?

TR: Well, I've learned that in asking how we can make love stay, I posed the wrong question. Romantic love moves around. That's what it does. Indifferent to misguided human cravings for permanence and certainty, it stages its glorious show, then folds its tent and leaves town. Or, at least, it stops buttering the popcorn. Perhaps it's both insulting and injurious to romance to try to hold on to it.

Ah, but there's another kind of love that does stay—and most Buddhists are familiar with it. When you "fall" into universal love, you're "in" love all the time, external events notwithstanding; you live and breathe in love. Even then, should your romantic partner decamp, you might feel sad or even angry for a while, but you won't sit up night after night swilling tequila and listening to heartbreak music.

It should be noted that there are relationships between mature, grounded, personally evolved individuals (people whole enough not to cling or be needy) that do last, and sometimes manage to embody both the romantic *and* the spiritual.

AM: In your latest book, *Wild Ducks Flying Backward*, you say that the word "spiritual" has become highly suspect. Why do you say that? How and why did the word degenerate?

TR: When a blue-collar, average Joe hears the word "spiritual," he'll frequently hee-haw and spit. It sounds sissy, elitist, and heretical to him, a threat to his masculinity and a contamination of the patriotic and religious detergents with which his brain has been thoroughly washed. When cool urban cynics hear the word, they sneer. It's an affront to their existential hipness.

For many others, it's a reminder of the legions of charlatans, frauds, and self-deluded dilettantes who are making money by hawking various brands of "spiritual" guidance. Then, too, there are the innocent airheads who go about broadcasting embarrassing streams of woo-woo in their everyday lives (and who are frequently the victims of the con-artist gurus).

These folks—some greedy, some ignorant, some just sweetly naive—have all contributed to the aura of suspicion that surrounds the word "spiritual" in contemporary American society. That's indeed unfortunate, because spirituality, when pure, connects us to the godhead with infinitely more efficacy and grace than does religiosity.

AM: What is the most spiritual place you have ever visited?

TR: An uninhabited savannah deep in Africa, a hundred miles from any artificial light, where, while lions coughed and night birds sang, I gazed at a dozen wheeling constellations and millions of ancient sparkling stars.

AM: If it were true, after all, that humans were made in the image of God, what exactly do you think God would look like?

TR: God is a carrot. Wait a second, that's not right. God is a radish!

HarperCollins Interview

Abigail Holstein/2009

From the HarperCollins Web site (HarperCollins.com), March 30, 2009. Reprinted with the permission of Abigail Holstein.

Q: So, Tom Robbins, you've gone and written a children's book about an alcoholic beverage. First, why the ode to beer?

TR: Why not? As ode fodder, it's got to have at least as much potential as nightingales and Grecian urns.

Beer is so universally beloved that 36 billion gallons of it are sold each year worldwide. Moreover, it's been popular for thousands of years, with origins dating back to ancient Egypt and Sumer. It has deep connections to the earth—and possibly to outer space, as well (I explain this in the book). Bittersweet, like much of life itself, it's exceptionally thirst-quenching and enormously refreshing; it's cheerful, accessible, affordable, lovely in color, and somewhat nourishing, being one of our few neutral foods: perfectly balanced between acidic and alkaline, between yin and yang. Best of all perhaps, beer makes us tipsy. What's not to ode?

Q: Well, it can make us fat.

TR: So can Coca-Cola, which lacks not only beer's impressive pedigree but—since they removed the cocaine from it in 1903—it's capacity for mischievous adventure as well.

Q: Okay, but what's the angle with children?

TR: Children see beer commercials every time they watch a sporting event on TV. In the supermarket, they pass shelves and coolers overflowing with the stuff. Neon beer signs wink at them as they're driven to school, to church, or the mall. And, if their own parents and older siblings aren't enjoying beer, then the parents and siblings of their friends surely are.

Kids are constantly exposed to beer, it's everywhere; yet, aside from wagging a warning finger and growling—true enough as far as it goes—"Beer is for grownups," how many parents actually engage their youngsters on the subject? As a topic for detailed family discussion, it's generally as taboo as sex.

It's a kind of largely unpremeditated side-stepping, and part of the reason is that most parents are themselves uninformed. Even if mommy and daddy have more than a clue about beer's ingredients and how it's brewed, they know nothing of its history, let alone the rich psychological, philosophical, and mythic associations bubbling beneath the surface of its wide appeal.

Q: Are you saying that in a sense, *B Is for Beer* is an educational book?

TR: In a sense. But it's also an entertainment.

Q: It's entertaining all right—and for adults, too, wouldn't you agree?

TR: Like the circus, it's intended for "children of all ages." That includes college campus keg cadets, Joe Sixpack's brighter sister, and geezers who're pretty darn tired of having to read their grandkids to sleep with tomes such as *Poopie the Pukey Puppy.*

Q: So, children need to know the "meaning" of beer?

TR: Well, at the very least they need a clearer understanding of why their dad keeps a second refrigerator in the garage, and why he stays up late out there on school nights with his shirt off, listening to Aerosmith.

Q: Moving on, your novels are known for their strong female characters. Would you say that Gracie Perkel in *B Is for Beer* is a childhood version of some of those memorable women?

TR: I suppose that's possible. Gracie is smart, upbeat, and spunky, and certainly not afraid of new experiences.

Q: She does have some unusual encounters, not only with beer but with her chronically hip Uncle Moe and with, you might say, the nature of reality.

TR: Children Gracie's age are still new enough on the planet to instinctively comprehend what mystics and advanced physicists mean when they speak of reality as though it were a bottomless dish of lasagna rather than a slice of toast. Extra dimensions and parallel universes seem perfectly natural to them—that is, until various institutions (familial, religious, academic, corporate, governmental, and military) outfit them with blinders, throw a beige blanket over their sense of wonder, and in the name of practicality, shoot out the lights in their imagination.

Q: You aren't overly fond of the way we educate our children?

TR: The brutal truth is, we're scarcely "educating" children at all. Even if you overlook the guilt, fear, bigotry, and dangerous anti-intellectual flapdoodle being funneled into young brains by schools on the religious right, what we're doing is training kids to be cogs in the wheels of commerce. Sure, vocational training is important, too, but it shouldn't be confused with education.

Education is for growth and fulfillment. A child's mind is its living room, it's going to be residing there for the rest of its earthly existence. What a tragedy to furnish that room as if it were only a cubicle in an office complex or a bay in a factory. There needs to be space for art and literature; a comfortable cognitive couch upon which to sit and contemplate the greater mysteries of life, death, be bop, and the space/time continuum. Presumably over a couple of frosty brewskies. Provided, of course, the imbiber is now eighteen or older and hasn't inherited the addict gene.

Q: Of course. How would you compare *B Is for Beer* to your previous nine books of fiction?

TR: At 126 pages, it's shorter. It's illustrated. And it's less complex, although considerably more complicated than *Poopie the Pukey Puppy*.

Q: One might suspect you're making that up. Over the years, you've proved to be wildly, often comically, inventive, and in terms of both style and content. Where do you get your innovative ideas?

TR: I don't have a good answer for that. I've been blessed—or cursed—with curiosity, imagination, and a love of language for as long as I can remember. When I sit down to write, I just let the goose out of the bottle. This time, it happened to have been a beer bottle.

Q: What will you possibly do for an encore?

TR: Not my problem. I've decided to take advantage of outsourcing. My next novel will be written by a couple of guys in Bangalore.

The Storyteller's Tale

Tania Ahsan/2009

From *Kindred Spirit Magazine*, May/June 2009, 32–33. Reprinted with the permission of Tania Ahsan.

TA: Your new fiction title is presented as a children's book for grown-ups and a grown-up book for children: what do you think of the way we educate children in the Western world today?

TR: The brutal truth is, we aren't "educating" children at all.

Education is for growth and fulfillment. By and large what we are doing is training kids to be cogs in the wheels of commerce. The emphasis is vocational rather than educational. Sure, job training is important too, but it isn't education. A child's mind is its living room, it's going to be residing therein for the rest of its life. What a tragedy to furnish that room as if it were a cubicle in an office complex or a bay in a factory.

In addition, much of American education has been usurped by fundamentalist Christians. The guilt, fear, bigotry, and anti-intellectual flapdoodle funneled into young minds by those sanctimonious, dangerously misguided apocalypse junkies amounts to nothing less than child abuse.

TA: How would you describe your own belief system? Are you a theist, atheist, or agnostic?

TR: I'm both a monotheist and a pantheist, which is to say I simultaneously believe in the one Infinite Divine and in the magic gods who inhabit rivers, tree trunks, storm clouds, and numerous other places, including certain neon lighting. There's no contradiction there: we can't impose human limitations on divinity. Moreover, since we can only speculate about the true nature of the Godhead, I am also—like everybody else on the planet, including the Archbishop of Canterbury and the Pope—de facto agnostic. Not one person knows for sure. As a character of mine once said, "I believe in everything, nothing is sacred/I believe in nothing, everything is sacred."

TA: Who has had the greatest influence on your spiritual life?

TR: Having abandoned my oppressive Southern Baptist heritage in my late teens, I began investigating Asian systems of philosophical liberation during my senior year at college. However, it wasn't until I ingested a heroic dose of pure LSD at age thirty-one that those teachings ceased to be mere abstract ideas and became as real to me as the ground beneath my feet.

In the years since, I've sipped heady spiritual nectar from the unorthodox goblets and radical teacups of Chögyam Trungpa, Bhagwan Shree Rajneesh, Gurdjieff, Rumi, Kabir, numerous anonymous masters out of the Tibetan "crazy wisdom" lineage and my idol, the fifteenth-century Zen poet and rebellious monk, Ikkyu Sojun. I don't follow any of those guys, understand, nor do I have an actual spiritual practice. What I do have is a life-affirming attitude. I choose love over hate, adventure over security, beauty over practicality, laughter over dogma, and jelly doughnuts over rice balls and communion wafers.

TA: Do you think people are generally more receptive to metaphysical ideas than, say, thirty or forty years ago?

TR: Indeed, that seems to be the case, although those who are genuinely interested in expanding their consciousness and enlarging their souls are still a tiny minority compared to those who live to expand their careers and enlarge their bankrolls. It doesn't really matter. As we saw in ancient Greece, only about 15 percent of a population need be enlightened in order to foment a golden age.

TA: How do you define happiness?

TR: In Zen, they define happiness as, "First grandfather die, then father die, then son die." That's pretty good, but I'd prefer, "Grandfather not die, father not die, son not die." If that's unrealistic, my idea of bliss would be to sit by a wild mountain stream with someone I love and a cold bottle of exquisite champagne, while woodpeckers hammer the nearby trees and foxes growl in their dens. A jelly doughnut for dessert.

TA: What's the best piece of advice you've been given?

TR: The first and only time I ever consulted the I Ching, it advised me (and I'm paraphrasing here) to "Be careful what goes into your mouth and what comes out of it." Had I been able to follow that wise counsel, my life would have been much easier—although, perhaps, not quite as interesting and certainly not as sweetened by doughnuts.

Nevertheless, it was such perfect advice that I haven't felt compelled to open the I Ching since.

TA: Are you content with what you've achieved so far in life?

TR: My goal has been to twine ideas and images into big subversive pretzels of life, death, and goofiness on the off-chance that they might help keep the world lively and give it the flexibility to endure. I doubt that I've been successful enough to feel content about it, but I'm still trying.

TA: Do you have any regrets?

TR: On a personal level, I've participated in a couple of ill-advised marriages. I should have known better but I couldn't help it. I was in a sex trance at the time. But, hey, romantic disasters are all part of life's rich pageantry.

In my work, I suppose I regret having given such a favorable impression of cocaine in my early novel, *Still Life With Woodpecker.*

It took me more than a year of weekend tooting (I never let it interfere with my work) to finally realize that coke is a pharmaceutical jackhammer that punches holes in the soul.

TA: Your books seem to portray a variety of different emotions felt by a number of diverse characters. Is there an emotion or trait you have trouble empathizing with?

TR: Well, willful ignorance is not really an emotion but I must confess I have a minimum of tolerance for it. It has a tendency to breed all manner of loutish behavior, including religious aggression, football hooliganism, and blind nationalistic zeal.

TA: Where do you get your wonderfully inventive ideas?

TR: I appreciate the compliment, but I don't have a good answer. I've been possessed by curiosity, language, and imagination for as long as I can remember. When I sit down to write, I just let the goose out of the bottle.

TA: The internet has made research for writers much easier. Do you welcome the change or do you still prefer to do your research the old-fashioned way?

TR: I'd be a fool not to take advantage of the internet for research. It's a handy fountain of depth-less knowledge and I drink from it greedily. For writing, however, I remain committed to pen and paper. There's something so organic, so substantial, so personal and private and soulful and friendly about watching one's handwritten thoughts soak into wood pulp. I say this even though my own penmanship resembles the nasty scrawls chalked on alley walls by Mongolian monster boys.

TA: From your writing and interviews, you seem to be very present, while others of your generation are mostly looking backward at their pasts. Do you do that consciously or is it just natural to you?

TR: I make an effort to live in the present moment, although the rent there can be rather steep.

TA: If you were marooned on a desert island and the entire works of three authors could be airlifted to you, what writers would you pick?

TR: I'd want every poem ever written by Rumi, for their incandescent imagery and industrial-strength spiritual example; I'd choose the novels of Henry Miller, for their exhilarating prose style and erotic stimulation (it gets lonely on a desert isle); and lastly I'd request the complete works of Georges Simenon. Frankly, I'm not a big fan of Simenon (the French mystery writer) but the guy published about two hundred books, which should keep me occupied until I'm rescued or die from coconut poisoning.

A Literary Conversation
with Tom Robbins

Liam O. Purdon and Beef Torrey/2009

Previously unpublished interview. Reprinted with the permission of Tom Robbins, Liam O.
Purdon, and Beef Torrey.

The following interview was conducted by email correspondence during the
months of July, August, and September 2009. Beef Torrey, editor and co-
editor of two other volumes in Mississippi's Literary Conversations series—
one with Tom McGuane and another with the late Hunter S. Thompson—
and co-editor of the latest Jim Harrison bibliography, approached me earlier
this year, in April, wondering whether I might be interested in joining him
to put together a volume with Tom Robbins as our focus, an author whose
works he knew I had been very much interested in teaching and examining
critically. When Beef told me Mr. Robbins would be in Denver the following week, on the latest leg of a book tour following publication of his ninth
and latest novel, *B Is for Beer*, I wasted little time getting on a plane, my
Argo, to meet the creator of such memorable characters in American fiction
as Amanda, Sissy, Switters, and now, even little Gracie. Though over three
hundred people had the same idea I had that day and were already ahead of
me in line in Denver's Tattered Cover Bookstore to listen to and meet this
one-of-a-kind, post-postmodern literary witch doctor, Lady Fortuna winked
at me, as she has done from time to time in my life, and somehow enabled
me to find a seat in the crowded great room of the store just a few moments
before Maestra's Maestro climbed the dais, made himself comfortable at the
podium, adjusted his sunglasses, and began his reading of excerpts from *B
Is for Beer*.

The crowd was mesmerized, motionless, like a tamed, sleeping dragon.
Then it came alive, joyously, as the question and answer session began. I

tried to catch Mr. Robbins's attention several times to ask a question, but to no avail: I was too far back in the cheap seats even to be noticed by the lethargic security guards. Several hours later, after I had secured a signed copy of the novel and a photograph with the author, a beautiful woman who seemed to be very knowing (was she Medea?) suddenly appeared right next to me as if ready to answer the question she knew I wanted to ask. When I did, she gave me the information I needed to reach Mr. Robbins at a later time at Villa de Jungle Girl, the consecrated Grove his wife, Alexa, and he have called home for many years in La Conner, Washington. Once in my hand, the *Golden Fleece* of Mr. Robbins's email address became the invaluable means by which Beef and I began the process of completing, for you, the following—the latest—literary interview to be conducted with Tom Robbins, one of contemporary American literature's most fearlessly original and imaginatively creative, engaging voices. Since Beef knew how much Mr. Robbins's literary art meant to me, he graciously invited me to initiate the conversation, and so it began with my establishing the first question's context by saying . . .

Many who have come before us to interview you, some of whose works comprise the earlier part of this Literary Conversations collection, have provided us, as well as other readers, with a rich array of insights into and facts about who you are and where you have come from, and about how you write and what you perceive the relation to be between your art and American as well as other cultural and philosophical traditions, especially those of the East. These subject areas are very important to know about, especially because you have just published your ninth novel, *B Is for Beer*, a children's book for grown-ups and a grown-up book for children.

We know we have been raised and borne aloft by the tireless efforts of nearly all of our predecessors to reveal the multidimensional nature of your creative outlook and to begin to understand the disarmingly simple surface appeal of your literary art, and for that reason alone, we intend initially to make most profitable use of what has been said about you and your work, by others, as well as by you, that pertains to our current principal interest, which consists of the exploration and elucidation of, in as many ways as our time with you will permit, the interchange between the reader and your novels.

Nowhere more incisively do you clarify that unique interchange than when you remind your readers you want them to experience, as the result of awakening, the wonder and joy of their own humanity, and of living authentically in the world. Despite Bootsy's "unfortunate vocabulary," for example, you indicate at the end of *Villa Incognito* she may have been on to something all along. You also emphasize it is never too late to have a happy childhood at the end of *Still Life With Woodpecker*. And now the title of your latest novel, *B Is for Beer*, offers anew that experience of joy since it reminds your readers of the initial wonder they felt when first exposed, as children, to the exciting mystery of language through the primers given them for the purpose of mastering words, those strange sound/image representations of simple facts, out of which more complex ones would eventually be constructed.

In reminding your readers of that erstwhile joy, and in developing this idea in the book through Gracie Perkel's imaginative encounter with the Beer Fairy, are you also asking your audience to consider the importance of memory itself, the importance of remembering to remember, and has this emphasis been an important consideration throughout your works and in your own life?

Tom Robbins: If there is a word that accurately describes my writing process, it's probably painted in Sanskrit on the wall of an obscure temple in the jungles of India—or else highlighted in a textbook for graduate students of abnormal psychology. One aspect of that unorthodox process involves, naturally, the selection and development of themes.

Invariably, I'll begin a novel with three or four themes on my countertop, which is to say, a smallish scullery of subjects—sociopolitical issues and/ or philosophical or scientific questions—that have intrigued me off and on for months, maybe years. At this point, none of the themes have been fully developed intellectually, let alone prepped for inclusion in a narrative stew, and I'm in no rush to do either. Rather, I deliberately submerge them in my deep subconscious, content to let them marinate in the dark juices of my imagination until which time events in the slowly unfolding narrative signal them into service.

The hope (switching analogies) is that when at last a single-celled theme crawls out of the green ooze at the bottom of my brainpan, it will have begun to sprout little legs, exchange gills for lungs; to gradually walk on dry land, breath oxygen and eat fruit; and eventually morph into something large, powerful, and graceful, if a trifle unusual looking, such as, say, a big-assed rhinoceros. And one should bear in mind that if my rhino charges one's personal Land Rover, it isn't necessarily intent on vehicular demolition: more than likely it's only wishing to mate.

Okay then, has memory—"remembering to remember"—been one of the themes that has undergone that sort of loosely calculated evolution in my work? I can't remember.

Beef Torrey: Is remembering to remember also a necessary step in the process of awakening or reawakening to the exciting possibilities of existence, possibilities that are often obscured or made to be forgotten, the result of the humdrum nature of everyday existence?

Tom: Even if remembering to remember hasn't been an overt or consciously expressed thematic concern of mine, you are doubtlessly correct in suggesting that something of that nature percolates none too quietly in a great many of my pages. I can see that I've encouraged readers to reflect upon the time in their younger lives when they were filled with a kind of wild, free energy; a sense of unity with the larger universe; back before various institutions subjected their innocent (yet subliminally aware) psyches to a battery of wire brushes and cauldrons of harsh detergents.

I'd submit, however, that any call to remember on my part goes well beyond the mere recollection and resurrection of childhood joys; that it attempts to evoke our connection to eternal principles, the unending flow of indestructible phenomena known in Hinduism as *samsara*. There are scientists who say everything that has ever happened, certainly in the past million years, is registered in our collective DNA, and if we can allow ourselves to remember to remember that we are infinitely more than the mere sum of our name, our occupation, zip code, political affiliation, net worth, and cell phone number; that—transcending such supposedly defining data—we share a common bond with all life forms (perhaps even with inanimate objects as suggested, fancifully, in a couple of my novels), well, remembering our grander, truer, identity kind of puts our everyday travails into a different perspective, doesn't it? And so what if such speculation, geneticists notwithstanding, should amount to little more than a load of woo woo poo poo? If one doesn't get overly hung up on it and turn it into dogma, it can greatly enrich one's life to remember to remember that each of us, every moment of every day, may be playing a role in a fascinating piece of on-going cosmic theater.

If nothing else, I do occasionally remind readers (and, simultaneously, myself) to remember to avoid the folly of taking themselves too seriously, the narcissistic ego being the source of most depression, discontent, and unattractive behavior in the world. But here let me pause to emphasize that I'm neither an aspiring guru nor in the motivation trade. My primary aim since I began writing at age five has been to entertain, surprise, and enliven myself and others by telling stories that have never been told in a style that defies categorization. For better or for worse, I've hitched my little red wagon to the Language Wheel. It isn't enough to describe experience, we must also experience description.

Beef: Describing experience is certainly what you do, what any novelist does. What do you mean by experiencing description?

Tom: It's just another way of saying that language is not the frosting it's the cake. Which is just another way of saying that words matter, matter as much or more than the things they're supposed to represent. I don't care that the butler did it. I don't care how or why the butler did it. What interest me are the descriptive words the writer has selected to evoke the butler's nasty deed.

Some years ago, in a review of a novel entitled *The Man Who Loved Cat Dancing*, a staff critic for the *New York Times*, wrote, "If you can overlook the language, this is whopping good yarn." Excuse me!?! If you can overlook the language? That's like saying that if you can overlook the grapes, this is an excellent wine. If you can overlook the fact that the person beside you in bed has been dead for two weeks, he or she is a stimulating companion.

Liam: Related to the issue of memory is also another matter that comes to the fore in *B Is for Beer*. This one has to do with the seam, the experience Gracie initially undergoes while holding on to the Beer Fairy's wand and "Blowing [the] Pop Stand" of everyday existence. Never a line of separation but always one of junction between two edges in your works (one has only to recall the described effect of Ellen Cherry Charles's febrile eye-gaming of profligate Spoonzy's ladle in *Skinny Legs and All*), the seam experience here showing the "picturing" relationship between word and object that can never be articulated, since it is neither fact nor object, invites your readers to behold and even feel, if only for the briefest moment, the vitalizing sensuousness, if not the sensuality, of physical existence, especially when the "seedy spikes at the tip" of the grass stems rub against Gracie's "elbows like the beards of affectionate billy goats." Wide eyed, Mrs. Grundy may be left speechless in response to the configuration and features of this "showing," but is this not the place to which we have to get if we are to re-experience, as we once felt (and knew) in our innocence, the joy and wonder of every breath we take?

Tom: If you're looking for action in this universe, the place you want to be is on a borderline. Whether it's the event horizon of a black hole, the frontier between Gaza and Israel; the troublesome demarcation separating (none too successfully) adolescence from adulthood, proton from neuron, ego from id; or that seemingly harmonious balance of opposites where yang rubs up against yin, it's on such borders where things get really interesting. That probably explains why I've chosen to pitch my little tent on that straddle between the Clear Light and the joke; why I'm moved to juxtapose and even mix together truth and fantasy, nihilism and comedy, mythos and logos, tragedy and fun. And it's why the Beer Fairy introduces young Gracie to otherness, to the interpenetration of realities. After all, both the dullest and most dangerous people on earth are super-nationalists and religious extremists, people who totally identify, to the point of death, with one and only one political subdivision or dubious conception of the nature of being. God knows (Satan, too) we wouldn't want Gracie to grow up to be dangerous and dull.

You're right to venture that awakening a reader's sense of wonder is probably a subconscious goal of mine. I don't mind yanking the rug out from under a reader in such a way as to shatter their belief system, but only if it leaves him or her feeling better than ever about being alive. Perhaps the best chance for achieving that is to operate in the borderlands, to learn to successfully transverse the "seam."

Beef: While other seam experiences beg to be considered at this moment, the connection between joy and memory by a vitalizing sensuousness and sensuality compels the question of influence on your artistic outlook and works by the fiction and nonfiction of Henry Miller. You have indicated in past interviews that Miller is a writer whose imaginative creations you greatly admire for their passionate intensity as well as stunning realism. Those works, no doubt, include *The Tropic of Cancer, Black Spring, The Tropic of Capricorn*, and each part of *The Rosy Crucificixion*, the controversial trilogy that probably still shocks Mrs. Grundy today. But do those influential works also include the stunning and joyous nonfiction, the essays and sketches, published by Miller in such later collections as *The Air-Conditioned Nightmare* and its second volume, *Remember to Remember*?

Tom: It's fair to say that I've never been a huge fan of Hemingway's hard pebbles of prose, but when I reread Hawthorne's *The Scarlet Letter* a couple of years ago, it struck me what a tremendous *relief* it must have been when readers came upon Papa's clean, bright syntax (clean even when stabbed onto the page with a hunting knife) after decades (centuries!) of rococo tutti con coco ornamentation marvelously impastoed and frescoed by Hawthorne and his verbally generous ilk. More recently, I tried to reread *Tropic of Cancer*, only to find it crass, harsh, unromantic, and aggressively sexist, rather unappealing and disappointingly so, yet all the while thinking what a *refreshment* Miller had to have been in the wake of all that euphemistic tea dribbled onto book paper by thousands of novelists too intimidated by professional smut-sniffers or by their own priggish selves to more than timidly suggest that men and women (let alone same-sex couples) might ravish one another in the hayloft or under the chenille. Prior to Miller, all of the steam in Western literature was wafting from those porcelain teapots. (*Lady Chatterley's Lover*, published six years earlier, was pretty tame stuff compared to *Tropic of Cancer*, and no one besides James Joyce and a handful of dissatisfied Irish housewives had any clear notion what Molly Bloom was going on about back in 1922.)

So, I salute horny Henry for his daring in smashing sexual taboos, as well as for his staggering vocabulary and incandescent language, and I readily confess that each of those attributes inspired me. However, he's now descended a few notches in my fiery pantheon. Moreover, while I was knocked-out by *The Air-Conditioned Nightmare* back in the day, I now remember none of it, and apparently I've never read *Remember to Remember* at all.

Beef: Consideration of how Miller may have had an effect on your literary art raises the related issue of possible influence by another twentieth-century American realist, Nelson Algren, the creator of such memorable characters as Kitty Twist, Dove Linkhorn, and Velma and Rhino Gross. In several previous interviews you have lamented the fact that his works, such as *The Man with the Golden Arm, Chicago: City on the Make,* and *A Walk on the Wild Side,* have either been forgotten or deliberately ignored especially by the academic community. Perhaps lacking the white-hot intensity of Miller's prose, Algren's nevertheless presents us with the same kind of lonesome monsters Miller's novels do. Is this aspect of Algren's literary art something that helped shape your conception and characterization of otherness?

Tom: I suppose it's mandatory to refer to Algren as a "realist," despite the fact that the gritty pyrotechnics—the mixture of funk and liquid hydrogen—that lit up his paragraphs rocketed him into a zone more real than either realism or surrealism. Yes, and although I would without hesitation place his name in contention for the title of Greatest American Author of the 20th Century, and although I wrote a weekly column entitled "Walks on the Wild Side" for my college newspaper, the presence of otherness in my work derives from my Asian and mythological studies, as well as from personal experience (psychedelic and otherwise), not one twig of it directly traceable to Algren's sooty urban elm.

If anything in Algren consciously influenced me, it would have been neither his characters nor his milieu, but the big jangling poetics, the deceptively sensitive slapstick humor, and the verb-surprises-noun bittersweet junkyard magic show of his *style*. That's not exactly traceable, either, although one could always do worse than apprentice oneself to a supreme stylist. A novel without style is like a swan without feathers: it's just another plucked chicken.

Anyone looking for early influences on my work, however, will need to shift their gaze beyond these shores. Specifically, they'll have to call out, in their best French accent, the names François Rabelais, Arthur Rimbaud, Blaise Cendrars, and most loudly, Alfred Jarry. Jarry's *Exploits and Opinions of Doctor Faustroll* infected me like a virus, a feverish pathology for which there would prove to be no cure save distance. It is with wobbly restraint that I've managed not to read Jarry again in forty years.

Doctor Faustroll is a quasi-novel, maybe even an anti-novel, and while my own novels may be a tad unconventional, they definitely don't breakfast in the experimental or avant-gardism camp. Obviously, I've taken liberties—at times outlandish—with the novelistic medium, but I've insisted on my work being at the same time completely accessible to any normally intelligent, open-minded reader. I've never played to little candy-box clubs of smug academic types or sympathetic friends. I crave more body heat than that. And if it appears that I'm trying to have it both ways—provocative yet friendly, esoteric yet inviting (not to mention playful yet deadly serious)—well, to have your cake and eat it too has always seemed perfectly reasonable to me.

Liam: While on the subject of otherness, a hallmark of your literary art, it is important to remember how in *Another Roadside Attraction* Plucky Purcell in the Pelican Tavern corrects the three barflies' misperception of the cast and band members of the Indo-Tibetan Circus & Giant Panda Gypsy Blues Band. While greatly agitated by their misperception of who these unusual performers are, the barflies are gently calmed by Plucky, as he turns to them and smiles, explaining, simply, "The ladies and gentlemen whom you desire to assault are showmen—jugglers, fire walkers and yogic acrobats—whose mission it is to entertain and enrapture children of all ages. They bring into the lives of ordinary Americans the color and splendor of the Orient, especially of those Asian cultures whose folkways have been abolished by Communist invaders. They are no threat to your freedom for it is in the name of freedom that they perform their magical feats." The point of Purcell's explanation is that there is always similarity in difference if one is willing to embrace and understand otherness, though, as a very wise old shaman once said, it is the difference, not similarity, that ultimately gives "life its fizz, its brew." Is this why, then, in each of your books the principal characters your readers are invited to meet and spend time with—Amanda and Ziller, Sissy and the Chink, Bernard and Leigh-Cheri, Alobar and Kudra, Wiggs Dannyboy and Marcel, Boomer and Ellen, Turn Around Norman and Can o' Beans, Larry Diamond and Twister, Masked Beauty and Today is Tomorrow, Maestra and Switters, Stubblefield and Dern, Elvis Suit, the Professor, Dickie, Miss Ginger Sweetie (or Cookie), and even little Gracie Perkel—have about them an otherness that elicits curiosity while compelling thoughtful, sympathetic response?

Tom: When a circus or traveling carnival rolled into one of the small Southern towns where I grew up, there were always righteous citizens (Pentecostals and hardshell Baptists) who would snort, frown, turn their backs, quarantine their kids, and hide in their clapboard bungalows, praying hard against the threat of contamination by godless frivolity.

Ah, but if you'd peek from behind the hydrangea bushes in their yard at night, you'd spy them at the window, shade pulled slightly aside, eyes fixed on the unfamiliar colored lights blazing on the show lot, ears cocked toward the festive pagan music, nostrils twitching to capture more (still more!) of the exotic (and strangely erotic) aromas a-swirl down there. Irresistible! Otherness is the Greatest Show on Earth and everybody secretly longs to run away with it. It's just that we're too damn scared.

Incidentally, in subatomic physics they work with concepts such as "forbidden spin," "strangeness numbers," and "the absolute elsewhere," which in a sense refer to otherness. Perhaps even absolute otherness.

Liam: Other than otherness and the length of a cheerleader's skirt, the next most conspicuous constant in your novels appears to remain the limiting and, in some instances, sinister nature of consensual reality in which your characters must participate. The principal cause of this unfortunate condition may ultimately be traced to the tyranny of the dull mind, as you suggest in *Even Cowgirls Get the Blues*, but you have also alerted your readers to other, more subtle influences symptomatic of the dull mind, such as consumerism and marketing, and symptomatic of plain, simple, Grade A pathology, such as forms of cultural enchantment usually deployed by proponents of authority culture and members of think tanks sponsored by corporatist interests. Are you suggesting through your fiction it is necessary for everyone to take stock of the various ways in which he or she may be controlled within society as a preliminary step in the process of change, a step which must occur prior to awakening, for example, to the importance of difference? In other words, is awakening as you understand and conceive of it a rational act at least initially?

Tom: In Asia, there are saints and gurus who profess to have become enlightened spontaneously. Wham! They just fall down in a swoon one Tuesday and wake up radiating like an amorous glowworm. Suddenly, they understand *everything*—and considering their subsequent behavior and wise teachings, there's no reason to doubt them. We Westerners, however, lack the potential, genetically and culturally, to receive or process that kind of wake-up call. Sure, we're bombarded with hints on an almost hourly basis, but the messages are too coded or we're too preoccupied or too inured to react in any lasting or meaningful way.

Not that, mind you, many more of us than could fit in a couple of suburban bowling alleys are interested in enlightenment as such, but anyone with a salted peanut of sensitivity must recognize that we're wrapped up 24/7 in the tentacles of commerce, manipulated outwardly by marketing forces in all their various guises, and inwardly by our narcissistic egos; dumbed down and larded up; and that's precisely why it feels so good to be drunk or stoned or momentarily lost in the all-encompassing raptures of orgasm: we get a brief glimpse of what it's like to be totally free of all that crap.

It's an ironic paradox that sometimes we can see more clearly when we're blind drunk. Of course, it quickly wears off. Those who desire to wake up and stay awake must work at it diligently. It all starts with recognition. If the burgers are tasty and you can't see the bars on the windows, it's hard to know that you're in jail.

We writers who are saying "yes" to life, saying it by means of stylistic élan as well as narrative content, are automatically saying "no" to those forces that would destroy life, exploit it, bridle it, or render it miserable. By composing texts that are neither brutal nor bland, by creating fictional alternatives to the effects of creeping meatballism, we may possibly achieve extra-literary results. If not, well, our novels and poems are less fattening than booze and more legal than drugs—although I doubt if they'll ever replace the orgasm.

Liam: The subtlety and even insidious effectiveness of cultural enchantment will remind all readers of your fiction of the metaphoric way in which you identify one kind of an internalized, coercive control "mechanism" through the idea of the veil of ignorance in your fifth novel, *Skinny Legs and All*. As the principal characters in that story, Ellen and Boomer, realign themselves in regard to each other, the philosophical profundity of each veil's "mechanism" is thoroughly clarified. But it is not until the actual Dance of the Seven

Veils on Super Bowl Sunday that the reader is shown at the I & I what he or she must do with the knowledge gained. Accordingly, are you suggesting by this fact in the book that having knowledge, ultimately, is not enough, and that acting upon one's knowledge is always necessary, frightening as that commitment might be? In other words, must each of us participate, as Salome models the action through her final performance, in a reverse ecdysiastic epistemological hootchy-kootchy for our knowledge to have effect?

Tom: An "ecdysiastic epistemological hootchy-kootchy." What a lovely phrase! It's a dance beyond Emma Goldman's wildest dreams, and there are no excuses for not learning it since you can hootchy this kootchy at your desk, in a wheelchair, or on a ventilator; the only place, in fact, where it can't be successfully practiced is in the numbing gray fog and money-mad miasma of Business As Usual. I'm alluding, of course, to a private, mostly mental version of the dance, since public decency laws still prevail.

There's much to be said for the wisdom of sitting quietly and observing. That is, until the music starts. Once you've heard the piper (or the DJ at that club on the edge of town), once that rhythm has entered your bloodstream, you've got to kick off your tight shoes, rise from your comfortable seat, and dance. Sooner or later, the piper will leave town and the club will be raided by the Thought Police. (They don't like that veil-dropping business.) At which point, you—familiar now with the beat—must make your own music and, veil-less, keep dancing your own steps until that day when you and your hootchy kootch are absorbed by the endless conga line of *samsara.*

In dropping at the very beginning, the veil that customarily would be saved for last, the skimpy silken curtain that conceals from vulgar eyes the wellspring of life, Salome may be pantomiming Einstein's daunting advice: "Go out as far as you can go and *start* from there."

Liam: In your interview with Nicholas O'Connell in 1987, you explain all of your works are like "cakes with files baked in them"—extraordinary confections that are "beautiful to look at and delicious to taste, and yet in the middle there's this hard, sharp instrument that you can use to saw through the bars and liberate yourself [with], if you so desire." That "hard, sharp instrument"—your elaborated versions, if you will permit the analogy, of the brick Krazy Kat, in George Herriman's comic strip, was always throwing at institutions, vested interests, traditions, dullards, etc.—mutates time and again with the publication of each successive novel comprising your canon. In *Still Life With Woodpecker*, for example, that instrument is dynamite *as* question or energetic skepticism, the type of skepticism in which Princess Leigh-Cheri finally participates, as it were, to eliminate the oppressive structure of control imaged by the monolithic pyramid in which she and Bernard are held captive. What are some of the other files, bricks, or "hard, sharp instruments" you have baked into your novel cakes to help the imprisoned reader make his or her escape?

Tom: Wow, that's a tough one. Tough first of all because I never read my books once they're published, by which time my attention has moved on to unexplored territory, new characters, and fresh concerns. I've told myself that in my golden years I'll sit down to scrutinize my oeuvre and decide then if I think it's any good. However, the golden years seem to have crept up on me when I wasn't looking, and I've yet to begin evaluating. Tough also because I've hidden no single file or hacksaw in any one book, but generally a whole tool chest of these instruments, a few rusty or made of rubber, is strewn throughout its narrative.

Taking a shot at it, let me focus on *Even Cowgirls Get the Blues*, my most famous novel albeit far from my best. In *Cowgirls* there's the liberating example of the whooping cranes, who prefer extinction to compromise. There's the defiance, in word and deed, of the pseudonymous Bonanza Jellybean, who risks her life rather than allow paternalistic pressure and chauvinistic stereotyping to prevent her from living out her girlhood fantasies. There's the dark angel Doloros, who comes to envision a wholly bipartisan brand of feminism. Then there's the ironically named Chink, who's a veritable hydrant of radical advice, encouraging us to take another look at paganism and admonishing Sissy, among other things, to be her own valentine, her own Jesus, her own flying saucer; to rescue *herself*; a toolbox of files that could enable any number of prison breaks—and/or also land one in a lobster boil of trouble. But the wages of liberation are trouble, I guess.

Beef: All this talk about cakes has created a thirst, which returns our attention now to your latest creative effort, *B Is for Beer*. In your most recent interviews regarding that book conducted by Tania Ahsan and the folks at HarperCollins, you say beer's potential as "ode fodder" is as good as any other subject, if not more so, since beer reintroduces the reality of taboo, one of many "mechanisms" deployed frequently as part of an on-going strategy of control through cultural enchantment. The subject of taboo is not one you have previously shied away from, as the issue of adolescent female sexuality illustrates in *Fierce Invalids Home From Hot Climates*. But what is unusual about beer as taboo is the implicit connection taboo has in this instance with a pervasive and accessible commodity whose history is inextricably tied in with the history of civilization itself. Is this evidence of a new form of corruption being exercised by the marketplace on an unsuspecting or oblivious citizenry, a new mutation of Puritanism, or both, and ought everyone be wary of mores defined by an unbridled predatory capitalism? Should Mr. Clean be defining our moral conception of purity, or any other moral conception, and what might Dickie Goldwire have to say about this trend if he could be persuaded to break his silence to respond from Boulder, Colorado?

Tom: Dickie Goldwire is probably making his way back to the tigerlands of Laos even as we speak. The florid cancers of advertising that shocked Dickie upon his return to the U.S. after years as an MIA have metastasized, and today every one of our institutions—political, cultural, educational, and religious—have been commercialized to the marrow. The civilized world is now one boundless bazaar, resonant with shills and teeming with pickpockets; a permanent round-the-clock medicine show where snake oil flows like wine, all major credit cards accepted. And the strip mall no longer ends at the corner, it extends into our skulls, our consciousness, our souls.

I'd be remiss not to at least acknowledge in my little entertainments the evils of insidious market-driven totalitarianism, a belching effluvium of psychological greenhouse gases detrimentally altering our moral climate. On the other hand, a novel ought not to be a soapbox. Despite the sundry unpleasantries it's obliged to periodically address, my fiction remains stubbornly resistant to angst, being more predisposed to wahoo than to boo hoo. I have zero interest in adding to the dreariness of the world.

In fact, in literature as much as in life, I'm weary of the dreary. Like, I suspect, a great many others readers, when I sit down to a literary repast I'd like a glass of champagne once in a while instead of a Styrofoam cup of tearwater. I'd like oysters Rockefeller, even a nice jelly doughnut, in place of yet another chunk of an author's bloody heart or his wife's cold tumor on toast. Sorry, I digress—but let me say one last thing about the overwhelming preponderance of suffering, of darkness, in contemporary fiction; while emphasizing that a steady diet of sunshine, especially when accompanied by side-dishes of jolly ho-ho overly optimistic inanities (I'm not channeling Candide here or dressing up as Pollyanna) is equally wearisome.

Some people prefer white meat, others prefer dark. That's fine, that's a matter of taste. It isn't important if you drool over the one while generally avoiding the other. A chicken, however, doesn't have that luxury. The hen needs both. A chicken with only white meat is a turnip and a chicken with only dark meat is a dead duck. The same can be said about a novel.

Okay, I just made an appeal for champagne but, hey, a glass of beer would be welcome, too. Being historic and global, ubiquitous and egalitarian, beer may be the ideal liquid, bubbles and all, upon which to float a barge of char-acters or in which to suspend ideas such as the ones we've been discussing. Yet, as you suggest, beer runs freely in every gutter along Madison Avenue, and due to its very popularity, beer and the image of beer is easily channeled by the marketeers into our habits and into our fantasies. A lot of how guys conduct themselves today—socially, sartorially, and ethically—is dictated by beer commercials. We're all being cast in the image of Joe Sixpack: fun-loving, sports-crazed, boorish, shallow, baffled by women, politically naive, and very, very thirsty.

Beef: Mention of Goldwire's name calls to mind the final acts of tribute he is purported to have made honoring the memory of his friend Stubblefield in *Villa Incognito*. The scrawling of the word "LIE!" across signs advertis-ing "Vine Ripe Tomatoes" throughout Boulder's metropolitan area should remind *Villa Incognito's* readers of Stubblefield's objection to an advertising illusion that has no basis in fact, a distortion of reality, like the notion of "genuine imitation leather" introduced in *Even Cowgirls Get the Blues*. But this challenge to the semiocracy of consensual reality fostered by corporate interests introduces a gestural politics reminiscent of that practiced by Bau-drillard and other theorists following the events of May 1968, and following the rise of the Situationist International in Paris. Is this insurrection of signs, this radical act of *détournement* practiced by Goldwire, an indication you were in any way affected intellectually back in the late Sixties by the new revolution that "would be symbolic or not be at all" that was being exported from France at the time?

Tom: To the best of my knowledge, my active resistance to the invasion and corruption of language, truth, and meaning by advertisers was homegrown, a product of the prevailing zeitgeist in Sixties America; itself a product of marijuana, psilocybin, and LSD (which at least partially explains why the Establishment is so frightened by the spectre of consciousness-expanding substances). True, I had my nose in French sauces back then, but I was un-der the spell of *la belle époque* and its madcap *fin de siècle* avant-gardists, not Baudrillard or Foucault, though I would have applauded their attempts to hack pathways through our dense foliage of sign and symbol, a jungle fertilized to excess by mass communication and rampant post-Marxist con-sumerism.

Liam: The beer taboo, coupled with this last thought about Dickie Goldwire, raises the issue of taboo as you treat it so insightfully and imaginatively in *Villa Incognito*. There, readers will recall, you present the problem created by Viet Nam War combatants who wanted to become and remain MIAs.

The taboo resulting from that decision, truly one of remarkable proportions, conceals how statist order has appropriated and even sanctified the condition of absence associated with the MIAs since war's end, not for the purpose of honoring the great sacrifice made by those who remained unaccounted for at the time of withdrawal from Viet Nam of all American armed forces, but rather for the apparently sinister end simply of propagating statist order itself and its control of the liberal state. Is this why Colonel Thomas, apparently only one of the few thinking members of the intelligence community, responds to the discovery of the three MIAs in Fan Nan Nan as if it were a national security issue? Is the illusion that keeps the military, more or less, in control of foreign as well as domestic policy so incredibly gossamer thin that the recalcitrance of three thinking and conscious conscripts might tear it asunder if their rejection and denigration of the order is not quickly and effectively silenced and covered up?

Tom: In a sense, every society is defined by its taboos. To remain lively and flexible, a society needs a few splinter groups or individuals dedicated to flouting if not actually smashing those taboos. Some cultures recognize and encourage this need. Think of the disorderly ritual clowns of the Hopi and Zuni, the backward-walking, urine-drinking tricksters of the Plains tribes; the *agorhi* sect of night-traveling outlaw babas in India, and the "crazy wisdom" shamans of Tibet. In pagan and newly Christianized Europe, well into the Middle Ages, entire villages would be granted temporary license to commit the most scandalous acts of sacrilege and licentiousness: their saturnalias and Feasts of Fools being the origin of Carnival and Mardi Gras. It was a safety valve, a way of periodically loosening the iron collar so that the community didn't strangle on its prohibitions, and it may explain why we yokels today are so titillated by (and probably secretly envious of) edge-living rock stars and intemperate artists such as Hunter S. Thompson.

Naturally, the military industrial complex, being obsessively dedicated to—dependent upon—herd control, will brook no breaks in its wall of taboos, and Col. Thomas could spot potentially widening fissures from considerable distance. Beer, however, while it may be taboo in some quarters (Sunday school picnics and day-care centers), is definitely absent from the Pentagon's *verboten* list. Military commanders condone and even facilitate the hearty consumption of brewskies (oblivious to any possible correlation with urine-drinking Winnebagos). At least that was my observation during four years in the air force, but my vision may have been blurred by beer.

Beef: The suggestion evoked by the cover-up in *Villa Incognito* that power is ephemeral and has no real basis in reality, a terrifying truth for statist order's apologists and ardent proponents, suggests on your part more than just a passing interest in the issue of power. Is it your understanding, perhaps like Michel Foucault's, that power is always already present in any social relation, though it is always capillary in nature? And if this is the case, do you also agree that power always implies resistance?

Tom: Foucault was spot on. Power is intrinsic in virtually every human transaction. We can no more eliminate it than we can eliminate death and taxies. (There's a cool band out of Seattle named Death Cab for Cutie.) What we can and must do, however, is to use every trick in our repertoire to prevent too much power from coalescing in any one person or place. My main man Switters and his fellow maverick CIA agents (taboo-busters one and all) address this matter directly and forcefully in *Fierce Invalids Home From Hot Climates*.

If power is intrinsic then resistance to power must also be intrinsic—or else the Second Law of Thermodynamics has a hole in it.

Liam: Any discussion of *Villa Incognito* has to lead eventually, as previous interviews with you indicate, to consideration of the function of the tanuki named Tanuki, the figure you have appropriated from Japanese myths of the Animal Ancestors, and the trickster fox Kitsune, the hermetic figure of the same tradition. The interaction of these characters at the book's beginning appears to remind us that we should never forget the role desire plays in our lives, and never forget also the need to moderate that desire according to our own law so that it does not have to be moderated for us. If this statement has any degree of accuracy regarding the book's seemingly introductory parabolic action, does this action, in turn, inform what happens in the remainder of the book, and if it does, is the audience being made aware that in the awakening process attainment of self-knowledge is as important as understanding rationally how the "mechanisms" of consensual reality's oppressive structures work?

Tom: Yes, well put: It may be less important to "know thy enemy" than to be aware that each of us is our own enemy as long as we are sleep-walking through life. The truth, though, is that at the moment I'm writing that stuff, I'm unaware that I'm addressing an audience. As much as I respect and am indebted to them, in the throes of composition, I'm talking not to readers but to the *page*.

Forgive me if this sounds woo woo, but the creation of imaginative fiction is such a mysterious enterprise that little can be said about it that isn't misleading. If I could explain what I do I probably wouldn't do it. I'd give it up and become an international jewel thief or something (although always tempted to leave an original love sonnet beside the contessa's bed after making off in the night with her emerald necklace). The great Nelson Algren once opined that "Any writer who knows what he's doing isn't doing very much." Well, I may not be the one to determine whether or not I'm doing very much, but I'll freely confess that when the Muse is present and we're locked in a tango, I don't really know what I'm doing—on a conscious level, at any rate. Moreover, I don't care to know. I've learned to trust my intuition. Oh, I'm fully, intensely engrossed, all right: it's quite the opposite of haphazard or slapdash and only occasionally spontaneous. I'm aware that I'm engaged in something larger but am content to just squeeze it out slowly, like radioactive toothpaste, one short squeeze at a time. I'm a little choo-choo train on a rainy night, just following the tracks.

Beef: The stylistic maneuvers engaged in by you in *Villa Incognito*, maneuvers you have elsewhere identified sometimes as "riffs," are frequent and contributory to the book's total effect. The reader certainly benefits from being *in Cognito* at times while understanding sometimes it is better, simply, to remain *incognito*. But the "riff" you perform that is most remarkable occurs when stylistically you modulate to the key of James Michener to contextualize the Lao people and their singular multi-tiered culture. Have you ventured over the years into many of Michener's imaginative reconstructions of the world, and has that experience of overwhelming plenitude affected your style as have certainly the passion and acuity of Henry Miller's prose?

Tom: Though I'd deny under waterboarding that I'm satirist, my riff on Michener does approach satire—while simultaneously proving to be a quite effective, painless way of imparting to the reader a rice bin of geographical, historical, and cultural information about Laos and its inhabitants. I'd bet the ranch dressing that I've never riffed on Michener before, but as I've mentioned, I don't read my books once they've gone on sale, so there's a slight chance I could lose that bet.

Liam: This playful use of Michner's style is reminiscent of what John Barth does in a number of his works, *Sabbatical* being one example coming readily to mind. You have never really said much about Barth as a contemporary writer, though characters with the name Barth do appear in *Even Cowgirls Get the Blues*. Is there a reason why the author of *Giles Goat Boy* has not been included in your consideration when discussing very distinguished friends and writers such as Tom McGuane, Jim Harrison, or the late Hunter S. Thompson? Is Barth's connection to the academy something that has made him suspect, as he was a member of The Johns Hopkins Writing Seminars faculty when the program was created and headed by the incomparable

John T. Irwin, author of *American Hieroglyphics*, and poet who has published under the *nom de plume* of John Bricuth?

Tom: You gentlemen give me credit for being more literary than I actually am. I was never an English major, you know.

Sure, I've glanced at Barth out of the corner of my eye; at Barth, Coover, Gass, and Barthelme; and found their dangerous verbal acrobatics thrilling at times, though a trifle cold for my taste, a trifle *sans coeur*—which could be unfair since I've spent so little quality time with them. (Maybe I'm like one of those sharks that refuse to eat sushi-grade tuna.)

And sure, I'm a sucker for a good story and can go a little haywire over picturesque prose. I love the novel, but the fact is, my thyroid has been set to pumping with equal frequency, equal force, by poetry, by movies (François Truffaut and Alan Rudolph), by music, by theoretical physics, by travel, by renegade mysticism ("crazy wisdom" for example), comic strips like *Terry and the Pirates* and *Krazy Kat*, and a whole museum of painters, including Andy Warhol.

Standing by my fully justified rants against the virulent swine flu of advertising, I'm nonetheless an aficionado of package design (recall the Camel pack motif in *Still Life With Woodpecker*), and I love Pop Art. While only a hobo would go for a soup-can novel, I do often wish that our writers possessed more of the unpretentious enthusiasm, vitality, humor, vision, and charm of Warhol, Johns, Rosenquist, and Oldenburg. (Pop Art, by the way, merrily turned the tables on the corporate pimps.)

I'm likely in a minority but I'm for writing that is willing to wrap itself in the chiffon of dream and the goatskin of myth, but that shuns the mummy bandages of good ol' earnest mainstream social realism because it can't abide the smell of formaldehyde. I'm for writing that has the wisdom to admit that much of life is indisputably goofy and that has the guts to treat that goofiness as seriously as it treats suffering and despair.

I'm for writing that glugs out of the deep unconscious like ketchup from a bottle: writing that can get as drunk on ketchup as on cognac—and then sing all the way home in the cab with Cutie.

I'm for writing that sings in the shower. I'm for writing that shoplifts sleazy lingerie from Victoria's Secret and searches the clear night sky for UFOs.

I'm for writing that quivers on your lap like a saucer of Jell-O and runs up your leg like a mouse. I'm for writing that knocks holes in library walls.

I'm for salty writing, itchy writing, steel-belted, copper-bottomed, nickel-plated writing, writing that attends the white lilacs after the heat is gone.

I'm for writing that can swing like Tarzan—on a vine woven from the nose hairs of Buddha. I'm for writing that rescues the princess *and* the dragon.

And so on and so forth.

Liam: The mention of John Barth and *Even Cowgirls Get the Blues* in the preceding question calls to mind one of Barth's earlier works, *The Floating Opera*, a work that appropriates Huck and Jim's raft in a novel way. Many of your works also appear to do the same thing with equally fascinating results. The Capt. Kendrick Memorial Hot Dog Wildlife Preserve, Siwash Ridge, the I & I, and even the oasis where the Pachomian Order is housed appear to function as a place like that famous raft where the subject space of the self is opened up in order that the process of self-overcoming might begin. Were you in any way influenced by the otherness of the place in which Twain chose to put his famous fugitives for the purpose of engaging in an affirmative anarchy of becoming?

Tom: Back when I was wee lad, I was gaga over a novel entitled *The Boxcar Children*. Written by Gertrude Chandler, the plot involved four orphaned siblings—two brothers, two sisters—who, to avoid being separated upon their parents' demise, run away. Fortunately, they chance upon an abandoned boxcar and spend the night there. The forgotten boxcar has been sitting some yards from the tracks, and a thicket has grown up around it. The children find it agreeable and set up housekeeping, the older sister serving as surrogate mother and schoolmarm. Thus concealed, they control their own lives together without interference from well-meaning though sometimes cruel authority figures.

Whether it was the influence of that book or our own instinctive compulsion to escape the domineering eye of adult authority—to create an adventurous alternative lifestyle—my young pals and I established, and at every opportunity occupied, any number of primitive hideouts in the wooded hills around the Appalachian villages where I spent my first eleven years.

So, now that you mention it, I can see that the hot dog stand in *Another Roadside Attraction*, the rebel all-girl ranch in *Even Cowgirls Get the Blues*, the blackberry house in *Still Life With Woodpecker*, the oasis in *Fierce Invalids Home From Hot Climates*, the jungle villa in *Villa Incognito*, et al, might each be interpreted as a version of that boxcar and those boyhood hideouts: a secret awakening place where one might escape the b.s. and become one's self to the fullest extent of one's self. To this day, I'm nourished and excited by hiding out, and I still resent and resist authority, so it's possible that all along I've been unconsciously creating those private nirvanas as imaginary refuges: clandestine sanctuaries for my characters, my readers, and myself.

If Barth viewed Huck and Jim's raft as such a covert retreat, a waterborne version of the outlaw sanctum, it was a stroke of genius. I must now read *The Floating Opera*.

Beef: Mention of the Capt. Kendrick Memorial Hot Dog Wildlife Preserve should remind any reader who has followed your work of Amanda and Ziller. Much has been said about the two, and most of it has reflected contemporary interests in anthropological understanding and mythological representations of fundamental human social relationships. Amanda has been characterized time and again as the Earth Mother or the Great Mother, the archetypal figure. Certainly there is much to be said about such characterizations. But there seems to be very little evidence over the years of anyone linking these two individuals to the definitions of style and content you develop in the book. Were you consciously or perhaps unconsciously personifying style and content through Ziller and Amanda, respectively? And if you were doing so, either consciously or unconsciously, is it possible their union constituted, for you, an effective expression of embodying the counter-idea since Ziller, always making his audience care, transmutes the seemingly disparate knowledge possessed by Amanda, making it always seem coherent?

Tom: Indeed, on one level both the lovers could be considered archetypes: the loinclothed Ziller an Orpheus figure, using his music, his art, to simultaneously charm the world and retaliate against it; all the while romantically identifying with another time, a distant place (*otherness* again); Amanda, a manifestation of the triple aspects of the universal goddess (maiden, slut, and mother/wife), as connected to the earth as any mushroom, though given to innocently flitting about in its blossoms like a butterfly. She's wise yet also naive, he's playful yet also dark; and something strangely meaningful seems to cling to them. Complementing one another, they embody both the silly whimsy and the serious transcendence that characterized the '60s, and, I hope, the book.

Liam: If in fact you did create a complete personification of the counter-idea through Ziller and Amanda in *Another Roadside Attraction*, does that creation then make Marx Marvelous really the principal focus of the book? After all, is not the preservation of the manuscript, which constitutes the book's conclusion, effected by Marvelous only after he has managed to overcome his former self, the post-Enlightenment rational man, and to find within himself, through the experience of an epistemological honesty, a new understanding that weds him in the special way to the counter-idea, to the thought of the outside?

Tom: Putting aside archetypal associations, there were in those years any number of young women and men who could have been real-life models for Amanda and Ziller. It was an amazing period—sometimes sacred, sometimes profane, sometimes impossible to tell the difference—and though I've long since put it behind me, I wouldn't have missed it for a billion bucks. At any rate, Marx Marvelous is hardly archetypal, unless Jung considered the accidental pilgrim an archetype, but M.M., too, had and still has counterparts aplenty.

He's a prime example of a rational, even stuffy, but bravely searching mind that has opened up and ventured afield to the point where it inadvertently finds itself in collision with minds that are less like scholarly lanterns than free-twirling pinwheels of rapture that sparkle mysteriously in every direction. (In his quixotic quest to foresee and neatly pre-assimilate the full scope of our religio-intellectual future, M.M. at least partially exemplifies what Baudrillard was getting at when he warned against the futility of seeking an all-encompassing epistemological Costco.)

Confirmed pragmatists caught in these seductively euphoric situations do often have their minds blown, but usually end up gluing the pieces back together with trembling hands and a durable industrial putty. Mr. Marvelous has been transformed by Amanda and Ziller: the question is whether he will remain transformed or, when the waters of Bohemia finally become too choppy for his conventionally constructed rowboat, he'll turn tail and retreat into one of those laboratories or academic think tanks where there's seldom enough breeze in the room to spin a glowing pinwheel of ecstasy.

In his favor, M.M. is genuinely curious, so perhaps the future will find him still skeptical—as well he ought to be—but willing nonetheless to bait his cognitive hook for some approximation of what Henry Miller meant when he referred to "a translucent fish swimming in a planetary sperm." If nothing else, his experience assures the reader that our lives are not as limited or prescribed as we may believe and there's always potential for radical change.

Liam: This alternative way of possibly considering Marx Marvelous's role in your first book suggests a consistent reaction on your part against the suspiciously unified subject of classical anarchism, the subject of post-Enlightenment thinking which is always implied in traditional anarchist critiques of capital and the state. Is this profound wariness of the Cartesian autonomous self traceable to your interest in and knowledge of Nietzsche, your interest in and knowledge of Hermann Hesse, or both, thinkers and literary artists whose works and ideas you have indicated in previous interviews you admire very much?

Tom: Yeah, I don't doubt that Nietzsche and Hesse, bless them, left their marks on me, though marks less like scars or cattle brands than faded shore-leave tattoos. They showed me, among other things (in his *The Joyful Wisdom* and *Human, All Too Human,* Nietzsche revealed a dry but mischievous comic sensibility), that conventional attacks on the authoritarian state, on the formidable fortresses of power, control, and avarice can be just as unenlightened and corruptible as the established order they seek to undermine.

Liam: Evident in the magic theater of all of your works is an implicit declaration, a declaration in a way reminiscent of Nietzsche's, of the *anarchy of the subject* to assure your readership that subjectivity as you conceive it must remain multiple, dispersed, and strictly provisional. Does this implicit insistence upon there being multiple strands of subjectivity within the individual characters you create permit you to preserve and cultivate difference and otherness? Equally important, does it put in play a prohibition in your works against the possibility of a totalitarian subjectivity? And does this ontological prophylaxis have the collateral benefit of insuring your treatment of the anarchy of the subject will have the status of a permanent revolution through the perpetual re-radicalizing of the subject?

Tom: At this stage of our developmental journey (and any dupe who believes that we today are the finished product, the *pièce de résistance* of three-million years of evolution, hasn't been watching the news), we simply aren't ready for benevolent anarchy and the freedom from manipulation, sneaky repression, and state-and-church-sanctioned herd control that true liberty would ideally assure. Anarchy can't flourish without love, without laughter.

Love and laughter can't flourish as long as Dr. Fear and Mr. Greed—spawn of the narcissistic ego—are operating the carousel.

The central dynamic of history has not been a conflict between good and evil but between ignorance and enlightenment. Our innumerable and interminable scenarios of good versus evil—in Hollywood, literature, government, and Sunday school—are too simplistic and misguided to accomplish much of anything beyond tightening the screws and padding our blinders. As counteraction to all that good guys/bad guys, cowboys versus Indians melodrama, Nietzsche produced a series of in-your-face reality shows, sometimes with a Wagnerian soundtrack, Valkyries singing the high notes. For his part, Hesse—with Mozart, mescaline, and the mysteries of the East in his repertoire—went deeper, staging a virtual neurological cabaret, though cautioning potential patrons that "the magic theater is not for everyone." And it is not. But maybe someday . . . ?

Beef: At the present moment the terminus a quo of your creative effort features a roadside attraction specializing in hot dogs and the terminus ad quem of that same effort features beer. With hot dogs and beer in each hand, and vegetables in between on the platter serving your imaginative repast, have you effectively ruled out any future gastronomic enticements to participate in the imaginative worlds you create? Have you, in other words, left your readers hungering in a way you perhaps did not anticipate?

Tom: Food—its procurement, preparation, and consumption—often figures prominently in the fiction of robust, non-establishment writers such as Jim Harrison and Tom McGuane. Personally, I seem to be more interested in the sheer sensual resonance, the imagerial poetic potentiality of foodstuff, as well as its wider cultural associations and metaphysical implications, though endeavoring to sidestep any indulgence in obvious symbolism. Let's face it: sometimes a hot dog is only a hot dog.

Considering the lengths to which I've gone in extolling the virtues—both gastronomic and aesthetic—of tomato sandwiches in my essay "Till Lunch Do Us Part" (included in the collection *Wild Ducks Flying Backward*); considering the hymns I've sung to mayonnaise, tequila, beets, stir fry, and beer, among other sapid sacraments, it may be time now for my readers and me to contemplate a temporary fast.

On the other hand, when I think of the literary possibilities of the jelly doughnut, that plump pastry Pantheon, that unbroken circle, that holy tondo, that doughy dome of heaven, that female breast swollen with sweetness, that globe of glorious goo, that secret round nest of the scarlet-throated calorie warbler, that sun whose rays so ignite the proletariat palate, that hub of the wheel of sustenance, that vampire cookie gorged with gore, that clown in an army overcoat, that fat fried egg with a crimson yoke, that breakfast moon, that bulging pocket, that strawberry alarm clock, that unicorn turd, that jewel pried from the head of a greasy idol (a ruby as big as the Ritz), that Homeric oculus (blind yet all-seeing), that orb, that pod, that crown, that womb, that knob, that bulb, that bowl, that grail, that . . .

Liam: Immutable mutability? But a final question, if I may? In previous interviews you have lamented the fact you have ceased to be as subversive as you initially intended to be as a writer. This may be why you characterized your work as "post-postmodern" in your interview with Russell Reising in 2001. But is this state of affairs really the case? Haven't you been involved in a trans-semiotic revolution from the start, a revolution of the symbol that has as its object the shaking of the system, as Jean Baudrillard so aptly put it, "down to the depths of its symbolic organization," creating a "catastrophic situation"? Haven't you, in other words, been repeatedly engaging in a symbolic critique of bourgeois semiotics, the very semiotics which has in part contributed to the engendering of the current massive social and cultural fact of simulation itself, this new reality or this "desert of the real itself," as Baudrillard describes it in *Simulacra and Simulation*? And thus, for example, is not Leigh-Cheri's creation of and participation in the simulation of Bernard's incarceration at McNeil Island Correctional Facility, the simulation that eventually leads to the memorable meditation on the Camel pack and becomes the source of the "princess prisoners" movement—is not that simulation ultimately rejected by Bernard as being nothing more than expression of Leigh-Cheri's "herding instinct" or inessential insanity rather than her appreciation for a human experience which should be authentic?

Tom: As someone who's convinced that human experience is becoming increasingly inauthentic, who believes that even our dreams, especially our nightmares, are weirdly wired electro-chemical simulation tanks; as someone who gets as incensed as Orwell over political and mercantile doublethink and Newspeak (though not to the point of letting it snow on my fiesta), I'm nevertheless reluctant to throw the first stone, particularly when that rock of mine could turn out to be papier-mâché. From a certain perspective, all artists are fakers—though as Picasso told us, art fibs in order to get at a greater truth.

If on the page I can persuade you that my visions are true, does that make them truths or are they merely a loftier, whiter, more amusing and original order of lies than the ones regularly spewed by the Pentagon, Madison Avenue, and Fox News? I don't know the answer nor can I accurately judge how successfully "subversive" my seriously playful fiction has been. Maybe I was indulging in self-deprecation in order to coax a compliment out of Dr. Reising. On the other hand—though I'm unsure if it qualifies as subversion—over the decades I've received literally scores of letters from readers who testify that my books have changed their lives, and at the risk of immodesty, I'm inclined to believe them sincere.

I cannot say with confidence that Leigh-Cheri's simulated experience in the attic was any less authentic than Bernard's experience in prison. Albeit a copycat affair, it nonetheless was poignantly heartfelt, bold, extreme, impulsive, and imaginative (conceptual art, in a sense), and therefore perhaps equally genuine and even more significant than Bernard's commonplace, involuntary incarceration. It's said that theatricality has the capacity to heighten reality, but I don't know if I can always tell the difference.

What I *think* I know is that ultimately all we can do in this life is hop on that strange torpedo and ride it to wherever it's taking us: ride it with gusto; cheerfully, even audaciously, never vicariously; ride it with open eyes and a warm heart; remembering to pack a handsome lunch and some poems by Neruda; riding it high, riding it tough, undermining the philistines, defending the wild, admiring the moon, copulating with willing mermaids (or mermen) along the way; singing all the while and praying for grace; ever bearing in mind what Switters came to realize at the conclusion of *Fierce Invalids Home From Hot Climates*, to wit: *It's always broke and we can never fix it. On the other hand, there's nothing to break, so what is it we imagine we're fixing . . .*

Index